World Population—
The View Ahead

INTERNATIONAL DEVELOPMENT RESEARCH CENTER SERIES NO. 1

World Population— The View Ahead

Proceedings of the Conference on World Population Problems held at Indiana University on May 3-6, 1967 —sponsored jointly by the School of Business and the International Affairs Center of Indiana University, and financed by the International Business Research Center, the International Development Research Institute, and the Human Resources Development Committee, all operating under a Ford Foundation grant

Edited by RICHARD N. FARMER

JOHN D. LONG

GEORGE J. STOLNITZ

PUBLISHED BY THE BUREAU OF BUSINESS RESEARCH
GRADUATE SCHOOL OF BUSINESS / INDIANA UNIVERSITY

HB
849
.C63
1967

PMC COLLEGES
LIBRARY
CHESTER, PENNSYLVANIA

89675

Copyright 1968

by

The Foundation for the School of Business

located at Indiana University

COVER DESIGN BY DAVID NOBLETT

Preface

THIS VOLUME is the product of the Conference on World Population Problems held at Indiana University on May 3-6, 1967. Problems associated with population might well constitute the most important challenge faced by mankind during the next half-century; therefore, they require the best professional attention the universities can muster.

Because the problems transcend all disciplines, yet include all, an effort was made to structure the conference and commission the papers on a truly broad substantive base. We hope that the findings summarized in this volume will stimulate fresh insight and a sense of urgency to all who grapple with the problems of population.

The conference was one of a series of events marking the dedication of the new School of Business building, and was sponsored jointly by the School of Business and the International Affairs Center of Indiana University. It was financed by the International Business Research Center, the International Development Research Institute, and the Human Resources Development Committee—all operating under a Ford Foundation international grant to the university.

Primary responsibility for planning the conference fell to Professor John D. Long as conference chairman and Professor Richard N.

Farmer as conference cochairman. Professor George J. Stolnitz gave extensive counsel in the choice of conference topics and participants.

Acknowledgments would be incomplete without an expression of appreciation to Professor Robert C. Turner, who conceived the idea of the conference; to Dr. W. George Pinnell, dean of the School of Business; and to Professor Robert F. Byrnes, former director of the International Affairs Center, for their support throughout this project. We would also like to thank the staff of the Bureau of Business Research, School of Business, for assistance in the production of this volume.

Our most obvious obligations extend to the distinguished scholars who participated in the conference—especially to those whose papers appear in this book. The editors have not attempted to make more than minimal changes in each manuscript.

RICHARD N. FARMER

Chairman and Professor,
International Business Administration Program,
Indiana University

JOHN D. LONG

Chairman and Professor of Insurance,
Acting Chairman, Department of Finance,
Indiana University

GEORGE J. STOLNITZ

Director, International Development
Research Center and Professor of Economics,
Indiana University

May, 1968

Contents

An Overview, *George J. Stolnitz*   1

The Outlook

The Long-Range Outlook—Summary of Current Estimates,
Milos Macura   15

Comments on Macura, *John D. Durand*   43

Economic and Technological Aspects

Economic Capacity and Population Growth, *Simon Kuznets*   51

Comments on Kuznets, *Gustav Ranis*   98

Agricultural Development is Not Enough, *Joseph J. Spengler*   104

Comments on Spengler, *Raymond Ewell*   127

Population Growth and the Potential of Technology,
Hans H. Landsberg   138

Food in the Future—Comments on Landsberg, *T. J. Gordon*   168

Sociological Aspects and Quality of Life

Urbanization—Problems of High Density Living,
Philip M. Hauser   187

Comments on Hauser, *Lowdon Wingo, Jr.*   218

Life Expectancy and the Life Cycle—Some Interrelations,
Harley L. Browning   227

Quantity and Quality in Populations of Man and Animals—
Comments on Browning, *Charles J. Krebs*   252

Death and Birth Controls

Death Control—the Implications of Increased Longevity,
R. L. Coigney   257

Prospects for World Population Control, *J. Mayone Stycos*   271

Comments on Stycos, *Christopher Tietze*   285

Ethical Issues of Control

The Ethics of Population Control
in the Light of Biology and Theology, *John Rock*   291

Playing God, *Robert C. Cook*   295

Birth Control—Ethical and Theological Implications,
Philip Appleman   301

Participants of the Conference   309

An Overview

GEORGE J. STOLNITZ

*Director, International Development Research Center
and Professor of Economics, Indiana University*

MY TASK of introducing this volume brings to mind the doctor who was so successful that he sometimes told his patients they were well. The reader can soon confirm the expert and timely quality of the contributions by the authors of the main papers and by their discussants alike. That the over-all orientation of the conference was remarkably cohesive, in terms of main questions raised and best available answers offered, should also be rather apparent. A clearly predominant major theme emerges from the papers and discussions, the more impressive in view of the varied topics and approaches treated by individual participants. The theme is one of confrontation throughout the rest of this century and beyond—between, on the one hand, enormous primal human needs still unmet and fueled by accelerating expectations, and, on the other, accelerating capacities for meeting such needs, both in scientific or technological realms and in our understanding of possible social, economic, and even moral pathways to change.

The basic form of the confrontation is age-old, but its substantive scale on either side of the equation is unprecedented, thereby blending a further reason for brevity here with an occasion to amplify. It seems best to summarize rather quickly, letting the papers speak for themselves, and to direct attention to some points that seem to have been relatively neglected. As with the doctor and his patients, euphoria concerning the outcome of a scholarly conference can also be self-defeating.

To begin with over-all impressions, the prevailing mood of the papers as of the conference itself (really the range of moods) seems relatively constrained. Only occasional hints are given of the pendulum swings to be expected in discussions of world population, more often in popular presentations, to be sure, but not unknown in scientific gatherings as well. On the "scare" side, the emptiness of slide-rule acrobatics is exposed in a single reference. Hans Landsberg jokingly cites the arithmetic whereby the weight of the world's population can eventually equal that of the earth, given only some positive growth rate and enough time. He could as easily have trotted out the vision, requiring no more assumptions, of a solid wall of human flesh surrounding the globe and moving out into the universe with the speed of light.

But even reasonable versions of calamitous possibilities have been relatively absent from the conference's deliberations. Only the presentation by Dr. Ewell reflects clearly the warnings by responsible agencies, such as the FAO, about the near-term threat of famine among hundreds of millions. During the years since the latest period documented in Professor Kuznets' paper, a mounting series of adverse events have occurred in world agriculture: lagging production increases or frequent short-run declines in areas where food supply per capita and agrarian productivity are low at best and the margins for even intermittent setbacks extremely meager; the drawing down of surplus stocks in the food-rich regions; and the unrelieved large uncertainties besetting the import capabilities of most low-income nations.

The conference made about equally short shrift of the opposite or soothing side of the opinion spectrum surrounding world population prospects. Only slight attention is accorded the view that dramatic fertility declines can bring an essential end to world overpopulation problems by the close of the century. As Dr. Macura's paper suggests, those holding this view may arrive at it from widely varying directions. Some see the main causal mechanisms for fertility declines as coming from general socio-economic progress; others stress the specific innovation of vigorous soon-to-be-successful programs of family planning.

The first opinion presumably rests on an assumed evolution of feedbacks, in which near-term high fertility would not prevent development from reaching a range beyond which further development could swing the tide to sustained declines in fertility. We know very little about the nature or magnitudes of such possible feedbacks, either in theoretical terms or even in the form of illustrative numerical models. The situation is inherently worse on the statistical front. No empirical counterparts exist to guide our analysis of the relevant feedback systems as they might apply to nations with current or recent high fertility. In any case, the question effectively remained outside the compass of the conference and is barely suggested in the papers.

With respect to family-planning programs and whether these may soon become a major new element in the population-development equation, we are still much like the child who was anxious to learn about her birthday gift and was told, "Wait and see." The emergence of balanced empirical judgments on this score within less than a decade may be possible but appears doubtful. Compilations of information on family-planning programs are just beginning to appear, and these are much more administrative or procedural in nature than demographic or economic. Both in theoretical and empirical terms, the linkages between activity levels of such programs and their consequences for fertility rates have yet to be established. Reports of glowing successes are almost daily intermingled with accounts of abortive or discouraging results: Korea and India, Taiwan and Pakistan, and no one knows about Mainland China. Part of the difficulty may be the usual one of bridging information gaps when facts and policies are changing rapidly. But I suspect that no small part stems from the circumstance that the facts themselves are in abeyance.

In short, I gauge the prevailing stance of the conference as occupying a kind of grimly realistic middle ground, not extending much beyond a subrange of bridled pessimism and qualified nonpessimism (with the possible exception of Dr. Ewell and one or two participants who foresaw a rapidly improving fertility picture in numerous high-fertility areas within the fairly near future). That this is so among such an expert group of observers (one, I might add, not known for excessive timidity) is itself an indicator of the magnitude of the confrontation referred to earlier. For, at least by historical standards, the drain of demographic demands on development prospects should be overwhelming.

It is well to recall some basic background facts in this connection. The maximum rates of natural increase among European populations during the nineteenth century rarely exceeded about

1.5 per cent per year. Today's growth rates in much of Asia, Latin America, and Africa frequently approach or exceed twice this magnitude. Agrarian densities in a number of major hardcore cases such as India go far beyond the levels that would have been viable for the development pioneers of a century ago, even with full allowance for international trade.

Or we can take another route. Suppose the populations of the underdeveloped regions ceased their growth today. Even then, the numbers whose ways of life would have to be radically transformed if they are to begin to approximate modern levels of living would far outstrip the populations of the regions that have already made the grade. Using the United Nations classifications in *World Population Prospects as Assessed in 1963,* today's underdeveloped areas ("less developed" in UN terminology and essentially Latin America, Africa, and Asia, less Japan and Temperate South America) have a combined population of some 2¼ billion. To an order of magnitude, this is 3 to 4 times the combined population of today's developed regions as of 1920 (some 675 million), when sustained economic development and social modernization had become entrenched in most of this part of the world. The figure 2¼ billion is also well over twice the corresponding number for the higher-income regions today (about 1 billion in 1965), when the question of assured development is no longer in doubt.

SUCH COMPARISONS, of course, are a starting point. The 1963 UN projections so ably summarized by Dr. Macura's paper suggest a "minimum" population rise in the underdeveloped areas of some 2 billion by the year 2000 (the so-called "low variant"); a "medium" possible rise of 2.5 billion; a "high" possibility of about 3 billion; and an "outside" possibility of some 3.5 billion. The population increment between each successive pair of these escalating versions approximates a half-billion, and some demographers would contend that the UN "outside" might be more appropriately regarded as "high"; the UN "high" as "medium"; and so on down to the "low" as "outside." Many of the specific uncertainties surrounding the UN projections are related in the Macura and Durand papers, requiring no further comment here. It is enough for our sense of the orders of magnitudes involved to summarize that the human components of the globe who face a dismal economic present and a still highly uncertain developmental future outnumber their historically successful predecessors elsewhere by a fourfold to eightfold factor, say sixfold as an average.

Given the constraints on development that such sheer demographic volumes will surely impose on the demand side, what can be said on the side of supply? What are the prospects that the sum of rising needs and rising numbers together can be accommodated?

A first key conclusion in this regard, which the Landsberg and Gordon papers illustrate in valuable if partially conflicting new detail, concerns the limited transferability or even relevance of Western-type technology to the low-income nations. Such limitations are especially serious for food and agriculture—at once the most critical and lagging sectors of the underdeveloped economies. A second basic proposition that occasioned no dissent at the conference concerns the critical extent to which specific technological progress in these sectors will be influenced by over-all socioeconomic and political conditions. Technological optimism as such is not enough even when justified, whether the technology in question can be imported from abroad or must stem mainly from indigenous sources. Spengler emphasizes that agricultural modernization interrelates at numerous central junctures with over-all modernization. Kuznets, after concluding that economic factors are probably adequate to accommodate considerable agricultural expansion without prejudice to nonagricultural modernization, cautions further that the weight of social and political influences can be decisive and may yet prove adverse on balance.

Landsberg illustrates the last aptly. The main research on agriculture in tropical areas (a large part of the low-income world) is still being conducted by foreign foundations, while the establishment of long-needed research institutes under domestic auspices is often still in the process of getting off the ground. The bottleneck here is surely political rather than lack of awareness. Landsberg's comments repeat what Stamp and many others have underscored for decades. Nor is the problem one of unavailable resources as such. If governments were willing, a generation or more of agricultural scientists could have been trained and launched by now in numerous low-income nations. Gordon's recital of a "brave new world" of longer-run and long-run technological possibilities is accompanied by the caution that "Education, patient teaching, can lead as almost no other innovation to increasing the world's food. . . ."

Despite all this, the supply side of the population-development confrontation remains highly ambiguous. For it is also true that income per capita has generally moved up, inchingly in some hard-core, high-density cases such as India (though it would appear at least upward even here) and often rapidly in a broad array of density situations. Industrial production has often shown remarkable uptrends. If the "big success stories" will be few in the coming decades, as Professor Kuznets has ventured, at least substantial and eventually sustained development seems probable in many parts of the less-developed world.

The big question marks, therefore, center about food and agriculture, which could still prove to be the conquering villain of the story. Kuznets' review of world food data since the interwar period suggests how precarious is the average international balance between food and population and how slender our factual basis for prediction. For the underdeveloped world as a whole, growth in food production has slackened appreciably during recent years while production per capita has apparently not moved at all. The averages may well conceal considerable deterioration in areas with perhaps well over a billion population. Moreover, as the food supply and trade data reported by Kuznets show, subsistence for much of the world's population depends increasingly upon agricultural performance and policies beyond their control. Even in areas where the longer-run trends in food output are upward, short-run or annual declines are frequent.

Nevertheless, both Kuznets and Spengler, as well as what I take to be the clear majority of conferees, are inclined to the view that the food supply requirements of the imminent demographic tides in Latin America, Africa, and Asia can somehow be overcome. This is not to rule out sharp regional differences, a distinct possibility already evident in the data. Adequate accommodation of food needs in many underdeveloped areas may well be accompanied by continuing crisis in others.

Professor Hauser presents a panoramic view of urban patterns through history and an extensive array of the mounting problems encountered throughout the world urban scene. He uses a simple size-density model for conceptualizing some salient interrelations over time and space between high-density habitation and its physical, economic, social, and governmental correlates. Interwoven in Hauser's discussion is the judgment, which he apparently regards as obvious, that "the underdeveloped areas of the world are over-urbanized." This leaves open the question of whether the urban problems confronting many underdeveloped nations might not be the lesser evil, despite their immensity, than the alternative of still greater numbers remaining on the land. The unavailability as yet of persuasive answers to this question and its important policy implications are underscored in Wingo's paper, which also critically reexamines the usefulness of a size-density approach to urban development analysis.

Here again a middle ground is suggested. As with development generally, unprecedented size and growth of urban populations in the low-income nations may be confronted by enormous capacities for accommodation.

The second half of the volume turns from population-development interrelations to more explicitly demographic issues. Mortality and fertility become the focus of attention, in which quality-of-life questions are often intermingled with quantity-of-population issues.

Dr. Coigney reviews the "mortality revolution" in the underdeveloped world over the past two decades, during which forward movements of survival chances and life expectancy have often far exceeded the speed of the corresponding movements in developed areas many decades earlier. Changes that typically required a generation or half-century in the West have been compressed into a few years or a decade among significant numbers of the low-income nations. As a result, the gaps between the developed and underdeveloped parts of the world have often narrowed greatly—probably much more so than for any other socioeconomic indicator of comparable importance—though the current differentials remain large to enormous and the differentials by causes of death even larger.

In the developed areas, where the Biblical "upper limit" of a 70-year life expectancy has become customary, large future gains must await scientific breakthroughs against the diseases of old age. A new range of longevity possibilities may emerge from our growing knowledge of the aging process and how it may be slowed. Should such possibilities be realized, enormous social and economic rearrangements would be required if greater longevity is not to deteriorate into mere prolonged survival.

Professor Browning turns the facts of high or rapidly rising life expectancy to other uses. In a frankly exploratory essay, he suggests how and why the social scientist should relate longer life to some salient aspects of the life cycle, giving his own special attention to marriage, the family, and childbearing. One among several intriguing hypotheses he advances is that social institutions in traditional, high-fertility societies tend to adapt slowly to sharply declining mortality if left on their own. Explicit policy efforts to educate individuals and families about emerging mortality facts might motivate them to reduce fertility through later age of marriage, increase the intervals between births, or to recognize that fewer births can assure the same desired size of surviving family. Demographers and sociologists have long speculated about these possibilities in the abstract, but little empirical research exists to guide us about either their behavioral dimensions or their implications for policy.

I would add that our knowledge is about as primitive with respect to numerous other mortality implications for the social scene: decisions to migrate, other mobility propensities, labor productivity, educational aspirations, or work career expectations, to name a few. So far as I know, the social scientist has rarely probed the ramifications of sharply declining mortality—and, by association, morbidity —in any of these directions. Rather, we have simply assumed that our sense of the plausible is sufficient proxy for the actual.

The last main subject matter of the papers centers about "birth control," a still bedeviled phrase in some quarters. The underlying empirical and policy question is easily stated: can socially engineered attacks on high fertility, spearheaded by major recent advances in contraceptive technology, be expected to bring rapid relief from population pressures in the world's impoverished nations? Fifteen years ago, the idea would have seemed a quaint new fad in science fiction—probably a dull one at that. Today it commands instant excitement internationally.

Professor Stycos' paper makes no attempt to forecast either the onset or the pace of the fertility changes that may result from family-planning programs or other causes in the high-fertility nations. On matters of prediction he prefers to stop with the observation that the spread of controlled fertility in these areas is no longer a question of "Yes" or "No" but only "When." Rather, his attention is to issues of infrastructure: the social, cultural, and ideational foundations that must presumably support the new technological possibilities if these are to attain widespread application in practice. Drawing mainly on Latin American experience, he reviews recent advances in the state of public communications concerning birth control, its growing legitimation by political and religious bodies, and the latent widespread demands for smaller families suggested by numerous surveys.

He also sees possible clouds on the horizon. Ideological alignments among conservatives and revolutionaries may be a deterrent or even subversive factor, at least in Latin America. Moreover, the going everywhere may become slower for family-planning programs in their second or later phases, once the groups most strongly motivated toward fertility control have been accommodated. The last is only one among a battery of major question marks. Since the subject receives little explicit attention in the papers, some amplification seems appropriate here.

Thus the main information we have as yet on actual family-planning developments is administrative or organizational in nature—number of IUD insertions, pills distributed, contraceptives sold, visits to clinics, numbers of participating technicians, and the like. The essential difficulty here is that there is no known reliable way of converting amounts of birth control activities into relevant numbers of births. Demographically—oriented data, such as births occurring or prevented among those adopting birth control practices, have been compiled only for very small population subgroups. Attrition rates from all sources, for example among IUD users, will have to become registered over a period of years before we can acquire any informed sense of their magnitudes. Fertility differences between acceptors of birth control methods and nonacceptor groups are poorly known. We still must learn the extent to which acceptors may be merely switching fertility control methods rather than increasing the extent of their control. All of the reported success stories combined come to a bare few, and we have yet to ascertain whether these speak mainly for themselves or as the vanguard for the future. In at least one such case, Taiwan, there are indications that fertility had already turned downward before the recent family-planning programs became effective.

SIMILAR questions abound on the input or economic side. We know very little about the probable costs of motivating persons to adopt birth control or, conversely, about the typical numbers of responses to expect from given total outlays intended for this purpose. To relate a given family-planning program budget to total population, thereby yielding a small number of cents per capita, tells us little if the program is in fact directed to a small segment of the population, yet the existing information is often presented in this fashion. Whether "externalities," in the form of unprogrammed social communication and persuasion, have a significant leverage effect relative to outlays focused on specific target groups has still to be established. The financial and real-resource costs associated with formal programs or their informal counterparts may well be much higher in many instances than the magnitudes on record.

In short, and unfortunately, it is still too early to say whether the rising tide of birth control expectations we hear so much about represents the thinking of the targeted beneficiary populations or the hopes of those doing the targeting. In fairness, it should be said that I have no idea what the response by the conference participants would be to these points, since time precluded their discussion.

Stycos' plea for "a comprehensive positive morality" in support of controlled reproduction anticipates eloquently the papers on ethical and theological implications. Dr. Rock sees a convergence between long-standing ethical justifications for planned fertility on biological-social grounds and the Catholic Church's liberalized redefinitions during recent decades of the goals of responsible parenthood. The convergence in terms of ethical goals is essentially completed, he believes, although the question of acceptable means is unresolved. Whether the Church will modify its position on licit methods of fertility control remains problematic. Professor Appleman makes a frontal attack on the "morality" and "natural law" arguments underlying the Church's traditional stand against contraception. Internal doctrinal divisions, coupled with rising external pressures, may portend an effective by-passing of the Church's conservatives, even if they should continue to prevail officially.

Robert Cook sees no meaningful choice if man is to control his evolutionary destiny. An international ethical code will have to be fashioned, one responsive to the exigencies of both sides of the "vital revolution" in the modern era, if sheer survival is to be assured. The nineteenth century acrimonies over the ethics of mortality control have long receded into history, but the outcome was incomplete. A rational ethics for fertility is yet to come, and may well face far greater obstacles and dispute before commanding comparable acceptance. But come it must, since the alternative over the evolutionary pull is extinction.

A notable omission from the conference should be observed in closing. All indications point to a drastic shift in the distribution of populations within and between the developed and underdeveloped parts of the world during the next half-century. Barring world-wide atomic holocaust, the emergence of very large or giant populations in a significant number of individual countries in Latin America, Asia, and Africa seems inevitable. It seems as certain that an enormous growth of economic, industrial, and military "muscle" will also occur in many parts of these regions—if not in per capita terms, then at least in the aggregate. That these prospects would have a profound bearing on the course of future international political relations seems obvious. Yet only Durand reminds us of the subject among the papers of this volume.

The explanation of the omission is simple: research in this area is so limited that the planners of the conference saw small promise of organizing a worthwhile, scientific-level discussion at this time. The explanation is of little moment as such, of course, but it does point to a pressing need. We are far from the state of professional attention required, on the part of political scientists and others, if diffuse speculation and journalistic alarms are to be replaced by sober, informed judgment on international political-population interrelations.

THE OUTLOOK

The Long-Range Outlook—
Summary of Current Estimates*

MILOS MACURA

Director, Population Division, United Nations

IN ASSESSING the relevance and mechanics of modern population trends, many authors are inclined to emphasize the importance of the eighteenth century. New elements in the growth of population, which began to appear in the mid-eighteenth century in regions of European settlement, were no doubt an overture to the spread of a more rational reproductive pattern all over the world. And it seems that the modernization of population reproduction, though still off-balance (due primarily to the persistently high fertility in large areas) and to some extent one-sided, is the most important aspect of current population trends. It would not be an exaggeration, however, within the modern period, to give the greatest attention to the twentieth century. It is expected that, when this century ends, the world's population will have grown from 1.6 billion to over 6 billion—a tremendous and unprecedented speed of growth which perhaps will never occur again. But demographic growth in the twentieth century has been neither stable nor equally distributed over time; it has undergone many changes during its short history.

The first third of the century was characterized by relatively high rates of population growth in the regions of European settlement; there were also great demographic losses during World War I and stagnation in many countries during the depression of the 1930's. It was not this third of the century that may be understood as the most challenging from the demographic point of view. The second third of the century, which brought World War II with its enormous demographic losses for many developed countries, also

---

* The views and opinions expressed herein are those of the author and do not imply the expression of any opinion on the part of the United Nations Secretariat.

brought new elements into the reproductive pattern of populations living in the less-developed regions. The improvements in medical, technological, and sanitary progress, and the improved world food situation, have so far induced a vast change in mortality trends, while fertility has remained high with virtually no change. It is anticipated that the last third of this century will follow the reproductive pattern already established, and the greatest rise in contemporary population growth will be during this time. Out of the 4.5 billion people who will have been added to the world's population during the twentieth century, about 2.8 billion will be added in its last thirty-five years.

Such an expansion of world population obviously emphasizes the quantitative aspects of the problem, although the structural and qualitative aspects seem to be of equally great importance. However, these questions are largely overshadowed by the growth problem and by the very simple fact that multiplying numbers of people means multiplying needs and requirements. In addition, the quantitative aspect of population trends in the last third of the century is the one that will influence the structure and quality of the population and of the world's future development. The inflow of people into schools, into the labor market, and into towns and cities will be unprecedented. This is a fact that should constantly be kept in mind when dealing with developments during the next thirty-five years.

The immensity of the anticipated population growth lends primary importance to the estimated number of future world population and therefore to the demographic projections. For any sound evaluation of the latter, it is important to make a valid estimate as to whether world population will be 6 billion or only 4.5 billion by the end of the century. Not only the number, but also the structure of population and its social and economic implications will differ, depending upon whether the assumption of 6 billion or 4.5 billion is accepted. Expectations of the degree of impact that economic and social change will have on population growth must also differ under the two assumptions.

From a technical as well as from a policy point of view, estimates of future population deserve full attention. If the population grows at a moderate rate, and if the annual increases are of a kind that have been experienced, then humanity will have problems of lesser magnitude to solve. However, if the growth of population remains at a high level and if the annual increases are much greater than those already encountered, then present thinking, planning and organization, and policy decisions should take new directions. For these reasons, a reexamination of population projections should be made continuously. It should help us to understand as fully as possible what the magnitude of future population might be and, consequently, what might be the range of problems to be faced.

Three Projections of Population by 2000

The estimates by Carr-Saunders and Willcox of past world population trends were among the most important contributions to modern demography, and they have also made interest in the growth of population more realistic and meaningful. Of course, the growth of population had been an attractive area of study for a long time. But, because of the lack of historical experience, early studies of population growth were either brilliant mathematical exercises of the Eulerian type or a Malthusian kind of theoretical speculation. The growing awareness of changing rates of population growth and the increasing understanding of its mechanics, together with postwar involvement in the world's development problems, encouraged the construction of population projections on a wider scale and with a longer prospect. For obvious reasons, the United Nations Secretariat was one of the leading agencies in developing new methods and techniques and in estimating future world population trends.

It should be mentioned that United Nations estimates of future population had to undergo a stage of marked uncertainty and much painstaking research.[1] The high variant of the 1980 world population as estimated in 1951 was 3,636 million; according to 1954 estimates, it was 3,990 million, and the figure estimated in 1957 was 4,280 million. The high variant of the 1957 study was lower than the medium variant as assessed in 1963, which gave a world population in 1980 of 4,330 million. Although the three variants (high, medium, and low) of the 1957 and 1963 assessments of world population for particular years differ substantially, the corresponding estimates, high and medium, for the year 2000 are rather close to each other (6,990 and 6,994 million, respectively, for the high

---

[1] For a good summary, see John V. Grauman, "Success and Failure in Population Forecasts of the 1950's: a General Appraisal," in *Proceedings of the World Population Conference 1965*, III (New York: United Nations, 1967).

variant, and 6,280 and 6,130 million, respectively, for the medium variant).[2] Without suggesting any definite conclusion, it may be said that we are still faced with varying predictions when dealing with the numerical assessments of future population trends. Could it also be noted that the gradual acquisition of new information and improvement in methods have usually resulted in higher estimates of future population?[3]

Assumptions for future mortality and fertility (for regional projections and assumptions for migration as well) were organized in the 1963 UN projections under three variants, already mentioned. Obviously, there are no stable relations between high, medium, and low projections. There might be a number of sets of assumptions regarding varying levels, onset of decline, pace of decline, and the effects of reduced mortality and fertility.[4] The results of the numerous combinations of factors involved may differ widely, owing particularly to the unfortunate fact that for large areas the selection of alternatives is rather subjective and not based on precise observation. But it might be of interest that the 1963 assessment of the end-of-century population provides for a smaller difference between high, medium, and low variants (12 per cent and 11 per cent) than the 1957 assessment (10 per cent and 22 per cent). Is this an indication of an increasing certainty in predictions that may arise from growing experience on the part of the UN staff in making projections?

---

[2] "The Past and Future Growth of World Population—a Long-Range View," in *Population Bulletin of the United Nations* (No. 1; New York: United Nations); *The Future Growth of World Population* (Population Studies No. 28; New York: United Nations, 1958), pp. *vii* and *viii*; *World Population Prospects as Assessed in 1963* (Population Studies No. 41; New York: United Nations, 1966), pp. 13-17. For India, Pakistan, Ceylon, and Nepal, see also Pravin M. Visaria, "Population Projections for Countries of Middle South East Asia During the 1950's," in *Proceedings of the World Population Conference*.

[3] This is true for all the regional projections for 2000 as well, with the exception of projections for East Asia, Europe, and the Soviet Union, which are, according to the 1965 assessment, lower than were estimated in 1957 *(World Population Prospects . . .*, pp. 16-17).

[4] Compare *World Population Prospects . . .*, pp. 44-47, and also p. 17: ". . . in the present report projects have been calculated with assumptions formulated separately for each region, despite admittedly large areas of uncertainty in many regions. The result of present assumptions for large parts of the world is an accelerated population growth which eventually slows down, sooner in some regions and later in others, the peak growth rates to be attained being higher in some regions and lower in others."

In addition to the three variants, a fourth projection was prepared that estimated the growth effects of constant fertility, as observed in the 1950's, combined with declining mortality.[5] The world population in the year 2000 was estimated, based on these assumptions, at 7,522 million. This estimate was to a great extent an intellectual exercise, but very impressive in many respects. It suggests, inter alia, what might be the differences in growth of population among the three alternatives that all hinge on a decline in fertility; it proposes a growth model that assumes stable fertility.

Among the population projections that were recently published, two additional ones merit our attention: Professor A. Y. Boyarsky's projections of world population in the year 2000, published in 1965; and Professor D. J. Bogue's estimates prepared in 1966.

Boyarsky's general assumption is that the future growth of population of world regions will differ according to social organization and levels of development and that, within the next few decades, the currently developing countries will gradually join the group of developed countries.[6] For the twelve regions he set up, Boyarsky employs the ratios of $(e_o^{2000} + e_o^{1920})$ to $(e_o^{1960} + e_o^{1980})$ to represent the varied pattern of future life expectancy. They were used for estimating the "conditioned stationary population" at the year 2000 for each region. Then allowance was made for the impact of fertility on population growth, assuming particular future fertility trends for each region. Finally, a differential margin of error was applied to the computed figures, giving the world population at the end of the century as $4,626 \pm 410$ million. In the last paragraph of his paper, Boyarsky considers 5 billion as a plausible estimate of total population, of which 3 billion may be labor force.

Bogue's understanding of the future growth of world population was first submitted to the 1966 Pacific Science Congress and then quantified in a paper entitled "The Prospects for World Popula-

---

[5] "Broadly speaking, though there are exceptions, the 1950's were marked by a near constancy in birth rates and by considerable rises in expectation of life in virtually all of the world's regions. It is this situation which furnishes the background for a 'constant fertility, no migration' variant" *(World Population Prospects . . ., p. 125).*

[6] A. Y. Boyarsky, "A Contribution to the Problem of World Population in the Year 2000," in *Proceedings of the World Population Conference.*

TABLE 1 WORLD POPULATION ESTIMATES
(in millions)

Author and Variant	Millions		Variability Index (UN Medium=100)	
	1980	2000	1980	2000
United Nations (1963)				
High	4,551	6,994	105	114
Medium	4,330	6,130	100	100
Low	4,147	5,449	95	89
Constant fertility	4,519	7,522	104	123
A. Y. Boyarsky (1965)				
Maximum	....	5,036	...	82
Main estimate	....	4,626	...	75
Minimum	....	4,216	...	69
D. J. Bogue (1966)	4,061	4,527	...	74

SOURCE: *World Population Prospects as Assessed in 1963* (Population Studies No. 28; New York: United Nations, 1958), pp. 134-37; A. Y. Boyarsky, "A Contribution to the Problem of World Population in the Year 2000," in *Proceedings of the World Population Conference, 1965*, III (New York: United Nations, 1967); Donald J. Bogue, "The Prospects for World Population Control," University of Chicago, 1966, mimeographed.

tion Control."[7] Considering that worldwide interest in birth control "has already reached a state where declines in death rates are being surpassed by declines in birth rates," he assumed that the pace of population growth had begun to slacken. He then assumed that the rate of growth "will slacken at such a pace that it will be zero or near zero at about the year 2000, so that population growth will not be regarded as a major social problem except in isolated and small, retarded areas." The figure for world population in the year 2000, which was derived by Bogue, was 4,527 million.

It is not surprising that the differences among all the variants of projections are great. But it is quite unexpected that the two opposite approaches worked out by Boyarsky and Bogue have yielded rather similar results (see Table 1).

[7] Donald J. Bogue, "Recent Developments in Family Planning that Promise Hope in Coping With the Population Crisis in Asia and Throughout the World," in *Population Problems in the Pacific, 11th Pacific Science Congress* (Paper No. 1; Tokyo: University of Tokyo, 1966), and Donald J. Bogue, "The Prospects for World Population Control," University of Chicago, 1966, mimeographed.

As regards their quantification for the year 2000, Bogue's "fertility control" approach is very near to Boyarsky's "social system and economic development" approach expressed in its main variant. Both projections are more than 15 per cent below the low variant of the UN projection, and about 25 per cent lower than the UN medium variant. The difference of 1.5 billion persons is perhaps just the difference that creates the concern over the future growth of world population.

The existence of several estimates of future population projections that substantially differ raises two questions. Which is the most plausible variant for demographic analytical purposes and for the study of future relationships between population and socio-economic phenomena? What are the proofs that the probability of assumptions for the plausible variant is such as to satisfy the minimum technical and scientific requirements?

Why the United Nations Medium Variant?

With all due respect for the projections of Boyarsky and Bogue, and keeping in mind their figures as a warning, the following analysis will deal primarily with the medium variant of the UN projections. The decision of selecting one alternative from among a number of equally hypothetical and, at least at the first glance, equally justified alternatives always seems arbitrary, and it definitely is. The decision may be supported by important reasons, such as consistency of assumptions, reliability of methods and techniques, convenience for analysis, preferences expressed by others, and so forth. But any selected projection has its own limitations and deficiencies. They must be known to the user, who should proceed with maximum caution and reservation, which are so necessary in any analysis of the future.[8]

---

[8] *World Population Prospects* . . . did give preference to the medium variant. Also, more space has been given to analysis of the medium variant in all instances where detailed three-variant analysis required more space. To some extent, this is also true for J. D. Durand, "World Population Estimates, 1750-2000," in *Proceedings of the World Population Conference*, II, pp. 17-22; he also takes the medium variant as the basis but also considers the ranges of low and high.

B. Bijchovsky and L. Rodina in a recent article in *Izwestya* (Jan. 25, 1967) also use the UN medium variant as the basis for their analysis. Some other docu-

As already mentioned, the UN population projections produced in 1963 were calculated on assumptions formulated for twenty-four regions.[9] The estimates for these regions were grouped and briefly examined according to the following criteria: (a) levels of development; (b) density of population; and (c) major geographical areas. It is indeed not possible to reproduce here all basic and working assumptions that were used for constructing the projections. But the most important ones will be briefly mentioned to give a general idea of demographic changes that have been taken into account in preparing the projections.

The decline in mortality as anticipated is obviously more intensive in regions with currently high mortality; it is also expected to reach the minimum in regions where mortality is already low. Expressed in life expectancy at birth, the assumptions accepted for the medium variant are shown in Table 2.

Measured by present standards, the expectancy of life is assumed to make marked progress in all areas of the world. This may be in continuation of past trends until a relatively advanced level of medical and health services is reached. Whether the next thirty-five years will bring additional substantial improvements in medicine and public health and extend the life expectancy beyond seventy-four years—at least in economically advanced countries—is

ments, however, such as the Statement by Heads of State of twelve countries (UN press release SG/SM/620/Rev. 1 of Dec. 9, 1966) have selected the high variant. It should be added that not too much use has been made of the low variant of the UN projections. Much was said at the 1965 World Population Conference concerning the prudence needed in constructing and using population projections. The essence of what was said is contained in the following statement: "It would appear that the meeting generally agreed with the very cautious statement by the Moderator to the effect that, although future populations cannot be predicted over the long run nor populations projected forward with a definable margin of error, what can be done only approximately must be done" (statement by the Rapporteur for meeting A.4, R. Bachi, *Proceedings of the World Population Conference,* I, p. 203; also statement by Moderator, Mrs. Irene B. Taeuber, pp. 191-200, 243-58).

[9] *World Population Prospects* . . ., p. 17 and Annex II and III (pp. 127-49). The following is a list of major areas and regions (* = developed): Eastern Asia—mainland region, Japan*, other; Southern Asia—Middle South Asia, South East Asia, South West Asia; Europe—Western Europe*, Eastern Europe*, Northern Europe*; U.S.S.R.*; Africa—Western Africa, Eastern Africa, Middle Africa, Northern Africa, Southern Africa; Northern America*; Latin America—Tropical South America, Middle America (mainland), Temperate South America*, Caribbean; and Oceania—Australia* and New Zealand, Melanesia, Polynesia, and Micronesia.

difficult to predict.[10] This may be considered an open question, at least for some years to come. Another question is whether the anticipated decline in mortality in eastern Asia and Africa is not slow in comparison to the progress which has been achieved so far in other less-developed areas. If the two questions are answered in the affirmative, life expectancy may be raised and the anticipated number of population increased accordingly.

Sex- and age-adjusted birth rates were used in the UN projections for quantifying the assumptions on fertility. As mentioned in *World Population Prospects,* the weighting adjustments system that was used in the 1963 assessment is outdated and is under revision. This is an area in which substantive improvements are needed, but these may be of more academic than practical value. The adjusted birth rates as used for projection work are shown in Table 3.

Except for a slight increase in the fertility of the populations of the U.S.S.R. and Japan (which seem to be generally admitted as a real correction of past fertility trends), there is a worldwide assumed decline of fertility. It is particularly marked in Southern Asia and Eastern Asia; according to the projections, the latter region should almost reach the European level of fertility as early as the end of this century.[11] Here again is a question which, if answered differently from that in *World Population Prospects,* may lead to a higher estimate of population in the regions concerned.

The estimated future sex and age structure of the population is an obvious product of the initial structure and of the assumed change in mortality and fertility. So are the ratios and numbers of the female population in the fertile ages from 15 to 44 years. But

---

[10] Professor Boyarsky in "A Contribution to the Problem . . ." accepted the following assumptions on life expectancy at birth to be achieved by the year 2000: for the developed capitalist countries, 80; for European socialist countries, 85; for many developing countries, 60; and so on.

[11] The fertility measure used in Professor Boyarsky's assumptions is a percentage addition to the "conditioned stationary population." He estimated the fertility allowance for the U.S.S.R. population at 20 per cent; for the populations of socialist European and capitalist countries and of the United States, 10 per cent; nothing for Japan; and 20 per cent for the populations of the developing countries. His assumption for the populations of socialist countries of Asia, with China being the main one, is ". . . a decline in fertility relatively not less than the increase in population . . . a roughly constant absolute number of births. . . ." ("A Contribution to the Problem . . .") The conditioned stationary population of this region was therefore increased by a minimum figure of 5 per cent.

TABLE 2   EXPECTANCY OF LIFE (e_0)

	1960-65	1980-85	1995-2000
Europe	68.7	73.7	73.9
U.S.S.R.	70.2	73.9	73.9
Northern America	71.7	73.9	73.9
Oceania	61.0	64.9	66.7
Eastern Asia*	46.3	55.8	62.7
Southern Asia	46.4	56.6	64.6
Latin America	57.9	65.0	68.7
Africa	41.1	48.8	54.7

* Japan: 68.2, 1960-65; 73.0, 1980-85; 73.9, 1995-2000.

SOURCE: Population Division of the United Nations (work sheets).

TABLE 3   SEX- AND AGE-ADJUSTED BIRTH RATES

	1960-65	1980-85	1995-2000
Europe	19.3	18.0	18.0
U.S.S.R.	20.3	22.0	22.0
Northern America	26.7	24.0	24.0
Oceania	28.7	27.3	27.5
Eastern Asia*	34.1	24.5	19.4
Southern Asia	44.6	36.9	26.6
Latin America	42.1	37.3	30.8
Africa	48.8	47.0	43.0

* Japan: 14.9, 1960-65; 15.5, 1980-85; 15.8, 1995-2000.

SOURCE: Population Division of the United Nations (work sheets).

TABLE 4   FEMALE POPULATION 15-44 YEARS OLD
(in millions)

	1960	1980	2000
Europe	88.8	99.6	106.6
U.S.S.R.	50.7	60.6	72.9
Northern America	39.8	55.9	75.5
Oceania	3.2	4.7	6.6
Eastern Asia	174.8	236.4	298.7
Southern Asia	185.9	299.1	513.6
Latin America	45.6	79.2	142.9
Africa	58.0	94.3	164.3

SOURCE: Population Division of the United Nations (work sheets).

the expansion of this segment may be very instructive for the assessment of the medium variant, since it is the main childbearing age group, whose increase should be understood in the light of differential changes in age structure throughout the period (see Table 4).

In relative terms, this age group is expected to grow faster than the total population in Africa, Northern America, and Eastern Asia, and, in Latin America and Southern Asia, even faster. It is an important factor, which may contribute to the anticipated large numbers of births and massive increments in world population by offsetting the effects of the declines in fertility rates. Perhaps the expansion of this female segment of the population may invite confidence, a confidence which may lead to acceptance of the medium variant of the UN projection as the plausible variant. Of course, as any other variant, this variant also has its own limitations, but these should not affect its acceptability and utilization.[12]

Twentieth Century Population Trends

The variety in growth pattern of the world's populations in the twentieth century is such that it can be generalized only with major reservations. The beginning, the intensity, and the combination of changes in fertility and mortality and their relationships to structural changes, as well as to their economic, social, and cultural correlates, do not encourage their being interpreted by a single hypothesis or a simplified set of hypotheses as generally valid. But for a broad understanding of the changes that have already taken place and that are anticipated for the next thirty-five years, a distinction between demographic trends in developed and less-developed countries may be useful.

This distinction is understood, indeed, to indicate the importance that is attributed to the association between the levels of development and the pattern of population growth. The distinction should

---

[12] To mention only some limitations: deficient statistics for large critical areas of the world; inadequate knowledge of reproductive behavior under various social, cultural, and economic circumstances; lack of knowledge on prospective improvements in factors encouraging declines in mortality; projection methods and techniques; and so on. It seems that particular problems are being met in estimating variables of large populations within the regions, a bias which can hardly be offset by a counterbias. In this respect, the estimates for some parts of Southern Asia and of Eastern Asia deserve special attention.

not be understood as static, though it classifies the same areas of the world into two basic groups over the whole of the twentieth century[13]—a long century in character, witnessing most profound demographic, economic, social, and political changes that affect the tempo of over-all development and the speed of transformation of less-developed areas into developed ones. This dual distinction should not underrate the importance of diversity in the pattern of population growth, especially in the less-developed stratum; this diversity may have, of course, a significant influence on many aspects of future life and relevant policy considerations (see Table 5).

The segment of the history of world population that is under discussion has been studied by many authors and under different circumstances. Nothing new can perhaps be added to what has already been stated or organized in a synthesis.[14] However, the fact that humanity has entered the last third of the last century of the second millennium suggests that this particular period be further considered. If the assumptions on future fertility and mortality could be accepted *grosso modo* as suggested in *World Population Prospects*, both the increment and the tempo of growth of population during the next thirty-five years would be expected to exceed those occurring during the last sixty-five years (see Table 6). Obviously, a strong accent is on all growth indices of the less-developed regions, where six-sevenths of the next thirty-five years' increment in world population will take place. This period's population growth will be more than double that of the last sixty-five years.

The upward trend of the world population growth rate, which has been in general the main characteristic of the last sixty-five

---

[13] A "nonstatic" classification which would reclassify each area from the less-developed to the developed group as soon as it reaches the criterion of developed would better satisfy some analytical needs. It could contribute to the study of the demographic transition of the world and to a better description of its particular stages. However, for the present analysis it seems that the classification of areas as published in *World Population Prospects* . . . meets the main purposes. It should be noted that level of fertility was used in this study as the criterion for defining the dichotomy between the developed and less-developed areas *(World Population Prospects* . . ., p. 3 and *Population Bulletin of the United Nations* (No. 7; New York: United Nations), pp. 1-3.

[14] Compare, for example, relevant chapters providing syntheses in *Determinants and Consequences of Population Trends* (New York: United Nations), the summary volumes of proceedings of the first and second World Population Conference; *Population Bulletin* No. 7; and others.

TABLE 5 POPULATION TRENDS IN DEVELOPED AND
LESS-DEVELOPED REGIONS, 1900-2000

	Population in Millions			Annual rate of growth (%)		
	World	Developed	Less-Developed	World	Developed	Less-Developed
1900*	1,650	550	1,100	...	...	...
1910†	1,740	600	1,140	0.53	0.87	0.36
1920	1,861	674	1,187	0.67	0.17	0.41
1930	2,070	759	1,311	1.07	1.20	1.00
1940	2,296	822	1,474	1.04	0.80	1.18
1950	2,516	858	1,658	0.92	0.43	1.18
1960	2,998	976	2,022	1.77	1.30	2.01
1970	3,592	1,082	2,510	1.82	1.04	2.19
1980	4,330	1,194	3,136	1.89	0.99	2.25
1990	5,187	1,318	3,869	1.82	0.99	2.12
2000	6,129	1,441	4,688	1.68	0.90	1.94

* J. D. Durand, "World Population Estimates, 1975-2000," *Proceedings of the World Population Conference, 1965,* II (New York: United Nations, 1967), p. 21.

† Interpolated between 1900 and 1920.

SOURCE: *World Population Prospects as Assessed in 1963* (Population Studies No. 28; New York: United Nations, 1958), p. 23.

TABLE 6 INCREMENT IN POPULATION IN TWO PERIODS

Period	World	Developed Regions	Undeveloped Regions
	Increment (millions)		
1900-65	1,630	482	1,148
1965-2000	2,849	410	2,440
	Average decennial increment (millions)		
1900-65	250	74	176
1965-2000	815	117	700
	Percentage increase over the period		
1900-65	99	88	104
1965-2000	87	40	108
	Average rate of growth (in per cent)		
1900-65	1.1	1.0	1.1
1965-2000	1.8	1.0	2.1

SOURCE: *World Population Prospects* . . ., p. 134.

years, will probably continue until the middle of the period under consideration. Then it will gradually take the reverse direction. As encouraging as this turn may seem, its practical value would be diminished by the continuous absolute growth of population over the period, with a marked increment in each successive decade.[15]

The main changes in the reproductive pattern of world population, as regards both the relations between the developed and less-developed regions, and mortality and fertility, have taken place —broadly speaking—since World War II. Of course, during the first half of the century, there were some short periods when the growth rates of population in less-developed regions exceeded the ones in the developed regions. These were the periods of wars and of the Great Depression, with substantial demographic consequences for many advanced countries. But, as a rule, the rates of population growth of developed regions were relatively higher, owing to the effects of differential fertility and mortality in both developed and less-developed regions.

A fast decline in mortality in less-developed regions, combined with almost stable fertility in the late 1950's and in the 1960's, was in sharp contrast to the declining fertility and mortality in developed regions. "La reprise démographique" in the postwar years brought the rate of births in developed regions to its peak at about 23 and the rate of natural increase to about 13 per 1,000, but this was substantially lower than the respective rates in the less-developed regions. The decrease in mortality in the latter was such (and will continue to be such) that it easily offset the slow decline in fertility. The peak of the rate of natural increase in less-developed regions may therefore be expected in the 1970's; by that time, it may reach 22.5 per 1,000 for the less-developed regions as a whole.

The interplay of fertility and mortality and of the sex and age structure may result in unexpected demographic features, as indicated by levels, trends, and relations of crude birth and death rates in the two regional categories (see Table 7). This interplay may be even more pronounced for smaller regional groupings where the factors involved may form a particularly unusual con-

---

[15] The absolute growth of world population is estimated for the 1960's to be about 590 million; for the 1970's about 740 million; for the 1980's about 860 million; and for the 1990's about 940 million.

TABLE 7 CRUDE BIRTH AND DEATH RATES
(per 1,000)

Year	World		Developed		Less-Developed	
	Births	Deaths	Births	Deaths	Births	Deaths
1965-70	32.9	14.4	18.5	8.5	39.4	17.3
1970-75	32.4	13.6	18.7	8.6	38.2	15.7
1975-80	31.6	12.8	19.4	9.0	36.5	14.4
1980-85	29.6	11.5	19.3	9.1	33.9	12.5
1985-90	28.5	10.7	19.0	9.2	31.8	11.2
1990-95	26.9	9.9	18.5	9.4	29.7	10.0
1995-2000	25.7	9.3	18.3	9.6	28.0	9.2

SOURCE: *World Population Prospects* . . ., pp. 34, 35.

stellation[16] with different growth effects. The attainment of highest rates of population increase in the less-developed countries may be dispersed over a period of fifty years and at varied levels. The peak increase of population (in terms of percentage decennial increase) was achieved in mainland Eastern Asia in the 1950's with an increase of 16.2 per cent. In Tropical South America and South East Asia it is anticipated at levels of 36.8 and 29.3 per cent, respectively, for the 1960's. At least seven regions may have their peak increase in the 1970's, ranging from 44.0 to 26.4 per cent (Polynesia and the Caribbean). Southern Africa may reach its peak increase of population in the 1980's (30.4 per cent), and the rest of South-of-Sahara Africa after the 1980's.[17]

The contribution of the areas of European settlement to the twentieth century population growth may not substantially differ from the contribution of the developed areas, for "European" and "developed" are rather close, and their geographical coverage overlaps. The assessment of the importance of the areas of European settlement for the growth of world population had primarily a theoretical value, and Professor Durand is right when he states that

[16] The crude death rates do to some extent contribute to the "unexpected features." Standardized rates obviously give a different picture; for example, in Latin America the crude rate for the 1990's is estimated as about 6 and the standardized rate (using the age distribution of developed regions) at about 12. These may be compared with the standardized rate for Northern America, which is about 9.

[17] *World Population Prospects* . . ., pp. 21 and 138.

they were not a dominant factor in the world population trend over the last two centuries. As for the future, the share in world population of areas of European settlement may well drop from 35 per cent in 1965 to 31 per cent in the year 2000. This is because their contribution to the increment of population may diminish from 35 per cent over the period 1900-65 to 26 per cent for the last third of the century.[18]

REGIONAL PROSPECTS FOR END OF CENTURY

The geographical distribution of the world's resources and world population, together with the regions' nonsynchronized trends, bring the regional aspects of world population growth into focus. The publication, *World Population Prospects*, has made data available on the world, the less-developed and developed regions as a whole, eight major areas of the world, and twenty-four regions up to the year 2000, and for all countries and some geographical areas to 1980. This is, perhaps, the most comprehensive source for the study of population trends and prospects. According to the medium variant of the UN projections, the last third of the century may bring the demographic changes in eight major areas indicated in Table 8.

The biggest absolute addition to the present population is anticipated in Southern Asia, which has almost one-third of the world population. The three largest countries are the main contributors to this huge growth of population: India, whose population is expected to increase from 483 million in 1965 to 981 million in the year 2000; Pakistan, with an increase from 115 million to

[18] Taking Professor Durand's estimates for the early periods and the UN estimates for the twentieth century, the long-range trends (in millions) are as follows:

Year	World	European Settlement	Share, in per cent
1750	750	165	22
1800	960	230	24
1850	1240	330	27
1900	1650	575	35
1965	3280	1146	35
2000	6129	1903	31

It may be observed that the 1750 figure differs somewhat from estimates made by Carr-Saunders and Willcox in *Proceedings of the World Population Conference*.

TABLE 8 POPULATION OF MAJOR AREAS, 1965 AND 2000
(in millions)

Area	1965	2000	Increment	In Per Cent
Europe	440	527	87	20
U.S.S.R.	231	353	122	53
Northern America	213	354	141	66
Oceania	17	32	15	88
Eastern Asia	852	1,287	435	51
Southern Asia	976	2,171	1,194	122
Latin America	245	638	393	160
Africa	306	768	462	151

SOURCE: *World Population Prospects* . . ., p. 134.

288 million; and Indonesia with a growth of population from 105 million to 152 million in 1980. It should be noticed that the volume of growth of population in this area is closely related to its tempo. The next in importance to Southern Asia is Eastern Asia, where the pace of growth is estimated as very moderate but with an impressive absolute increase. This is due to the slow growth of the population of Japan (from 97 million in 1965 to 122 million in the year 2000), and also the relatively slow but large growth of population of China (from 695 to 1,034 million). It is evident that the bulk of the increment in population of this area is due to the growth of China's population, and that future demographic changes in the area will closely follow the changes in that country's population.

Latin America and Africa are both expected to have large increases in population, coupled with a very fast rate of growth. In fact, the relative growth of the Latin American population may be the highest, followed immediately by the relative growth of population in Africa. Brazil and Mexico will probably contribute the largest share to the growth of population of Latin America (Brazil, from 81 million in 1965 to 211 million in the year 2000). In Africa the largest increase is anticipated for Nigeria, from 58 million in 1965 to 91 million in 1980. But in contrast to the two areas discussed above, neither Latin America nor Africa may be dominated by the growth pattern of a particular country or of a couple of countries.

A substantial growth in population is also estimated for Northern

America (in which the estimated growth for the U.S.A. is from 194 million to 322 million) and for the Soviet Union. The relative growth of these regions is moderate but much higher than the growth of European population, which is in relative terms the lowest.

Among the countries that were mentioned in the preceding analysis, no fewer than six have many common signs of serious economic underdevelopment, though their social structure and political organization differ greatly. Their aggregate population was about 1.5 billion in 1965, representing 47 per cent of the total world population. On the other hand, not more than three of the countries listed may be considered highly industrialized and technologically advanced. Again, they differ substantially in social structure and political organization. Their aggregate population was about 520 million in 1965 or one-seventh of the world's population, and one-third of the population of the six large economically less-developed countries.

ANTICIPATED STRUCTURAL CHANGES

Emphasizing the structural and qualitative problems of the future "development" of population perhaps has its strongest justification in the fact that there is no growth of population that does not have its own structural features.[19] As a matter of fact, all or almost all economic, social, cultural, and political functions have their "demographic framework," which is the stratum of population that is supposed to perform a given function; this is also how population becomes defined and structured economically, socially, educationally, and so forth. Differentiation of the functions is usually related to differentiation among sex and age groups; this is why the sex and age structure of the population has not only demographic but also economic and social meaning. This dif-

---

[19] "Development" of population is understood as a process which is simultaneously quantitative and qualitative, consisting of the growth of population (natural increase and migration) and of its structural changes (changes in biological structure as well as in economic, social, educational, and other relevant structures). For additional comments see Milos Macura, "Réflexions sur les éléments de la théorie démographique," *Economie et Société, publication jubilaire éditée à l'occasion du 70ème anniversaire de M. Le Prof. D. E. Kalitsounakis,* Athens, 1961, pp. 439-62.

TABLE 9 AGE STRUCTURE, 1965 AND 2000
(in per cent)

Area and Year		0-4	5-14	15-24	25-44	45-64	65
Europe	1965	8.5	16.6	14.9	27.6	21.8	10.6
	2000	7.7	15.2	14.5	27.0	22.5	13.1
U.S.S.R.	1965	10.3	20.6	13.8	30.7	17.7	6.9
	2000	9.3	17.8	15.8	26.3	19.6	11.2
Northern	1965	10.6	20.4	15.8	24.2	19.9	9.1
America	2000	10.6	19.2	17.1	26.3	17.9	8.9
Oceania	1965	11.1	20.1	16.5	25.7	18.9	7.7
	2000	11.5	20.1	17.1	25.4	17.4	8.5
Eastern	1965	12.9	22.7	18.0	26.6	15.3	4.5
Asia	2000	9.0	17.5	17.2	29.7	19.2	7.4
Southeast	1965	16.8	25.3	17.8	24.5	12.4	3.2
Asia	2000	12.0	22.5	20.0	27.7	13.2	4.6
Latin	1965	16.6	25.7	18.3	23.8	12.2	3.4
America	2000	13.8	24.2	19.8	25.6	12.3	4.3
Africa	1965	17.1	26.0	19.4	33.9	10.9	2.7
	2000	16.4	25.9	19.5	23.8	11.2	3.2

SOURCE: *World Population Prospects* . . ., pp. 127-31.

ferentiation is also a province in which many changes may be expected during the next thirty-five years (see Table 9).

According to the medium variant, all regions may face a more or less marked relative decline in the young age-group (0-14 years) by the end of the century, while the share of the old-age group (65 years and over) may increase.[20] The Soviet Union and Europe particularly may have a high relative growth of old-age population; perhaps the aging of population will acquire the most imposing characteristics of the growth trend in these two areas. An important relative increase in the working-age group is evident in all regions, but with emphasis on the younger or more mature working-age population, depending on the stage of demographic maturity of particular areas.

Expressed in functional contingents, the anticipation of a change in age structure is, no doubt, very instructive. For lack of space, only estimates for the two large groupings of regions will be given,

---

[20] The proportion of young and old age groups in Northern America and Oceania is somewhat unexpected; it may be understood, however, if assumptions on fertility and mortality are taken into consideration.

TABLE 10. FUNCTIONAL CONTINGENTS, 1965 AND 2000

	World	Developed Regions	Less-Developed Regions
Preschool contingent (0-4 years)			
1965 (millions)	452.0	97.0	355.0
2000 (millions)	705.0	127.0	578.0
Increment (millions)	253.0	30.0	223.0
Per cent increment	55.8	30.9	62.8
Average annual rate of growth	1.28	0.77	1.40
School-age contingent (5-14 years)			
1965 (millions)	751.0	191.0	560.0
2000 (millions)	1,284.0	242.0	1,042.0
Increment (millions)	333.0	51.0	482.0
Per cent increment	71.0	26.7	86.1
Average annual rate of growth	1.55	0.70	1.77
Working contingent (15-64 years)			
1965 (millions)	1,908.0	652.0	1,256.0
2000 (millions)	3,751.0	908.0	2,843.0
Increment (millions)	1,843.0	256.0	1,587.0
Per cent increment	96.6	39.3	126.4
Average annual rate of growth	1.95	0.95	2.36
Old-age contingent (65 years and over)			
1965 (millions)	169.0	91.0	78.0
2000 (millions)	389.0	165.0	224.0
Increment (millions)	220.0	74.0	146.0
Per cent increment	130.2	81.3	187.2
Average annual rate of growth	2.41	1.73	3.06

SOURCE: Population Division of the United Nations (work sheets).

though they might have more meaning if estimates for an eight-area world breakdown could be given. As the expected growth of the female contingent of reproductive age has already been discussed (Table 4), only other major functional contingents will be considered here (Table 10).

The fastest expansion, far beyond what is anticipated for the total population, may be reached by the old-age contingent. Its growth in the less-developed areas, if compared to the present situation, may be particularly fast; but it probably will not constitute more than 6 per cent of the increment in total population between the years 1965 and 2000. In the developed stratum, the relative growth of this contingent is moderate, but economically and socially very important, since it will constitute almost 18 per cent of the increase in total population.

Slower, though even more serious, may be the growth of the working contingent—for well-known reasons arising both from the present employment situation and the capital requirement for new openings. In the less-developed regions, this contingent may rise from 1.2 billion in 1965 to 2.8 billion by the end of the century. Since the already overpopulated agricultural sector could not provide additional employment opportunity, the nonagricultural sector would have to give employment to over 1.2 billion new workers within the next thirty-five years, on the assumption that 80 per cent of the working contingent will enter the labor force.[21] It should be added that, in the developed regions, the working contingent may grow at a slightly lower rate than total population, and that its increase of 260 million amounts to only 60 per cent of total population increment to the end of the century. This, as well as the fact that the structural reserves of labor are almost exhausted in developed countries, may contribute to a growing demand for labor, which may be partly met outside the developed regions. If this happens, it may be a stimulus either for an increase in interregional migration or for growth in mobility of capital.

The next structural problem of population prospects—the fast growth of school-age population—is again concentrated in the less-developed areas. It is true that its relative growth is under what is anticipated for total population. But the absolute number of new students in primary and secondary schools may exceed 1 billion; this would call for a tremendous extension of education facilities, which even now fall far short of needs. No doubt the developed countries may also encounter new educational problems, but their demographic component may be far smaller, even almost negligible.

As an illustration only and without any intention to discuss the complex issues of future education further, the growth of illiteracy will be briefly mentioned. According to the latest UNESCO estimates, the rate of illiteracy was reduced from 43 per cent to 39 per cent from 1950 to 1960. At the same time, the number of illiterate

---

[21] Compare with the average relative increase in nonagricultural employment as suggested by Ansley Coale on the assumption that the increment in the labor force is to be employed outside agriculture—Ansley Coale, "Population and Economic Development," in Philip Hauser, ed., *The Population Dilemma* (Englewood Cliffs, N.J.: Prentice-Hall, Inc.), pp. 66-68.

adult population increased from 700 million to 740 million. Allowing for deaths, among which the aged illiterate population is a large proportion, an estimate of 290 million new illiterates was made for the period under consideration.[22]

If a broad generalization concerning demographic prospects over the next thirty-five years is permitted, it could be said that the average annual rate of growth of population of 1.8 per cent would call for a faster expansion of all kinds of consumption than during the last twenty years. It might also be suggested that the long-range problems of the employment and investment complex would need an even speedier and more energetic solution, since the working contingent is expected to grow by almost 2 per cent. A faster expansion in education and training may also be needed to meet not only a high 1.5 per cent rate in growth of school-age population, but also to accommodate the large numbers of new students emerging from the large increments in population. An extremely high growth of the old-age contingent, over 2.4 per cent, would open new questions both of an economic and a social nature. A final general observation must underline the fact that the greatest and most profound changes, not only in numbers but also in the structure of population, will take place in the less-developed parts of the world, where needs and resources are even now considerably out of balance with one another.

Hopes and Expectations

As a kind of relief from the somewhat gloomy outlook indicated above, and a transition to more optimistic hopes and expectations, a brief mention may be made of the virtually tacit set of hypotheses on which the UN study of future population is based. Neither the UN projections nor the projections worked out by individual authors allowed for the possibility of disturbed growth of population during the next thirty-five years. Detailed series indicate that fertility and mortality, as well as the sex-age structure and the total population, follow a continuous trend shaped by the logic of assump-

---

[22] *Statistical Yearbook, 1965* (New York: United Nations, 1966), pp. 32-33. Critical situations are being encountered in Africa, where the illiterate population grew by 20.3 million in ten years; Eastern Asia by 16.9 million; and Southern Asia by 7.2 million.

tions, which have already been mentioned. The possibility of war was excluded, and its demographic consequences were not considered at all.[23] This assumption and its attendant implications seemed feasible for many reasons, not all of them necessarily of a technical nature.

Also excluded were the possibilities of great famines and pandemic diseases, which in the past have been important checks to population growth.[24] The effect of malnutrition was perhaps taken into account in assuming higher mortality with slower declines in the less-developed regions. But, as already pointed out, there were no signs of excessive mortality, and therefore no excessive mortality that might be the consequence of either famine or pandemic diseases. The no-war, no-famine, and no-pandemic assumptions, together with the assumption of improving health and medical conditions, seem to be realistic. The last twenty years have provided a sound basis for such hypotheses, since none of the three factors has occurred to influence mortality, except in a few unfortunate and tragic instances of local importance. There may therefore be hope that, in view of mankind's growing awareness, responsibility, and concern for his own well-being, addi-

[23] Demographic war losses were not given adequate attention in many recent publications despite their importance for several countries. Frumkin has estimated that Europe's second war losses exceeded 15 million, to be compared with a "normal" mortality of 38 million in the period 1939-45 and a 1938 population of 380 million. The heaviest losses were in group III, consisting of Poland, Czechoslovakia, Romania, Yugoslavia, Bulgaria, and Greece: 8.7 million war losses, 10.5 million "normal" mortality in relation to a pre-war population of 97 million. The losses of the Soviet Union were estimated at 17 million, to be compared to a pre-war population of 193 million. See Gregory Frumkin, *Population Changes in Europe Since 1939* (New York: A. M. Kelley, 1951), pp. 15-164 and 168-173.

[24] The famine factor is hardly mentioned in recent literature and is replaced by the malnutrition and hunger concept. Before World War II, it was widely discussed, particularly by Indian authors. Wattal states that "The rate of increase from 1872 to 1881 [Wattal says 1.5 per cent for ten years] was effected by the great Indian famine of 1876 to 1878. Famine was again responsible for the low figure [1.4 per cent] for the period 1891-1901. Similarly, the figure for 1921 [1.2 per cent growth from 1911 to 1921] was unduly low owing to the influenza epidemic of 1918, which was responsible for 12.5 million deaths. . . . The increase recorded during the period 1921-1931, namely 10.6 per cent, or 1 per cent per annum, may be regarded as normal in the sense that there was no great natural calamity to check the growth of the population." See P. K. Wattal, *The Population Problem in India* (New Delhi: Minerva Book Shop, 1958), pp. 7-8. Compare B. M. Bhatia, *Famines in India and Their Effect on Administration and Economic Policy (1860-1908)*, (Bombay: Asia Publishing House, 1963).

tional efforts may be made to avoid war and its destruction and to eradicate famine, as the two major possible sources of suffering and unjustified increase in mortality.

In *World Population Prospects,* the broad economic, social, and cultural considerations that underlie the assumption on fertility decline are perhaps also tacit. All three variants of projections allow for a decline in fertility; the magnitude of that decline may be measured by the difference between the numbers of population estimated by "constant fertility" and the medium variant, which is about 1.4 billion people by the year 2000. This is an important change in reproductive pattern, the greater portion of which is anticipated in the less-developed regions. This change is expected to occur following a "continuing substantial progress in economic and social development" that is "implicit in the assumptions on which the estimates are based."[25]

The difficulties in studying the relationships between the trends in fertility and the relevant social, economic, and cultural processes are many and well known, and they do not need to be mentioned here. Owing to diversified demographic patterns and to different models of economic and social development, these difficulties are even greater in the less-developed countries viewed as a single stratum of the world, with implications of the highest importance for the subject under consideration. Since, however, these relationships have to be discussed, despite possible bias or oversimplification, they may be classified under three broad headings: economic development and social change; cultural and psychological adjustments; and family planning programs. For the sake of convenience, recent experience will be examined first and future prospects later.

In the study of fertility, economic and social progress is usually taken to mean the combination of factors and processes that induce change in the reproductive behavior of individuals and in reproductive patterns of the population as a whole. Emphasis may differ according to the definition given to "economic" and "social," but there is no question as to their relevance; on this there is general agreement. The modest 5 per cent rate of economic growth of developing countries established as a goal by the United Nations Development Decade is not likely to be achieved, owing to inadequate progress during the first half of the decade.[26] Produc-

---

[25] *World Population Prospects* . . ., p. 6.

tion (understood here also as the pattern of employment of individuals and families) and consumption (conceived in terms of standard of living) did not attain such levels as to produce accompanying elements of a noneconomic nature, which would induce an automatic decline in the number of children in families. Female employment in nonagricultural industries, which is important in this context, failed owing to the high pressure of the male labor force on employment opportunities. Despite a high rate of urbanization in the less-developed regions (4.7 per cent in the 1950's), almost two-thirds of the population constituting the increase in rural population remained in the countryside, thus creating an additional imbalance between population and agricultural resources.[27] As previously mentioned, the relative improvement in literacy was to a large extent offset by rising numbers of illiterates. Many other signs of economic and social progress, which initially were highly promising per se lost much significance when viewed in per capita terms. This is an extremely paradoxical situation, in which the real results and achievements of man's efforts were diminished because they do not keep pace with man's rapid reproduction.

Under such circumstances, it is very hard to say to what extent social institutions and cultural values in general, and those in particular that have relevance to reproductive behavior, have changed. During the last few years many encouraging studies have

[26] Report of the Secretary-General, *The United Nations Development Decade, Proposals for Action* (UN publication 62.II.B2; New York: United Nations, 1966), pp. 7 and 25-38. "But the hard fact remains that the output of developing countries as a whole increased more slowly in the first half of the nineteen-sixties than it had during the nineteen-fifties. The slower progress in development, moreover, has been accompanied by the emergence or aggravation of major imbalances which imperil future growth. Instead of receding into the past, the age-old scourges of famine and epidemics have recently returned to haunt the minds of men; in some areas of the world, these are threats which have begun to assume critical proportions"—Interim Report prepared by the Secretary-General, *United Nations Development Decade* (E/4196; New York: United Nations, 1966), p. 5. "It is not surprising, then, that uncontrolled acceleration of population increase and rural-urban migration are now considered major deterrents to real economic progress in many countries" (p. 85).

[27] The growth of nonagricultural industries in the less-developed regions had hardly surpassed the growth of the urban population of 4.7 per cent per annum. The rate of growth of 1.5 per cent of the rural population was either equal to or slightly lower than the agricultural production in less-developed countries (Milos Macura, "Demographic Factors in Urban Development, *International Conference of Social Work*, XIII (1966).

been carried out in less-developed countries; the findings indicate that there is a preference towards having a smaller family, approval of birth control, and a need for education in contraceptive techniques.[28] It seems, accordingly, that the cultural values that have tended to encourage high fertility in the less-developed countries are being gradually abandoned, and that new social norms concerning fertility are being established.

There is no indication, however, how this important change will fit into the cultural context of a society that has limited resources and a low level of living, or how the new social norms regulating reproductive behavior of individuals will fit in with other social norms, which have not yet changed because of lack of external encouragement. There is also no indication whether and to what extent subjective psychological factors exert an influence upon change in social institutions that have relevance to questions of reproductive behavior.

The influence of social and cultural values is, indeed, a difficult and complex subject, which, if interpreted inaccurately, may mislead theoretical thinking and also family planning programs now under implementation. A spontaneous change in reproductive behavior would be very slow under prevailing circumstances in less-developed countries, and also ineffective in coping with the fast-growing and excessive fertility. If new trends are desired, they have to be stimulated by educating people and by creating circumstances in which they may decide the size of their family. Family planning programs have therefore been launched in not less than thirteen countries with a total of 1.5 billion population.

So far there has not been a comprehensive evaluation of the per-

---

[28] Bernard Berelson, "A Review of Major Governmental Programs," in *Proceedings of the World Population Conference*, II. See also "Studies Relevant to Family Planning" and statement by rapporteur, I, pp. 103-113; also Bernard Berelson and others, eds., "KAP Studies on Fertility," *Population and Family Planning Programs: A Review of World Developments* (Chicago: University of Chicago, 1966), pp. 657-64.

Berelson's generalization "with regard to attitudes toward family planning . . . in developing countries" is as follows: practice family planning now, 5-20%, say 10%; have some detailed information about reproduction and contraception, 10-40%, say, 20%; want no more children, of families with three or more, 40-60%, say, 50%; interested in learning about family planning, 50-70%, say, 60%; and approve of birth control, 65-80%, say, 75%."

The findings of the surveys conducted by the UN Latin American Demographic Center in seven cities of Latin America, communicated to the Economic

formance of national family planning programs. Many recently published papers deal with early aspects of population programs, such as the need for family planning, social and cultural acceptability, evaluation problems, and so on, while other studies discuss particular problems of a demographic or biomedical nature. The first comprehensive assessment of a large-scale family planning program was made by a UN technical assistance mission two years ago.[29] It drew the attention of political and technical circles to a series of problems, which were preventing the program from achieving greater success. Perhaps these and similar problems may be met when analyzing the implementation of population programs in other countries as well.

IN CONCLUSION, it may be pointed out that the recent years have not favored the development of conditions needed for a rapid change in fertility in the less-developed regions. Economic growth has been rather slow and insufficient; social change is still in its early stages; the idea of a small family gained support but has no firm place in the institutional framework; population programs appeared and expanded with many accompanying difficulties; finally, it should be noted that individual developments, which for a while may have encouraged a progressive change in fertility, were neither always synchronized nor mutually supporting.

As for the future, production must grow to meet the needs of the fast-growing population and to provide it with productive employment. The mobilization of resources and the adaptation of different types of society in ways that will more than double world production during the next thirty-five years—with emphasis on the less-developed regions—will be the most challenging tests of mankind's ability. It will also be necessary to supplement production programs by other programs; by the end of the century, there will

Commission for Latin America, are similar. They indicate that "urban women in general would prefer to have fewer children than they actually have, and that they resort to contraceptive methods, usually ineffective, with which they are familiar, to a much larger extent than was previously believed. Indeed, the findings of these surveys indicate that the peoples of Latin America are ahead of their leaders in their receptive attitude to population control"—Economic Commission for Latin America, *Official Records, Economic and Social Council of the United Nations* (Annual Report; New York: United Nations), p. 34.

[29] Report prepared for the government of India by UN Advisory Mission, *Report on the Family Planning Programme in India* (Document TAO/IND/48; New York: United Nations, 1966).

be over 6 billion people to be fed and nearly 3 billion to be employed. Sound and efficient population programs organized as integral parts of economic and social development should help to keep future population trends far below the potential 7.5 billion people by the end of the century. These programs should also help the family to complete its transformation into a modern form in a rather short time. By moderating the growth of population, the programs will also prevent excessive young age-structure, and thus facilitate the implementation of economic and social programs that deal with particular functional contingents of population.

It may also be expected that rapid economic growth, accompanied by progressive social change, will bring about new elements in institutional setting, cultural values, social norms, and behavior of individuals. Within a broad framework of transition from traditional to contemporary society, from primitive to modern technology, from an exclusively agricultural to an industrialized economy, from rural to urban community, from a life of want to one of abundance—a transition that the less-developed regions must undergo on an accelerating scale—the establishment of modern reproductive behavior will no doubt be an important element of progress. It will be an element that will not arise *post factum,* but will emerge as a part of popular emancipation and as a contributing factor to genuine development.

Comments on Macura

JOHN D. DURAND

*Professor of Economics and Sociology
  and Chairman, Graduate Group in Demography,
University of Pennsylvania*

DR. MACURA's paper is like the Kennedy Airport with its many runways inviting the reader to take off in a dozen different directions. I am going to yield to the temptation to take at least one flight despite the hazards involved, but first I will make a few observations on the aerodrome and its construction.

Dr. Macura makes it plain that these population projection runways are built on land that is swampy in many places—the great swamps of China and Africa are especially treacherous—and he warns us about the frailties of the aircraft being such that even those launched from the firmest ground cannot be guaranteed to follow a true course over any great distance. It is one of the marks of quality in the work of the United Nations demographers that these frailties, which are inherent in all long-range population projections, are clearly pointed out in the publication of the projections as a warning to the users. Dr. Macura adds emphasis to the point by referring to two other sets of world population projections (made by Professor Bogue and Professor Boyarsky), which give totals considerably below the "low" variant of the UN projections for the year 2000. While I agree that these have to be included in the range of possibilities, I think they are rather far from the center of plausibility within that range.

In their different ways, Professor Bogue and Professor Boyarsky are great optimists. Our respected colleague, Professor Bogue, looks forward to early total victory in the family-planning crusade. He sees reason, armed with pills and coils, triumphing over the folly of excessive reproduction within a few years or at most a decade or two, in the most obstinate fortresses of the world's poverty and ignorance. The possibility that this vision will come true cannot be denied, but in trying to assess the probability we have to take account of the experience up to the present time with efforts to promote family planning in areas of high fertility, low income, little industrialization, and a low level of popular education. In terms of effects on national birthrates, the results in most cases are scarcely perceptible as yet. It is true that decreases of fertility have been recorded in some areas, notably in Taiwan and Korea, and possibly these may be interpreted as signs of a turning tide—although it is not sure how much of the credit in these cases is due to the family-planning programs.

Also in Mainland China, the government's antinatalist policies may have produced some effect on the birthrate, but if so, no measure of it is available. In India, the birthrate seems to be unmoved as yet by a decade of rather gradually intensifying birth control promotional activities, although some pavement has undoubtedly been laid on which the bandwagon may begin to roll at some future time. The declaration of India's new health minister in favor of sterilization as the main instrument for the national population policy does not inspire much confidence in the early achievement of rapid control. Likewise in Pakistan, Indonesia, the Philippines, the Arab countries, and the tropics of Africa and America, what has been done so far in the direction of moderating fertility does not provide much basis for predicting early decisive downward movements of the birthrates. In fact, with regard to most of the underdeveloped world, such a prediction appears to be founded more on hopeful speculation than on any objective precedents.

Professor Boyarsky's optimism is of a different and still more appealing brand. The early victory that he anticipates is not in family-planning campaigns but in the greater war on poverty, ignorance, technological backwardness, and archaic social institutions. In formulating his projections, Professor Boyarsky takes it for granted that before the end of this century the presently underdeveloped regions will all graduate to the developed class and that their vital rates will automatically be assimilated to those of industrialized societies. This is a brighter vision than Bogue's, since it relieves us of the worry that the advantage of controlled fertility might not be enough to enable the underdeveloped countries to make very rapid progress in economic and social advancement. It is more optimistic also in its contrast with experience up to the present time. So far as the prospect of victory in fertility control is concerned, it can be argued that high optimism should be permitted simply because the relevant experience is so limited.

In the fields of economic and social development of underdeveloped countries, on the other hand, we have the record of two decades of widespread and diversified efforts in the postwar era, and, by any candid appraisal of the results, we have to recognize that they have been, on the whole, discouragingly small.

CONTRARY TO the views of Professor Bogue and Professor Boyarsky, many demographers are of the opinion that the UN projections, at least in the "medium" variant, understate the amount of increase in the world population that is likely to take place between now and the year 2000. Dr. Macura will remember the debate on this question at the last session of the UN Population Commission, where he was the representative of Yugoslavia and acted as the rapporteur. While Podyachichk, representing the U.S.S.R., criticized even the "low" variant of the Secretariat's projections as running too high, Dr. Ansley Coale, representing the United States, and some other members of the commission thought that the "medium" variant was too optimistic in its assumptions as to the dates at which fertility declines would begin in various underdeveloped regions and the speed with which fertility would be reduced. In fact, the previous versions of world population projections issued by the UN have consistently undershot the short-range if not the long-range marks, and the test of time might well prove this latest version again to be too conservative an assessment of the growth that is in store.

I think the "medium" variant of these projections represents a moderately optimistic assessment of expectations for success both in the family-planning movement and in economic and social development of the less-developed countries. The essential features of the projection framework can be summed up quickly. It is assumed that there will be no great wars, no major famines, no deadly pandemic, and that steady progress will be made in economic and social development of less-developed areas. In other words, failure and disaster are ruled out, as it is appropriate to do if one wishes to represent the demographic magnitudes involved in the tasks of avoiding disaster and achieving success. On the other hand, major breakthroughs in science, technology, and social organization that would radically alter the conditions of economic and demographic development are likewise assumed not to occur; this assumption, too, is appropriate to the purpose. The pace at which economic and social developments will go forward is not specified, but it is presumed to be sufficient to create favorable conditions for a steady and moderately rapid demographic transition in the less-developed regions; such a transition is presumed to be promoted at the same time by national measures of population policy. The transition envisaged is such that, upon its completion, the pattern of vital rates in the presently less-developed parts of the world would resemble the pattern now prevailing in more developed areas: universally low mortality rates and fertility rates in a low to moderate range, generating population growth at annual rates in the range from less than 0.5 per cent in some areas to 1 per cent or more in others. Meanwhile, this kind of demographic pattern, which has already been established in more developed countries, is assumed to continue there with some modifications but no very great change on the whole. The idea is that the fertility transition in more developed countries has been mostly completed and that there is not a great deal of room left for further progress in mortality reduction; the outlook in these parts of the world is then, on the whole, one of relatively flat long-range trends of mortality and fertility rates with population growth continuing at slow to moderate rates for an indefinite time.

In fitting specific assumptions for future mortality and fertility trends to this framework, the principal questions that arise relate to the timing and magnitude of the fertility decreases anticipated in less-developed countries. The UN projection architects have drawn up a model of the fertility transition in which the sex-age adjusted birthrate is reduced in thirty years to one-half its original level and is stabilized thereafter. The assumption of a reduction by one-half is just a rule of thumb; while it does seem to correspond to the magnitude of fertility reductions that have been experienced in a number of Western countries, it has to be admitted that past experience provides no sure guideline in this respect. The assumption that the transition takes thirty years is meant to allow for the expectation that improved means of communication, improved techniques of birth control, and organized programs for promoting the practice of it will speed up a process that took much longer in most of the countries in which the fertility transition has already been experienced. The projected population figures as of the year 2000 for several of the less-developed regions would be changed appreciably by substituting different assumptions, particularly as to the length of the transition period. The more critical question, though, is the date at which the transition is assumed to begin in each area. Various dates have been selected for its beginning in the different regions of high fertility, depending on economic, cultural, political, and other conditions. According to these assumptions, the transition would already be beginning in some areas, whereas it would be delayed one or two decades or even longer elsewhere. There is ample room for differences of expert opinion with regard to the specification of these dates, and different specifications have important effects on the projected population trends. To a large extent, the deviations of the "low" and "high" variants from the "medium" in the UN projections represent effects of differing assumptions as to these beginning dates.

Dr. Macura notes a narrowing of the range between the variants in successive revisions of the UN projections and asks whether this can be considered as an indication of increasing certainty in assumption building, with increasing experience in the making of such projections. Possibly so, but I do not think that this kind of experience is the most important factor in the degree of assurance with which one can use the projections. I think the main hope of increasing assurance in future revisions lies in the opportunities that the future may afford for observing the responses of fertility trends to continuing economic and social developments, and to expanding and improving population policy programs. Also important in this connection is the widening and deepening knowledge of demographic, economic, and social interrelationships, which can be gained from better data collection and more research in this sphere.

While we cannot avoid and should not wish to avoid being concerned with the uncertainty of the projections and the need to strengthen their basis, we should not let these concerns distract our attention from the picture of the future that these projections present, however tentatively. With due respect to Professors Boyarsky and Bogue, as Dr. Macura says, we should be prepared for the fact that massive population growth in the less-developed regions of the world may continue for some time. Our thinking and planning should be geared to the expectation of larger and larger additions each year to the number of mouths to be fed, families to be housed and provided with medical services and other essentials, and hands to be trained and employed. I do not think that our thinking about these matters should be limited to the period of these population projections. We should bear in mind that it appears likely, according to present indications, that this proliferation of humanity that we are witnessing will continue well into the next century if not beyond. Despite the anticipated decreases of fertility, the "medium" UN projection shows population in the group of less-developed countries as a whole increasing during the 1990's at a rate only slightly lower than the present rate, and it does not seem likely that this momentum would be quickly spent. It is not at all out of the question that the twenty-first century might outdo the twentieth in the magnitude of its addition to the world population.

We will be discussing various implications of this prospect in the course of the conference. I should like to mention one aspect of the matter that I do not see in our agenda, but which I think deserves the most thoughtful consideration, if not actual discussion on this occasion. I have in mind the implications of this population expansion for the problem of world political as well as economic order. When we think of the problems of the future, we tend to project our accustomed concepts of the world in terms of its institutional and organizational arrangements along with the population, the per capita production figures, and other such magnitudes, but these accustomed concepts may be incompatible with the changed orders of magnitudes we are envisaging. I invite you to contemplate a world in which the Indian nation might number eventually at least 1.5 billion and the Chinese perhaps still more, according to a reckoning that is not out of line with the figures Dr. Macura is presenting for the year 2000, and to consider that these mammoth nations would have a *developed* economy, in keeping with the basic premises of our projection model. That is to say, they would have per capita income perhaps ten times greater than they have at present, or more, with the mighty industrial complexes that such a condition implies.

Are we to imagine our present system of national allotments of space on the earth's surface and shares of its resources being maintained in such circumstances? And what of the anarchical system of organization of the world in sovereign states to which we are clinging? Can we conceive of the demographic and economic conditions of the future world that we are contemplating coming into evidence or being maintained under such an organization of national sovereignty? I do not think so. It seems to me that the population expansion is one of the primary forces that are driving humanity relentlessly to the choice between unity and self-destruction.

ECONOMIC AND TECHNOLOGICAL ASPECTS

Economic Capacity
and Population Growth

Simon Kuznets

*George F. Baker Professor of Economics,
Harvard University*

Given the sharp rise in the rate of growth of world population over the last two to three decades and the concentration of this growth in the less-developed countries, we are faced with the question of whether world economic capacity is equal to the strain thus imposed on it. Production of an adequate supply of the required goods, while not the *only* function of the economic system, is surely the first priority goal. Therefore, we concentrate in this paper on the economic capacity to produce enough to satisfy the needs of the rapidly growing population projected for the future.

Capacity to Produce (With Special Emphasis on Food)

This review is limited to the period to the year 2000 and emphasizes the requirements for and supply of food. These two limitations are easily justified on grounds of expediency: the authoritative world population projections terminate in 2000, and the easily available analyses of requirements and of the capacities to satisfy them deal largely with food and other natural resource industries. There are, however, more illuminating reasons for so circumscribing our review. The time limitation reflects the difficulty inherent in projecting over a longer period the process of technological and institutional change, since the latter moves at a rapid rate, and the cumulative interaction of its effects over a long period is not measurable in tolerably acceptable quantitative terms.[1]

The emphasis on requirements for and supply of food limits our view to only *one* complex of natural resource-based industries, but it is clearly the most important; we can supplement our detailed consideration of this complex with brief reference to other resource industries, largely mineral. At any rate, our discussion must stress the capacity to provide the necessary basic goods rather than dispensable goods (unless for some country or region, under conditions of international division of labor, the dispensable goods can be used to purchase the necessary).

Two sets of estimates of food requirements for the prospectively much larger world population have been published recently by the Food and Agriculture Organization; we will consider these, with special attention to the underdeveloped, low-calorie regions (Table 1). The population projections shown here for the less-developed regions are fairly close to those of the United Nations, being between the "medium" and "high" variants of the latter.[2] The definitions of these variants, which differ largely with respect to

---

[1] This rapidity of technological and institutional change is a function of the greatly increased technological power of mankind; the latter also means the increasing control over death, which has led to acceleration in the rate of population increase and thus paradoxically intensified the concern with the adequacy of our productive capacity while making it impossible to gauge such capacity beyond a relatively short span. Were we to pose the same question for the premodern centuries, when technology changed at what was relatively a snail's pace, a longer time span could be projected—with the emphasis on the stock of available nonreproducible resources and a barely changing stock of technology.

[2] The decadal rate of growth of the population of the low-calorie regions assumed in Table 1 for the period 1958-2000 is 24.0 per cent for the earlier estimate and 24.4 per cent for the later estimate (see Table 4, line 12, columns 1 and 2). For the period between 1960 and 2000, the decadal rate of growth in the UN population projections, with a rough allowance for the shift of the River Plate countries from Latin America and hence from the underdeveloped regions, works out to 23.5 per cent in the medium projection and to 28.1 per cent in the high projection.

See *World Population Prospects as Assessed in 1963* (New York: United Nations, 1966), Table A3.2, p. 134; Table A3.3, p. 135; and Table A3.8, p. 144. The trends in Tables A3.2 and A3.3 for temperate South America, which includes Chile in addition to the River Plate countries, were applied to the 1960 totals for the latter countries in Table A3.8, and the results were subtracted from the totals for the underdeveloped countries in Tables A3.2 and A3.3.

the date of the onset of the expected decline in fertility, are given in the original source. Here it suffices to say that "the 'medium' estimates are intended to represent the future population trend that now appears most plausible."[3] Hence the allowances for population growth in the low-calorie regions, made in the FAO estimates of requirements, appear to be adequate—although, as will be indicated in Table 4, the rates are slightly lower than those observed over the last quinquennium.

The detailed discussions of per capita food requirements in the year 2000 in the FAO, Freedom From Hunger Campaign, Basic Studies Nos. 10 and 11, dismiss any need to match the dietary patterns of the high-calorie countries in Group II, in which "the problem is often one of overeating rather than undereating, though malnutrition is still to be found in certain social groups and in certain areas" (Basic Study No. 10, p. 21). No targets are set for Group II countries in Basic Study No. 10, and to complete the picture we assumed per capita food requirements for that group in 2000 equal to per capita supplies in 1958. The later FAO study does allow for increases in food supplies per capita in Group II countries, but they are minor.

The more important task of setting the food requirement levels for the low-calorie countries involves estimating (a) calorie supplies necessary to sustain life and provide for the work energy needs, while allowing for the unavoidable wastage between production and consumption and for some inequalities in distribution; and (b) protein supplies, particularly in animal but also in vegetable form, necessary to assure a minimum quality of diet. In the earlier study, the per capita daily requirements in year 2000 for the four major regions in Group I are put between 2,400 and 2,500 calories, between 42 and 57 grams of vegetable proteins, and at 20 grams of animal proteins (see Basic Study No. 10, Table 2, pp. 24-25). In the second study the calorie requirement remains the same; animal protein requirements vary (among the four regions) between 20 and 25 grams; and vegetable protein requirements are within a more limited range from 46 to 54 grams (see Basic Study No. 11, Table 20, p. 57).

More important than the minor differences between the two sets

---

[3] *World Population Prospects as Assessed in 1963*, p. 6.

of estimates is the fact that both fix the food targets in the low-calorie countries in year 2000 at modest levels—at least in comparison with the levels now prevailing in the developed countries in Group II (granted the difference in climatic conditions). In 1958, per capita daily consumption in the developed countries was over 3,000 calories and 134 grams of proteins of which 44 grams were animal (see Basic Study No. 10, Table 1, p. 14). As Table 1 shows, even attainment of the targets would mean an economic value in year 2000 of per capita food consumption less than half that of current per capita food intake in Group II countries. But the requirements are meant to represent a "sufficient" nutritional goal, and if attained would constitute an adequate level of per capita food consumption and one significantly closer to that of the Group II countries than today.

We come now to the main question: are these targets attainable? Are the natural resources and the technological knowledge at hand sufficient to assure the attainment of the required food supply levels —considering that they mean a rise of 67 to 70 per cent in per capita food supplies in the Far East and of between 30 and 50 per cent in Africa and, with the prospective population increases, a tripling or quadrupling of total food supplies (see Table 1, lines 8-11, columns 2, 5, and 6)? The answer in Basic Study No. 10, devoted primarily to this problem, is, on the whole, in the affirmative; so is the one based on the later estimates, given in the paper presented at the 1965 UN World Population Conference (see footnotes to Table 1).

In Basic Study No. 10 the answer is given region by region, rather than for the world as a whole, because "it is unlikely that imports of food from the wealthier to the less wealthy regions can ever provide more than a small part of the needs. This would still remain true even if commercial imports were supplemented by substantial grants-in-aid through free distribution of surplus foodstuffs" (p. 221). In this consideration by regions, no serious question arises about Europe, North America, and Oceania. Here one can repeat what the study says about North America: "Resources, or future production capacity, are certainly capable of taking care of any probable requirements, with capacity to spare" (p. 221). The question then is about the four underdeveloped regions.

In Latin America and Africa, the physical resources are unquestionably ample, without approaching their full utilization, to meet the estimated increases required. . . . in the Near East, an increase in production in excess of threefold [required; see Table 1] would push utilization of resources much closer to the limits set by present technical knowledge than would be the case in either Latin America or Africa . . . it is an area in which there may be cause for some disquiet from the point of view of the natural resources. Water is strictly the limiting factor. . . . Of course, all this might be changed by the desalinization of sea water at costs which would be economic for irrigation, though transportation costs to areas far removed from the coast could still remain a problem. . . . In the Far East the balance between future food needs and known potentialities for production may well prove to be delicate. . . . If governments go about their task of planning agricultural development, armed with a clear and realistic knowledge of the feasible goals, the chances of bringing about a better balance between needs and production before it is too late will be considerably enhanced.[4]

The general conclusion is thus to affirm technological feasibility of the food requirements assumed for year 2000. Basic Study No. 10 concludes by saying that "the existence of large untapped resources of nature and knowledge represents a challenge to the ability and good will of man to solve a problem which is capable of solution" (p. 223). And this conclusion is repeated, with reference to somewhat higher food production targets for 2000, in the paper prepared for the 1965 World Population Conference: "It would appear that within the next twenty years (and even up to the end of the century) the technical possibilities for increasing production are more than adequate to meet the full needs of the growing population" (pp. 31-32).

The general grounds for inferring technological feasibility of the food supply targets given above, and the more specific meaning of the feasibility conclusions, will be discussed in the following section. Before doing so, we present a summary of the trends in food production and supplies, total and per capita, observed in the recent past—so that the targets for year 2000 and the rates of growth required to reach them can be viewed against the background of recent growth rates.

Table 2 summarizes the trends in food production since the late 1920's—a period of three and one-half to four decades, the longest for which food and population estimates for the world

[4] Freedom From Hunger Campaign, *Possibilities of Increasing World Food Production* (Basic Study No. 10; Rome: Food and Agriculture Organization, 1963), pp. 221-23.

and the low and high calorie regions, are available.⁵ Four aspects of the trends merit explicit mention.

First, for the world as a whole, food production grew rather slowly between 1925-29 and 1948-52, probably as a result of the depression and the war.⁶ Indeed, for the world, including Mainland China, the rate of growth of food production, 9 per cent per decade, was lower than that of world population, 10.7 per cent per decade— so that per capita world food output declined almost 2 per cent from 1925-29 to 1948-52 (Table 2, lines 20, 23, 26). In the post-war period growth in world food production accelerated to 33 per cent per decade; thus, despite the marked rise in the rate of growth of world population, per capita food production rose 9 or 10 per cent per decade (column 3). On balance, however, in the full span of some thirty-six years (from 1927 to 1963, the midpoints of the two terminal periods) the growth of world food production per capita was less than 2 per cent per decade (column 4).

Second, while *total* food output grew over the full period at about the same rate in the low-calorie and in the high-calorie regions (16.8 and 17.7 per cent per decade for the longest period,

---

⁵ The League of Nations estimates of "foodstuffs" include "food crops, meat, sea fish, milk, beverages, tobacco, as well as part of the group of oil materials and oils; this group thus includes partly crude foodstuffs ready for consumption and partly raw materials of the food, drink and tobacco industries" (see *World Production and Prices, 1936-37* (Geneva: League of Nations, 1937), Appendix I, p. 98). The index is an aggregative one, using quantities multiplied by "representative 'world' prices ruling in 1930, expressed in terms of gold dollars according to average annual rates of exchange" (p. 98).

The FAO food production indexes include "grains, starchy roots, sugar, pulses, oil crops, nuts, fruit, vegetables, wine, livestock, and livestock products. To avoid double counting, allowances are made for commodities used for livestock feeding; these include products fed as such, and semi-processed feeds such as oilcakes and bran. In addition, to the extent that adequate estimates are possible, allowances are also made for imported feeds, seed, and production waste." See Freedom From Hunger Campaign, *Third World Food Survey* (Basic Study No. 11; Rome: Food and Agriculture Organization, 1963), p. 80. The indexes are constructed by applying regional weights, based either on 1934-38 or 1952-56 farm price relationships, to the production figures.

Although the League of Nations and the FAO indexes differ somewhat in scope, the former can be used for rough extrapolation of the latter.

⁶ The findings for the world and the low-calorie regions including and excluding Mainland China are fairly similar. Mainland China was excluded so that the estimates in Table 2 could be used in conjunction with those in which the four low-calorie regions are distinguished, and in which the Far East omits Mainland China.

and 19.3 and 20.9 per cent for 1936-63; see lines 18 and 19, columns 4 and 5), population grew at much higher rates in the former than in the latter (18 or 20 per cent per decade and about 9 per cent respectively; see lines 21 and 22, columns 4 and 5). As a result, from 1936 to 1963 food output per capita grew much less in the low-calorie than in the high-calorie group—either declining 0.5 per cent per decade (including Mainland China) or rising 0.4 per cent per decade (excluding Mainland China), compared with a rise of 11 per cent per decade in the high-calorie regions (lines 24, 25, and 31, column 5). But in both groups, the postwar period witnessed a much higher rate of growth of total and of per capita food production than the prewar years.

Third, as a result of these differences in trends in per capita output, the relative disparity in per capita food production between the low- and high-calorie regions widened over time. The ratio of per capita food output in high-calorie to that in low-calorie regions, including Mainland China, rose from 2.8 in 1925-29 to 3.8 in 1962-64 (line 16); in the comparison excluding Mainland China, the ratio rose from 2.8 in 1934-38 to 3.7 in 1962-64 (line 17).

Finally, since the low-calorie, underdeveloped regions are our primary interest, the trends in their per capita food output should be noted particularly. From 1925-29 to 1948-52 this per capita food production dropped about 11 per cent—a decline not quite made up in the next eight years (from 1948-52 to 1957-59)—and in the last observed quinquennium, 1957-59 to 1962-64, it was at a standstill (line 7). In almost four decades per capita food output in the low-calorie regions showed no significant rise.

This discussion relates to observable trends in food production, not in food supplies, and does not distinguish the four major regions within the low-calorie group. We supplement it by distinguishing these four regions and providing estimates of both food supplies and food output (Table 3).

Table 3 is, however, subject to several qualifications. First, we calculated supplies by adjusting domestic production by the net balance of exports and imports—disregarding the possible contribution of net changes in domestic inventories. Second, in deriving the net balance of imports and exports, and hence the shift from output to supplies, for the high-calorie group we relied on weights and indexes for Western Europe, North America, and Oceania—thus omitting Eastern Europe (and the U.S.S.R.)—and included the River Plate countries with Latin America and the low-calorie group. Third, at several steps in the calculations, we had to introduce adjustments to assure conformity of the weighted averages of indexes for the individual regions with the indexes for the low- and high-calorie groups as wholes (from Table 2), and to make the world net balance of exports and imports equal zero. But all these qualifications are minor, because net changes in inventories cannot affect long-term trends appreciably, because the weight of Eastern Europe and of the River Plate countries in output and trade of the high-calorie group is limited, and because the conformity adjustments were all small.

The additional detail reveals that it was in the Far East and in Latin America that the per capita food output declined over the full period from 1934-38 to 1962-64 (line 11, columns 1 and 4). In the Far East, marked by the lowest per capita food production in recent years, the decline from 1934-38 to 1948-52 was as much as 13 per cent; and the level in 1962-64 was still 3 per cent below the prewar (lines 10 and 11, column 1). Yet the rate of population growth in the Far East was distinctly below that of the other low-calorie regions.

However, the major new finding in Table 3 relates to the trends in food *supplies*, as distinct from food production. Here we observe that the net export balance of food relative to domestic production, marked in 1934-38 in all the low-calorie regions, either shifted to a net import balance, as in the Far and in the Near East, or declined perceptibly, as in Africa and Latin America (lines 1-3, columns 1-4). Hence for the low-calorie regions as a whole a significant net export balance in 1934-38, 10 per cent of domestic food output, had virtually disappeared by 1962-64; correspondingly, the net import balance in the high-calorie regions declined from 7 per cent of domestic output before the war to zero in 1962-64 (lines 1-3, columns 5-7).

This means that in the low-calorie regions per capita food supply rose more, or declined less, than per capita food production—either because food output for domestic consumption rose more than that designed for exports, or because the ratio of exports to output of foods both consumed domestically and exported declined, or because imports (relative to domestic food output), increased—or for all three reasons. Thus while in the low-calorie regions (excluding Mainland China) food production per capita in 1962-64 was barely above that in 1934-38, food supplies per capita were 12 per cent higher—and even in the Far East the index was 6 per cent above that for 1934-38 (lines 11 and 13). Conversely, in the high-calorie regions per capita food supplies in 1962-64 were 25 per cent above the 1934-38 level whereas per capita food output was 33 per cent higher.

Yet even in terms of per capita food supplies, the rate of growth in the high-calorie regions was almost double that in the low-calorie regions. In 1934-38 the ratio of per capita food supplies in the high-calorie to those in the low-calorie regions was 3.3 to 1, higher than that for output per capita (2.8 to 1) because of net imports of food to the high-calorie and net exports of food from the low-calorie regions. By 1962-64 the ratio of per capita food supplies rose to 3.7.

We may now ask how the rates of growth implicit in the food requirements for the year 2000 compare with those for the recent past. Table 4 shows the rates of growth needed if the food requirements are to be satisfied—for two periods, one to 2000 and the other to 1975, the terminal dates in the presentation of the requirements—and the observed rates for the quinquennium since 1958.

The rates in columns 1-3 are to be viewed largely as required rates of growth in production—as in the analysis of feasibility quoted above, which treated the food production potentials region by region. To be sure, the possibility of trade and transfer of food among regions is not ignored. But it is assumed that they contribute relatively little to the needed growth in domestic supplies. This assumption will be noted in a later section when we deal with what might be called differential aspects of the projections, requirements, and feasibility. For the present, one may be justified in viewing the implicit rates in Table 4 as those in food production —to be compared with the observed growth rates in total food production in Tables 2 and 3.

The results of such a comparison depend largely upon the period in the past used for reference. As Table 4 shows, the required rate of growth in food production is between 37 and 41 per cent per decade for the low calorie regions, and between 24 and over 27 per cent for the world as a whole (lines 5 and 7, columns 1-3). But per capita food production and supply also depend upon the rate of population increase.

In the observed past, the period favorable to growth of food output was between 1948-52 and 1962-64—to take a time span long enough to warrant use in the comparison. Over that period, world food production grew 33.2 per cent per decade (see Table 2, line 20, column 3). *If* the growth experience of that decade to decade and a half is indicative of the long-term potential to year 2000, the growth rates of world food production implied in the requirements (24 to 27 per cent per decade) can apparently be met. But two difficulties emerge. First, the food requirements for the low-calorie regions imply an appreciably higher rate of growth (as high as 41 per cent per decade, if the later estimate of requirements is used) if the need for a higher rate of growth in the earlier phases (that is, from 1957-59 to 1975, compared with 1975 to 2000) is to be recognized, as given in an FAO later projection. Yet the rate of growth of food output for the low-calorie regions even from 1948-52 to 1962-64 was 35 per cent per decade—over a tenth lower. Second, the population projections implicit in the FAO estimates of requirements have been exceeded in all the low-calorie regions in the last observed quinquennium (lines 8-12, column 4). If these higher rates of population growth were to be assumed for reference purposes, total food requirements would have to be raised above the levels in column 3; the excess of these required rates over those observed in the presumably favorable period of 1948-52 to 1962-64 would be even greater.

The high level of the targets for the low-calorie regions, particularly the Far East, generates disturbing doubts which are only compounded by the question of whether the growth experience in the post-World War II decade to decade and a half is a valid reference base for judging the accuracy of the measures of long-term growth potentials. It may be considered too favorable a base, because the slowdown during the depression and the war may have left a backlog of easily tapped sources of growth, which cannot be expected to remain available for the long period ahead to 2000. Some justification of this view emerges when we find that the growth rates in food production for the low-calorie regions as a whole and for the world (both excluding Mainland China) in the last quinquennium are 28.6 and 27.3 per cent (Table 4, column 4)—distinctly lower than those for the full period 1948-52 to 1962-64, 33.2 and 32.4 per cent respectively (Table 3, line 15, columns 5 and 7). An even more telling factor is that the growth of food output in the low-calorie regions depends on expansion of area (or increase in number of cattle), rather than, as in the high-calorie regions, on higher yields per area or per cattle unit. The FAO estimates show that of the growth in the output of nine major food crops between the prewar period and 1962-63 in the low-calorie regions, over seven-tenths were due to expansion in area and less than three-tenths to rise in yield—whereas in the high-calorie regions, the former accounted for less than one-third of total growth and the latter for over two-thirds.[7]

Similar contrasts between the high- and low-calorie regions, although not as wide, are shown regarding the growth of output of cattle products dependent on increases in number of cattle and on the rise in yield per unit. The implication is that, since expansion of land under cultivation in the less-developed areas is not likely to continue in the future, the recent growth of food output in these areas, impressive as it may appear, provides little assurance for the future. On the other hand, it may be argued that in many low-calorie countries the postwar period was still much affected by political changes and uncertainties, which depressed production, and that the realistic potential would be underestimated if no allowance were made for these elements in using the postwar period as guide.

Obviously, past growth rates, particularly those for a period as short and as affected by major disturbances as even the longest time span in our tables, are a rough and uncertain guide to potentials for the future. We summarized the trends in the recent past, not because we expected to find sure guides for the future, but to observe what actually happened—since our interpretation of what might happen if the food targets are or are not met depends largely upon our knowledge of what occurred in the recent "untargeted" past. But while Table 4 suggests that the projections and requirements are *not* unrealistically high when we compare

---

[7] See P. V. Sukhatme, "The World Food Supplies," *Journal of Royal Statistical Society*, CXXIX (Series A, General, Part 2, 1966), Table 7, p. 235 (for the food crops) and Table 8 (for cattle products). The crops covered include wheat, rye, barley, oats, maize, rice, potatoes, groundnuts, and soybeans. In the case of cattle products, the yield accounted for only one-eleventh of the total rise in the low-calorie regions, and for over four-tenths of the total rise in the developed regions (the products were meat and milk, with one unit of meat converted to 10 units of milk).

them on a worldwide scale and refer to the relatively favorable post-World War II period, rather substantial excesses and probable shortfalls emerge when comparison is made for individual low-calorie regions. Furthermore, the record of the last quinquennium clearly indicates no progress in the low-calorie regions toward higher food production per capita—so that the accumulated shortfall, added to the originally set requirements for 1975 or 2000, raises the targets even further.

TECHNOLOGICAL, ECONOMIC, AND SOCIAL ASPECTS OF CAPACITY TO PRODUCE

Conclusions as to the capacity to provide other natural resource-based products for the population in year 2000 (and even somewhat later) are generally similar to those for food. Thus in a recent review of the supply and demand for natural resources to the year 2000, Joseph L. Fisher and Neal Potter concluded, concerning prospects of the underdeveloped countries, that:

> We are not persuaded that the next few decades will see any general or marked deterioration of living levels because of increasing scarcity of raw materials.... We venture the view that living levels in most countries can increase over the coming years, with diets improving slowly and energy and mineral use more rapidly.... We do not believe that shortages and inadequacies of natural resources and raw materials are likely to make modest improvements in levels of living impossible of achievement.[8]

In a paper prepared for the 1965 UN World Population Conference Joseph J. Spengler writes:

> Supplies of many nonfuel minerals will be depleted within a century or two, and it will become increasingly necessary to resort to substitutes or to synthetic production. Fossil fuel reserves may be used up in two centuries or less though the use of fuel cells could extend this period. Improvement in fission procedures and enlargement of sources of fission materials could meet energy needs for several millennia, while the development of feasible, economic ways of using fusion materials would virtually remove limits imposed by shortage of energy. Given adequate supplies of energy, exploitation of sources of heavy-volume minerals, or of substitute materials, which abound in the surface of the earth (iron, aluminum, crushable rock, *etc.*) would be economically feasible and the costs of desalinization and transportation of sea water would be reduced.[9]

---

[8] Joseph L. Fisher and Neal Potter, *World Prospects for Natural Resources* (Baltimore: The Johns Hopkins Press for the Resources of the Future, Inc., 1964), p. 68.

[9] See Joseph J. Spengler, "Population and Natural Resources," Background Paper B.10, United Nations World Population Conference, 1965, p. 31.

Finally, in an introductory paper for Session B-10 of the World Population Conference, a session that dealt with possible problems in the supply of natural resources, Edward A. Ackerman contrasts the "technologic optimism view" (according to which "the potential resources of the earth are so large when man's creativity is applied to them that it is meaningless to set arbitrary limits for future world population for an indefinite period in the future") with the "planned population equilibrium view" (according to which "the world population-resources problem must be viewed as one of unstable equilibrium, with the demand of population eventually having the capacity to outrun the supply from resources"). He then writes:

> There can be no doubt that the technologic optimism position is correct if we are to consider the world as a whole for . . . about 50 years. The world has the resources to support the population which would be attained by a projection of the 2 per cent growth rate that has recently prevailed, and probably at a higher average standard of living than now . . . The evidence for this conclusion can be drawn from many sources. It is considered to be enough a matter of public record so that no restatement or documentation is needed here. However, as we shall see later, the same conclusion is not necessarily applicable to all regions of the world, individually considered.[10]

In dealing now with the general grounds for feasibility conclusions for food requirements, we may assume that they are similar to those underlying the parallel conclusions for the production capacity of other natural resource-based products. The following discussion of the several aspects of these feasibility conclusions must perforce be general, since no economist has the competence to judge these estimates in technical detail—even if all the necessary details were available. Rather, the attempt is to define the general bases of the conclusions, to distinguish as clearly as possible the technological, the economic, and the social aspects of these judgments, and thus be in a position to recognize the questions that arise in a critical scrutiny of these judgments and underlying estimates.

Technological Aspect The technological content of the conclusions concerning productive capacity for the future may be put in the following general terms. The known stock of tested

---

[10] Edward A. Ackerman in *World Population Conference, 1965,* I (January Report; New York: United Nations, 1966), p. 260.

technological knowledge relevant to the field (whether it is food or other natural resource-based products) can, with the other production factors (labor, reproducible capital) assumed available, be applied to the known natural resources (used and unused) to increase the volume of production at a higher rate than the projected rate of population growth, and thus assure a higher output per capita. Given the projected populations and their requirements (targets), this statement clearly implies that we can evaluate the production equivalents of existing technological knowledge (which can be used more extensively than it is currently) and the availability of natural resources (or of their substitutes).

While natural resources and population trends and requirements must obviously be evaluated region by region because they differ so much from area to area, technological knowledge is a worldwide complex presumably available to all. Setting aside for the moment problems of different potentials for individual regions in the world, to be noted in the next section, we shall proceed here with an approach that, while recognizing regional differences in resource and population requirements, summates the production potential for the world, or for the large underdeveloped, low-calorie groups and developed, high-calorie groups.

The emphasis on both the stock of tested technological knowledge and the known natural resources is unique to the analysis of production potentials of natural resource-based products. For goods not directly dependent on these nonreproducible natural resources, we need only know the available stock of technological knowledge; if it permits wider than current use, no further questions arise. Thus if we were considering the capacity to supply a greater volume of barbers' services, or even of those of physicians, all we would need to know is whether the relevant stock of knowledge can be acquired by a larger number of practitioners, or whether the arts involved permit greater efficiency even within the existing stock of knowledge, or both. No question of natural resource availability arises, unless we assume that the services under discussion depend upon some exceptional genetic endowment and that the prospective rise in population will reduce or fail to increase the proportional supply of this limited genetic resource.

How can the existing stock of relevant technological knowledge and the inventories of known natural resources be translated into feasible productive capacity? How can one judge the detailed examination in the FAO, FFHC Basic Study No. 10 of the available but not fully used land and related natural resources; of the ways to increase yield per land unit by seed selection, pesticides, fertilizers, and so on; of the ways to increase the food supply from fishery resources? As already indicated, examination of technical detail is out of the question. But two characteristics of this and similar evaluations of technological feasibility and potentials may be noted, since they require no technical expertise. First, the data on existing natural resources are almost necessarily incomplete, and the understatement is likely to be especially great in the less-developed countries. Second, the estimates and evaluations relating to a long period ahead are based almost exclusively on the *existing* and tested stock of technical knowledge. In the nature of the case it would be difficult and well-nigh impossible to take account of the additions to the stock of knowledge that will be made in the near future; yet the application of this *new* knowledge may affect the production potentials, if not early then late in the period for which projection is attempted.

Knowledge of available natural resources is perforce incomplete because an up-to-date inventory, conforming to modern technology standards, requires relatively large inputs of capital and highly skilled labor, is beyond the means of the less-developed countries, and is not readily undertaken even by the developed countries, unless it holds out promise of prospective use. Furthermore, since the definition of a resource and its accessibility are both functions of current technology, changes in technology require continuous re-evaluation; even developed countries do not possess up-to-date knowledge of all their natural resources—ranging from the quality of soil to the subsoil wealth in coastal waters or in some backward region. Such omissions are relatively greater in the less developed countries, since their knowledge and indeed their whole view of natural resources are largely set by their own, rather than by modern, technology—qualified by intervention or assistance of economic units from the developed regions. This situation is amply illustrated by continuous discoveries—once growth quickens or contacts with the developed regions intensify—of natural resource deposits or potentials (for example, oil in Libya and the Arab peninsula, and various export crops in Africa) in many underdeveloped countries formerly assumed to be barren of such wealth.

Given the known resources, ascertaining the productive potential afforded by the existing technology, capable of wider than current use, is even a more complicated matter. The productive potential is essentially derived from comparisons of practices pursued in some parts of the world with those of a more advanced character—tried, tested, and adopted on a substantial scale in the latter. The gaps between current practices and the better practices, let alone the best, are numerous and wide. Such gaps may exist even in the developed countries because current activities may have been the best possible under the older technological knowledge and may have become so entrenched that a shift to a different and more efficient practice, permitted by recent technological change, faces structural obstacles.[11] In the less-developed countries such lags are necessarily greater, since the prevailing technology originated even earlier and was less affected by modernization and industrialization, despite the substantial carry-over value of modern technology evolved and applied in the developed countries—differences in climate and natural resource endowments notwithstanding. Disparities in technological level are marked even *among* the less-developed countries, all of which are employing premodern technology in agriculture, as is evident in a comparison of much of Africa with much of East Asia; traditional intensive agriculture in East Asia reached a high level of efficiency that permitted the emergence and long-term growth of a large and dense population.

But granted these numerous and substantial lags of current behind better practices, which make estimates of large additional productive capacity plausible, the question here relates to the extent to which these estimates take into account *further* developments in technology that may occur within the long span projected, in this case almost forty years. In trying to answer this question, one may usefully distinguish among various probable changes in technology that differ in magnitude, as well as in the time span required for their emergence, testing, and sufficiently wide application to affect productive capacity significantly. Assuming realistically that at any given time a stock exists of probable technological changes, with a full distribution along the scale of magnitude and of duration of the period of maturity to a significantly spread innovation, an evaluation of production potentials over a forty-year span could hardly take full account of those changes whose effects

---

[11] See, for example, the discussion of the vast potential of more effective land utilization in Australia in *Possibilities of Increasing World Food Production*, Basic Study No. 10, pp. 52-54 and 75-85.

may be realized toward the end of that span. And, indeed, for obvious reasons of caution, evaluation of the type indicated cannot assign significant weights to technological changes as yet untested, let alone those unborn. Those future changes that are explicitly recognized, but are not made the basis for a sanguinely optimistic technologic view, are seen as "escape hatches from any tendency toward increasing scarcity" of natural resources, but their possible effects are not directly included in the evaluation—in an effort to avoid confusing the possible with the conjectural and merely probable.[12]

If, all other conditions being equal, the evaluation of the technologically feasible productive capacity is subject to downward bias because of omissions in the inventory of known natural resources and because of the unavoidable exclusion of future technological changes that are likely to affect capacity *within* the time span of the projection, it would be difficult to attach a reasonably precise weight to the bias. This difficulty is due to lack of knowledge, and could be resolved only if some analogy could be drawn with the past, when similar evaluations may have been understated for the same reasons. No such comparisons are at hand, and the dangers of such analogies are patent. Review of the available literature suggests that there is wide disagreement; all one can safely state is that the downward bias is there, and *may* be significant.

In this connection one speculative observation may be of interest. Table 3 in the preceding section indicates that in some low-calorie areas the long-term rise in per capita supplies of food has been slight. Over the twenty-seven years from 1934-38 to 1962-64, this rise was only 6 per cent for the Far East excluding Mainland China (line 13, column 1); judging by the evidence in Table 2, the same small rise would probably characterize the longer period back to the second half of the 1920's. Yet over the same three and one-half decades the mortality rate in that region dropped sharply, which also suggests a decline in the morbidity rate; *aggregate* output, if not food production, total and per capita, also increased —while inputs of hours per head probably declined.[13] If so, with minor rises (and in some areas perhaps even slight declines) in

---

[12] The term is from *World Prospects for Natural Resources,* footnote 6, pp. 49-51.

per capita food supply, as measured by the economic weight of food, the countries managed to lengthen the life span, probably reduce morbidity, and achieve a significantly higher product per capita and presumably per unit of effort.

If this finding remains after adjustments for possible biases in the measures of national product, it suggests that the same slightly greater, or perhaps even slightly smaller, *economic* value of food per capita permits sizable improvements in the life and work that food is supposed to sustain. On the technological level, this suggests a trend toward greater efficiency of food, supplemented perhaps by products and services of modern medical care activities—greater efficiency in that the contribution of food and supplements to health, life, and work per unit of economic cost rose over time. This hypothesis may have significant bearing upon the meaning of food requirements for the future, measured as they are in constant price values; to pursue it further would require analysis of nutrition and health values of different food products compared with their economic weight—which is beyond our competence and the scope of this paper.

Economic Aspect Productive capacity in the field of our concern depends not only on the stock of tested technological knowledge and known natural resources, but also on the input of labor and reproducible capital—which in our formulation of technological feasibility were assumed to be available. But to say that it is technologically possible to provide a larger food output for the larger population in the year 2000 means one thing when labor and capital needed for this task are so large relative to total supply that assurance of food would mean scarcity of other goods; it means a different thing if the technological knowledge available for wider use requires only a moderate input of labor and capital, leaving an adequate supply of these resources for sustained growth in other areas of the economy. The problem of scarcity and opportunity costs is clearly economic; we may refer to these costs as the economic aspect of the judgments of productive capacity.

The distinction between technological and economic aspects is, in good part, false, for if the technological possibility of providing food, minerals, or some other limited group of goods can be realized only with a heavy draft upon labor and capital that would starve other important goods categories, it is not likely to be defined as technologically feasible. For technology is distinguished by a positive relevance to the satisfaction of human wants, and a production possibility that satisfies some needs but starves others can be viewed as technologically feasible only in a narrow and misleading sense of that term. Hence, a properly defined technologically feasible situation is necessarily economically feasible in that its requirements in the way of economic resources do not prevent needed and desirable growth elsewhere.

These comments are not made as a semantic exercise, but to emphasize that evaluations of productive capacity of the type already discussed necessarily imply economic feasibility even as they assert technological feasibility. And sometimes the implication is made explicit—as illustrated by the following quotation from Basic Study No. 10 (pp. 7-8):

> It would, of course, serve little purpose to consider the technical possibilities for increasing production without bearing in mind that many things which are technically feasible may be uneconomic. . . . Increases in production achieved in this way [uneconomic] would result in the human race growing poorer. Man would be producing more food and other agricultural products only at the expense of other things. The objective of this study is rather to consider the possibilities for raising agricultural production within the framework of, and as part of, a rising standard of living.[14]

In other cases no explicit statement is made, but it is clear from the general context that economic feasibility—in the sense of a sufficient supply of labor and capital for other required and desired results of economic growth—is meant. Indeed, even the population projections are based on and imply technical and economic feasibility assumptions. The following statement accompanying the recent UN projections of world population to the year 2000 is revealing: "Continuing substantial progress in economic and social development, however, is implicit in the assumptions on which the estimates are based. Without this, even the increases projected

---

[13] Gross domestic product per capita (in constant 1958 prices) in the Far East (East and Southeast Asia, excluding Japan and all the Communist countries) rose 25 per cent from 1950 to 1963; the rise in Latin America over the same period was 30 per cent; and in all non-Communist less-developed countries it was over 35 per cent. See *Yearbook of National Accounts Statistics, 1965* (New York: United Nations, 1966), Table 8B, pp. 488-90. The decline in average hours is characteristic even of moderate industrialization.

[14] *Possibilities of Increasing World Food Production*, Basic Study No. 10, pp. 7-8.

on the 'low' variants for some of the most crowded and economically less developed regions might be impossible. . . ."[15]

In short, if we ask whether the larger population numbers estimated for the future in the authoritative projections of the UN can be sustained, the answer is bound to be in the affirmative—at least by the authors of these projections; in *that* sense it is predetermined.

Two types of findings are implied if, in general terms, the economic aspect of productive capacity for the future larger population deals with the supply of capital and labor, and if "economically feasible" means that the larger volume of food or minerals calls for inputs of material capital and of labor (of various skills) which the economy can supply over the projected future while still allowing for growth in other areas. The first finding is that the *specific* material capital and the *specific* labor skills required for the greater output of food and so on can be provided by the country's economy or secured in trade (and other intercourse) with the rest of the world. Since these specific inputs are only a limited part of total inputs and since their availability in the world is assured because the demand for them was derived, in the technological analysis, from an existing technology, no serious questions attach to this implied finding of economic feasibility.

The second finding—that the capital and labor resources required for larger output of food and so on, combined with those needed for growth elsewhere, do not exceed the capacity of the economy—is a much broader judgment and subject to less certain tests. How does one judge the capacity of an economy (or nation) to generate

---

[15] *World Population Prospects as Assessed in 1963*, p. 6. An even more explicit statement is made in the *Provisional Report on World Population Projects* released in 1964: "A three-fold increase in the world population during the last hundred years has been made economically possible by technological inventions, investments in improvement of production equipment and in the use of natural resources, increasing skills, and heightened efficiency of economic organization, including the organization of international co-operation. *It is taken for granted in the projections presented here that developments along these lines will continue and indeed will be accelerated in the future.* [Italics added.] Otherwise even the increases projected on the 'low' variants for some of the most crowded and economically least developed regions might be impossible. . . ." [Because of continued high death rates and so on.]

The "high" and "low" variants in this report are thought to be wide enough to accommodate both a moderately optimistic and a moderately pessimistic view in these respects [production possibilities, for example], so far as prospects up to the end of the century are concerned (pp. 7-8).

sufficient material capital formation and to provide sufficient labor force with the skills needed by required economic growth, *including the growth of output of the particular goods that are of prime concern here?* Such judgments are necessarily crude, and rest essentially on analogies with the past. If in the past, several countries with differing historical heritage, natural resources, social and political structures, size, and so on managed to generate material capital formation of, say, 15 to 25 per cent of GNP, and to provide labor with adequate training in needed skills (all of this permitting growth of x per cent per year per capita), it seems plausible to assume that other countries, not too far beyond the range of past experience, could do likewise. This should suffice to satisfy the requirements of the projection. Of course, this type of analysis can easily be refined with respect to the scope and measurement of various kinds and vintages of material capital, skills of labor, and disaggregation of the total product by components.

The intention here is not to deal with the specific aspects of such analysis, but to suggest the general structure of the economic side of the evaluations being discussed. This general structure is particularly important because it points directly to the dependence of the economic aspect of these evaluations upon what, for lack of a better term, may be called the social structure, the social aspect. Clearly, all economic activities and relations depend upon (even though they affect in turn) the political and social structure of society as well as the beliefs and scales of values of its members; the latter affect the capacity to generate savings and capital, the capital-output ratios, the integration of modern education and higher skills, and all that we usually classify as economic.

Social Aspect   By social we mean here the political and social framework of the society, including the historically inherited beliefs and scales of values, which set the *conditions* for economic activity and hence for application of technology but are themselves not directly modified by the latter. An attempt at an economic innovation will not immediately and automatically effect changes in the social structure that will assure that innovation's spread and success. Insofar as such a social and ideological framework—one that conditions economic activity and application of technology—does exist, changes in it may constitute necessary requirements for modern economic growth, that is, for growth at a high minimum rate per capita, accompanied by rapid shifts in the industrial allocation of labor, capital, and product.

And, in the present connection, the existence of such a social structure means that the finding of technological and economic feasibility implies the feasibility of the changes in the social framework that are needed to permit economic performance to develop to the full extent that supplies of skilled labor and material capital warrant, given the existing technology and known natural resources. Such necessary and desirable changes in social structure and guiding views may be termed the social aspect of judgments concerning capacity to produce.

Here, too, a sharp line between the economic and social, like that between the technological and economic, is not easily drawn. Some institutions (for example, village credit cooperatives) may seem to be purely economic, yet they may perform governmental functions or may require the support of the central political structure to operate properly. Some government actions, like the fixing of exchange rates or income taxes, are purely economic in intent, yet they imply a specific relation between the government and the governed. Where, in these cases, is the line of division between economic and social? Nevertheless, the distinction appears significant when we deal with the *broad* political and social framework, which channels economic activity and which, by that token, cannot be identified with it.

That social preconditions of technological and economic feasibility exist and do not *automatically* follow from the availability of technological knowledge and economic resources, can hardly be doubted. After all, a viable political framework that assures a minimum of peace and equity in the process of modern economic growth—which like any process of change is provocative of conflicts—is indispensable for sustained growth. And the effects of failure of the political framework are all too obvious in recent experience (in Indonesia and Nigeria, for example) to be stressed. The limiting effects on economic growth of a system of beliefs inherited and adjusted to a preindustrial past, as in India, are also patent. And one must note, particularly, the relevance of international relations in their range from peaceful and planned trade and investment to armed conflict and pressure to divert resources to nonproductive armaments.

Social feasibility *must* be assumed if technological and economic feasibility are to be justified; that assumption would also rest on an analogy with the past, referring to changes in the social and ideological framework of many presently developed countries in the process of their economic growth. But unlike the technological aspect of the analysis (which rests upon tested applicability of devices and processes under specific physical conditions) and unlike the economic aspect (which deals with productive resources and their functional relations that can be at least statistically tested), the social aspect of the analysis is not amenable to measurement and hard tests. In particular, we do not know whether many of the presently underdeveloped countries are so far beyond the range of the social, political, and ideological framework within which modern economic growth could be observed in the past (all among Western European areas and their descendants overseas, with the single exception of Japan) that the lessons of the past, indicating feasibility of the needed social changes, may not apply. Even if we argue, as we should, that no region of the world, no human community, is so unique that lessons from the observable past of a large part of mankind are irrelevant or inapplicable, the *specific* application may still be impossible. We may have no tested analysis at hand of the amount of social change that did occur and was needed in connection with various magnitudes of economic growth in the past—in the light of which social feasibility could be explored for the less-developed regions for which technological and economic feasibility were otherwise assumed to warrant prospective growth in productive capacity.

There is, consequently, a question about the social aspect of productive capacity that does not apply with the same force to the technological and economic aspects. Can we gauge the probability that the required social, political and ideological changes will be made? And since technological and economic feasibility will not materialize unless the social changes are made, the question affects the whole judgment regarding productive capacity. In other words, this judgment specifically assures the attainment of this capacity *only* if social and related changes are made—often not fully specifying what these would be since there is no firm basis for doing so. And thus the whole matter is presented as a challenge to mankind—a challenge that is real because the technological and economic potentials are there if only the broad social changes are made.

This interpretation may be illustrated by two quotations from Basic Study No. 10. In discussing Africa and Latin America, for which, as already cited, physical resources are adequate for the required rise in food production, the report adds the *caveat:* "The outcome will depend primarily upon the establishment of progressive and stable governments that are willing and able to mobilize their own resources and make effective use of foreign aid" (p. 222). And concluding the summary for the world as a whole, the report adds:

> It seems probable that a sustained and satisfactory rate of progress will require the allocation of appreciably greater resources for the education of peoples, for research, for physical investment, and for international leadership and co-ordination than the nations of the world are making available at present. It will also require a greater willingness to move toward the institutional changes which would provide a more generally favorable climate for productive investment and application of technology.[16]

One should add that the weight of the required social changes as conditions of technical and economic feasibility is all the greater because, as suggested earlier, the extensive growth of food output and agriculture in the less-developed regions would have to give way to intensive growth with emphasis on yields. The implied shift in technology requires greater education, different patterns of organization of land and agriculture, and a variety of changes in both agricultural and nonagricultural institutions that would not be required if the same technology could be pursued broadly with some hope of meeting the targets.[17]

The emphasis on the need for social change is so obvious as to seem tautological; it is important to point out that it is *not*. One can easily imagine a situation in which technological and economic feasibility would be assured *without* any changes in the political and social framework or in the prevailing views of the population—for example, in many presently developed coun-

---

[16] *Possibilities of Increasing World Food Production,* Basic Study No. 10, p. 223.

[17] This need to shift to a new technological and hence institutional base is the main thesis in Theodore W. Schultz's *Transforming Traditional Agriculture* (New Haven, Conn.: Yale University Press, 1964). See also Lester Brown, *Increasing World Food Output: Prospects and Problems* (Foreign Agricultural Economic Report No. 25, U.S. Department of Agriculture; Washington: U.S. Gov't Printing Office, 1965), in which considerable emphasis is placed on educational and institutional changes required for a "take-off" in yields.

tries with respect to sizable growth in productive capacity. That the less-developed countries are characterized by political, social, and ideological structures that *must* be changed significantly if the technological and economic potentials of greater productive capacity are to be realized is a fact of major importance. To the extent that the technological and economic feasibility of supporting a larger population at a higher standard of living depends on a variety of relatively major changes in the political, social, and ideological cast of many underdeveloped societies or on the evolution and maintenance of a world system of international relations radically different from the present, all statements concerning capacity to provide for larger populations are challenges that may or may not be met. Insofar as such challenges are a matter of decision by individual nations and regions, we must shift from the more aggregative views and consider the *differential* aspects of the feasible trends in productive capacity in response to larger population.

Differential Aspects of Capacity to Produce and Supply The above discussion and quantitative illustrations have treated the major regions, and the low-calorie and the high-calorie groups, as wholes. Consequently, the requirements, as well as past production and supplies, were added for the several countries within each region or group; greater rises or declines in some countries offset lesser rises or declines in others. While such summation is indispensable in economical presentation, the implicit assumption that food production and supplies move easily and at no cost among countries within a region, and that the requirements for them can be added without distinction, is unrealistic. Besides, our conclusion in the preceding section that decisions relating to the broad social aspect are of key importance in validating technological and economic feasibility of production prospects would direct our attention to individual countries. They are the loci of major decisions concerning changes in social, political, and economic institutions, granted the mitigating effects of relations with other members of the concert of nations and various international organizations.

If we distinguish among countries and disaggregate the broad categories used in the preceding discussion, differential aspects of the capacity to produce emerge. These are associated with: (1)

differences among countries with respect to natural resources, historical heritage, and productive patterns and requirements; (2) differences between long-term trends and projections and short-term fluctuations in production and supply; and (3) the possibility that *within* the individual countries (particularly the larger ones) several areas and several social groups may fare differently with respect to per capita production and supplies; hence, long-term trends in prospects as well as short-term fluctuations may have different impacts on the different areas and population groups within a country.

1 Even when a low-calorie region is defined by a distinctively low-calorie consumption per capita, the several countries within it are likely to differ with respect to food consumption and production, rate of growth projected for population, and magnitude of required growth in food output to meet future requirements. Above all, the likelihood that the projected growth of food production or supplies will be realized is not the same for the several countries, since their capacity to make the needed social and political changes and mobilize the required economic resources is far from uniform. Unless the estimates of requirements and of productive capacity are carefully prepared on the basis of data specific to each country, and unless some account is taken of the relative probability of the required changes being made in each country's institutional framework (a nearly impossible task) we can hardly assume that growth in each country will conform to the feasibility projections.

Population projections are provided for individual countries, and presumably food requirements and targets can be approximated, but the latter cannot be identified with food *production* targets as was done for the world and the large regions within it. Individual countries need not aim at high food production if they can attain a higher level of other output more economically, and if they can use their comparative advantage to secure food in exchange for other products. Indeed, a productive capacity estimate for an individual country cannot be limited to food, but must include exportable goods for which food can be exchanged. Therefore, the estimate must approximate capacity to generate almost all products, not food alone. Many developed countries could, and did, rely on imports to cover their food deficits, as the data in Table 3 on net balance of food imports and exports suggest. Many underdeveloped countries possess resources other than food in which they have a large and lasting comparative advantage, and on which they can rely for a large and growing volume of food imports (for example, the Arab oil sheikdoms and several ore-rich countries in Africa).

We cannot spell out the food production targets implicit in the food requirements for individual countries, and compare current production records with these targets, country by country. Nor do we have the country production targets in the more general form of some required rate of growth of per capita total product, or of some limited but broad part of it (that is, exportable commodity product). Still, it may be argued that in the larger underdeveloped countries coverage of any substantial food deficit (relative to food requirements) by imports is not likely to be feasible. If food output and requirements at adequate levels amount, say, to 30 per cent of gross product (a not unrealistic figure for an underdeveloped country) and if the deficit is, say, one-sixth, the required food imports would be 5 per cent of gross product.

Given the low foreign trade propensity of large countries, particularly the underdeveloped ones, such a food import requirement might absorb the total import capacity of the country, leaving no resources for other indispensable raw material imports. Even the smaller underdeveloped countries cannot afford a gap between domestic food production and requirements (or a reduction in the excess of the former over the latter) unless they possess another export product or can produce import substitutes without excessive cost. The former usually requires some natural resource other than food as a basis of comparative advantage, and the latter assumes efficiency of industrial production not usually found in the less-developed countries.

However, the main argument here is that distinguishing the many individual countries, disaggregating the analysis, requires many more tests of the capacity to introduce the social, political, and institutional changes needed for the realization of technological and economic potentials—the latter assumed to be broadly given. In some underdeveloped countries, the social and institutional changes required for tapping the technological and economic potentials would have to be radical and far-reaching; the probability of such changes occurring would be low. The ensuing failure may be in food production or in the capacity to export in return for more food, or in the capacity to substitute efficiently for industrial products formerly secured by food exports no longer feasible.

The form of the failure is less important here than the likelihood of its occurrence, although it would be critical in its consequences if it involved a shortfall in food production and supplies in a large underdeveloped country, where food supply and reserves per capital are low to begin with. The point is that attainment of over-all food targets for a region does not exclude the likelihood that *within* the region there may be substantial failures to reach production and supply levels, failures that may be the source of continuing crises in a changing list of the less-developed countries.

2 A long-term goal and projection of the type discussed may be reached by a constant rate of increase or by an allowance for systematic changes in the rate of growth within the time span of the projections. But whether the rate changes systematically or is constant, the long-term targets do not allow for short-term fluctuations; yet the latter may occur even if the long-term trends are satisfactory. Such fluctuations are particularly common in food and agricultural production, and are often associated with weather and other factors not easily controlled. Low-productivity, premodern agriculture is particularly subject to these short-run disturbances by weather and other natural factors; it is in the less-developed, low-calorie countries that such fluctuations may be especially disrupting, since a short-term decline in domestic food output per capita may, because of small reserves, cause a supply crisis.

Table 5, limited to the three low-calorie regions for which continuous indexes of food production per capita are available for a number of countries, provides ample illustration of the susceptibility of food production per capita to short-term fluctuations, particularly in individual countries compared with the total for a larger entity such as a region. First, by comparing column 1, based on three-year averages, with column 2, based on seven-year averages, we can see how much the rate is affected by the brevity of the period. For the region, the effect is small: about a tenth for the Far East (line 1), even less for the Near East (line 13), and relatively sizable only for Latin America (line 20), because the low regional rate reflects a combination of upward and downward trends among the several countries. For the individual countries the shift from three- to seven-year averages results in much greater differences in a preponderant proportion of countries. Second, the average deviation from the straight line fitted by semiaverages, using the seven-year averages employed for column 2, is appreciably larger for each country than for the region of which it is a part (column 3)—a measure of variability which we calculated only for those countries in which per capita food output rose over the full period. This variability means that the upward trend is not at a uniform but at a variable rate, probably including absolute declines. Finally, the number of absolute declines is given in column 4, again for the countries with upward trends; it can be observed that most countries with upward trends were affected by absolute declines at least four times out of a total of twelve possible year-to-year changes, that is, in at least a third of the period.

There is no reason to assume that such short-term variability will vanish in the next two to three decades—even for countries in which the long-term rates of growth will be up to the targets. To be sure, if the rate of growth of per capita output is unusually high, as it was in Israel (line 16), absolute declines are infrequent. But as the evidence in Table 4 (column 3) shows, required rates of growth in per capita food production range, even in the period from 1957-59 to 1975, from 8 to 17 per cent per decade. Several countries in Table 5, with growth rates in column 2 within that range (Burma, Japan, Thailand, Turkey, and Venezuela) show four or more absolute declines. If experience is any guide, we should expect absolute declines in per capita food output to continue with some frequency in individual countries, even if the long-term projections are approximated.

Short-term declines in food production could, of course, be compensated by special imports or, if the long-term trend is satisfactory, by domestic stockpiling that would help to even out supply over time. But in the latter case—one reason for calculating the measures of variability in Table 5 only for the countries with an upward trend in per capita food production—the additional task requires a long-term policy which in its consistency and even approximate accuracy implies an efficient central government. As has been said, such a government is *not* characteristic of underdeveloped countries. The main point here is that short-term instability in production, even when trends in productive capacity are favorable, constitutes an additional burden and intensifies the need for political and institutional changes that are essential in the long run.

3 Area differences within a country are likely to be particularly wide in natural resource endowment, and hence in agriculture and other natural resource-oriented industries. Within agriculture, other conditions being equal, internal area differentials in long-term trends and particularly in short-term fluctuations would tend to be wider in the less-developed than in the more-developed countries. Thus, the comments above on the frequency of disturbing fluctuations in less-developed, low-calorie countries can be repeated for areas within these countries—with the significant additional suggestion that such disruptions are likely to be more frequent if we consider the impact on any important area within the country rather than that on the country as a whole.

Indeed, in some large underdeveloped countries, the several areas may be so distinct, the means of transportation and communication among them so limited, and the degree of coherence and resulting power of the central government so weak, that a local area crisis cannot be alleviated by domestic resources and may have international repercussions (as is the case with India currently). Furthermore, diversity is possible even in long-term trends among the areas, and is only reduced slightly by internal (within the country) flows of resources.

Consequently, conformity for the country as a whole to the food requirement targets (or any other set of production goals) may be accompanied by a long-term lag or failure of some areas within the country that is *not* adequately compensated by the flows between them and the other more prosperous and more rapidly growing areas. While such diversity in internal area trends will be compensated for eventually by increased mobility in the process of growth, there may be delays and frequent area crises—particularly if even the more prosperous areas lag behind the country-wide production targets.

In addition to the wider divergence among internal areas in the less-developed countries than in the developed countries in susceptibility to different short-term fluctuations in food production (or production of other natural-resource products) and even to different trends, there is the wider inequality in the distribution of the population among income-size and level-of-living classes. As a result, the country-wide averages of food output or supply per capita may be raised much more by the high level of consumption of the small top income class in the less-developed countries than in the developed.[18] Even though the share of the lowest income groups (say the bottom quartile) is no lower relative to the country-wide average in the less-developed than in the developed countries, the absolute levels are much lower in the former than in the latter. If we add somewhat higher economic status groups (still not including those at the very top), the share does become a lower relative of the country-wide average in the less-developed countries.

Consequently, absolute declines in production or supply per capita associated with short-term fluctuations, for internal areas or the whole country, and the diversity in the conformity of the trends in individual countries to the required targeted levels have a much greater impact on the numerically dominant groups within the underdeveloped, low-calorie countries than they could have in the more developed countries with their high supply levels and larger reserves. Even perceptible rises in the countrywide supply of food per capita may not mean a significant increase, or *any* increase, in the per capita supply of the lower economic groups, whose shares in the total may decline.

This last point is of particular importance if the failure to raise per capita food output or supplies also reflects a high rate of population growth. In the underdeveloped countries, as in many

---

[18] See, for example, *Possibilities of Increasing World Food Production*, Basic Study No. 10, pp. 24-25: "The figures . . . are . . . based upon national averages and thus ignore the fact that a proportion of the population already has a diet which exceeds the proposed level, while for the greater part of the population the deficiencies in diet . . . must be greater than indicated by the national averages. . . . This probably applies to Latin America, where there exists quite a large middle and wealthy class, including foreigners as well as indigenous population, whose dietary habits have little in common with the millions of Indians and Mestizos who are found in the rural areas; and to Africa, where in certain areas of the Mediterranean littoral, in East Africa and in South Africa, there exist several million people of European origin, whose consumption of the higher-priced foods must weigh fairly heavily in the regional averages" (pp. 24-25).

See also the discussion of differences among families in calorie supplies per consuming unit in Burma and India and differentials in other Asian countries in P. V. Sukhatme, "The World's Hunger and Future Needs in Food Supplies," *Journal of the Royal Statistical Society*, CXXIV (Series A, General, Part 4, 1961), pp. 483-88.

developed countries, fertility rates are negatively correlated with income and level of living. Urban population, with its higher per capita income level, has a lower fertility rate than rural population with its lower per capita income, and within urban population, the lower income groups have higher fertility rates.[19] Differentials in fertility and in the rate of natural increase tend to be associated positively, because mortality differentials—which run counter to those in fertility—are too narrow to offset them. This means that if rates of population growth are high, the rate of natural increase of the lower income groups is likely to be higher than that of the upper income groups—and the differential is greater than when planned family limitation or other factors lower the over-all rate of population increase. Hence unless changes, by policy design or otherwise, reduce economic inequality within the country, such inequality will tend to be wider with a high than with a low rate of population growth. The impact, under these conditions, of any failure to provide the same or a growing amount of food per capita is likely to be all the more painful for the lower economic groups, whose shares in total product, for reasons indicated, may decline.

Here again we could list various policies that could be used domestically to assist the lagging areas or the depressed lower socioeconomic groups, policies that have been used and are still being used in the more developed countries. But the required transfers of resources from the more prosperous areas or groups within the country, and the systematic movement of people from the less to the more rapidly growing internal areas, again imply the existence of an effective central government, of a consensus within the country that would permit such transfers, and of ingenuity in fitting the remedy to the specific conditions of the problem. None of these is easily found in the less-developed countries.

Summary Comments

This paper dealt, somewhat discursively, with the question of whether the productive capacity of the world could sustain the

---

[19] See George W. Roberts, "Fertility," Background Paper A.1, United Nations World Population Conference, 1965, pp. 61-62, on rural-urban differentials and p. 66, on income status differentials in fertility, both for the less-developed countries.

prospective growth in population—a question urged by the concern in recent years over the possibly catastrophic consequences of the population explosion. In considering this problem for the limited time span to year 2000 it proved necessary to distinguish the several aspects—technological, economic, and broadly social—of the evaluation of productive capacity; to examine the evidence and reasoning that underlie judgments relating to these aspects; and to emphasize the difference between capacity for the world, or for a large region taken as a whole, and for the individual countries, which currently and in the foreseeable future are the loci of major social and economic decisions. The discussion, particularly the details, related to capacity to produce and requirements for food, but it applies in large part to other natural resource products as well. Much of it is relevant also to the capacity to produce and requirements for any major good viewed as basic rather than as an easily dispensable luxury.

We may now summarize the conclusions, briefly and perhaps dogmatically. The only useful qualification is the obvious one that all the judgments are fairly crude, since they are not based on a relatively complete body of "hard" evidence, properly tested.

1 If we deal with the world, or its large regions, or even with individual countries (excluding those on the fringe of human settlement and in extraordinarily difficult natural surroundings, for example, the Arctic wastes), and with a period extending to year 2000 (or say fifty years ahead), the available and tested technological knowledge and the known natural resources are adequate for sustaining the projected population numbers at moderately rising standards of living. If requirements of natural resource products, like food and minerals, can be satisfied, the potential for goods not directly dependent on limited natural resources is even greater. This appraisal of technological feasibility is subject to a downward bias, since the inventory of known natural resources is necessarily incomplete and any evaluation of existing knowledge does not take account of new knowledge that may emerge and mature within the long projection span.

2 As usually evaluated, technological feasibility implies economic in the sense that the possible increase in food, fuel, and so on is provided by a technology that, when applied to known natural resources, requires a limited input of labor and reproducible capital, and leaves adequate supplies of both productive factors for growth elsewhere. This conclusion as to joint technoeconomic feasibility follows from the assumption that only those technological possibilities that are "economical" of labor and capital are pursued, and from the observation that aggregate requirements for capital, material or invested in labor skills, are not only a moderate proportion of total product, but are also moderate relative to the growth in product that they can generate.

3 It should be emphasized that the technoeconomic feasibility of sustaining a growing population at a moderately rising level of living does not imply that, with a *lower* rate of population increase, higher rates of growth in per capita food supply or per capita product would not become feasible. The judgment is merely that the available technology, natural resources, and economic resources (labor and capital), can preclude the subjection of the expected larger populations to the Malthusian "positive" checks (famine, disease, and so on).

4 The technological-economic potentials can be realized in many parts of the world, particularly the underdeveloped, low-calorie regions, *only* if the political, social, and economic institutions are changed, with consequent changes in the scales of values and priorities guiding the population. Land reform, a stable and viable central government responsive to the long-term needs of the community, a pattern of behavior that assigns sufficient weight to material welfare, and possibly other social changes are, in varying degree, indispensable to an effective and economic application of modern technology. Obviously, the variety and depth of these required social changes will be wider and greater if the food or agricultural targets cannot be attained by extension or slight modification of the old and traditional technology, but call for a shift to a different and modern technological base.

5 The capacity for making the required social changes and hence what may be called "social feasibility" cannot be appraised in general and yet testable terms. Whatever the cause and whatever the effect—whether the difficulty of measurement makes for ignorance, or ignorance makes for difficulty of measurement—our present knowledge of the precise social changes required for differing rates of economic and technological advance from different bases is poor. We have no inventory of the known political and social resources and their capacity for change. This aspect of the future is therefore usually presented as a "challenge" in response to the promise extended by the technoeconomic potentials, but one

that may or may not be met—with the result that the economic growth potentials may or may not be attained.

6 Since the individual country is the locus of decisions on changes in social, political, and economic institutions, the feasibility problem must be examined not only for the world and major regions, but also for individual countries. Furthermore, a distinction must be drawn between trends and short-term fluctuations. It should be recognized that the several areas within a country and the distinct socioeconomic groups within the population may differ in their growth potential and in their response to population growth.

7 Distinguishing the individual countries increases the number of points at which social and institutional difficulties may limit otherwise satisfactory technological and economic growth potentials, not only for food but also for other products. A single country may use some of these in international trade to obtain essentials. This means that, even if the world and the broad regions manage to raise output to provide for a growing population, some countries may fail. The loci of the resulting supply crises may shift over time from one underdeveloped country to another.

8 Distinguishing between trends and short-term fluctuations and recognizing the susceptibility of agriculture in the underdeveloped countries to vagaries of weather and natural calamities, one may expect that, even if the long-term growth trends are satisfactory, absolute declines in per capita production would be frequent. The task of dealing with the crises that would probably result emphasizes the need for a stable and effective central government capable of pursuing a long-term policy aimed at stabilizing supplies over time.

9 The same consideration is suggested by the recognition of the different impact of lagging trends or short-term declines on various areas or socioeconomic groups within a country. Diversities among areas and inequalities in income and levels of living are particularly conspicuous in the underdeveloped countries. Bridging interarea differences or relieving the impact of short-term declines on the lower economic groups may prove to be acute problems, since the average level of living is low and the central government is weak—particularly in the larger underdeveloped countries.

The above conclusions indicate that the failure to provide adequately for the prospective population numbers to year 2000 is likely to stem from the inability of society in underdeveloped countries to introduce the possibly major changes in their social and political organization and in their economic institutions that may be needed to exploit the otherwise adequate technoeconomic potentials. Such failure may also stem from the slow pace of improvements in international relations that would optimize the use of resources in furthering economic growth, particularly in the underdeveloped, low-calorie regions. In view of the long-recognized and repeatedly commented upon lag in the adjustment of the social and political structure to the technoeconomic potentials, particularly in modern history when technical change and economic innovation are so rapid, such conclusions are neither novel nor surprising.

What they mean in terms of the possibly calamitous consequences of the high rate of population growth projected to year 2000, particularly in the less-developed countries, depends largely upon one's judgment of the capacity of the underdeveloped countries to make the necessary social and political changes. Their meaning also depends on the capacity of the world to minimize wasteful strains in international relations (whether among the developed countries, among the underdeveloped, or between the two groups) and to further economic growth where it is most needed.

My own judgment is that neither wholesale calamity—widespread starvation and devastating epidemics—in the populous underdeveloped countries, nor widely successful social and political modernization permitting a rapid and effective exploitation of the large technological and economic potentials which many of them possess, will eventuate. But it is a judgment that does not reflect tested experience in a recognizably explicit fashion. The prospects for change in the social and political structure of the underdeveloped countries and in the framework of international relations can hardly be explored by the methods of economic and quantitative analysis; they require data and tools that are beyond the scope of this paper.

TABLE 1 FAO ESTIMATES OF FOOD REQUIREMENTS IN YEAR 2000
(Low-calorie regions; absolute values)

	Food Supplies in 1958			Food Requirements in 2000		
	Population (mill.) (1)	Food Supply per Capita (index) (2)	Total Food Supplies (index) (3)	Projected Population (mill.) (4)	Required Food per Capita (index) (5)	Total Food Requirements (index) (6)
1. Asia and Far East	1,498	88	1,318	3,639 *6.3*	147	5,349
2. Near East	125	159	199	327	186	608
3. Africa	208	101	210	421	129	543
4. Latin America (excl. River Plate countries)	170	155	264	548	163	893
5. Total, low-calorie regions (Group I)	2,001	100	1,991	4,935	150	7,393
6. Total, high-calorie regions (rest of world, Group II)	858	333	2,857	1,332	333	4,436
7. World	2,859	167	4,848	6,267	189	11,829

Relatives of Projections and Requirements in 2000;
Population and Food Supply in 1958 or 1957-59 = 100

	1961-63 Estimate			1965 Estimate		
	Population (mill.) (1)	Food per Capita (2)	Total Food (3)	Population (mill.) (4)	Food per Capita (5)	Total Food (6)
8. Asia and Far East	243	167	406	245	170	417
9. Near East	262	117	307	257	130	334
10. Africa	202	128	259	223	151	337
11. Latin America (excl. River Plate countries)	322	105	338	315	114	359
12. Total, low-calorie regions (Group I)	247	150	371	250	157	393
13. Total, high-calorie regions (Group II)	155	100	155	160	119	191
14. World	219	113	247	223	123	274

SOURCE: Lines 1-7, columns 1 and 4, and lines 8-14, columns 1 and 2: from Freedom from Hunger Campaign, *Possibilities of Increasing World Food Production* (Basic Study No. 10; Rome: Food and Agricultural Organization, 1963), Table 1, p. 14 and Table 2, pp. 24-25. Near East includes Cyprus, U.A.R., Iran, Iraq, Israel, Jordan, Lebanon, Libya, Sudan, Syria, and Turkey. Asia and the Far East, and Africa correspond to the usual definitions of the two continents, minus the relevant countries listed under Near East. River Plate countries excluded from Latin America and included under the high-calorie regions are Argentina, Uruguay, and Paraguay. The entry in line 6, column 4 is from P. V. Sukhatme, "The World's Hunger and Future Needs in Food Supplies," *Journal of the Royal Statistical Society*, CXXIV (Series A, General, Part 4, 1961), Table 18, p. 500. All other figures in this paper are identical with those for low-calorie regions in *Possibilities of Increasing World Food Production*, Basic Study No. 10.

Lines 1-7, column 2: from Freedom from Hunger Campaign, *Third World Food Survey* (Basic Study No. 11; Food and Agriculture Organization, 1963), Table 9, p. 20. In this table, percentage distributions among the several regions of world population and world food supplies are given for 1957-59 (which we identified with 1958). From these we derived an index of per capita supplies, to the base of an average for all low-calorie regions as 100. The calculations yield an index somewhat less than 100 because the population distribution among regions in Basic Study No. 11 is slightly different from that in Basic Study No. 10. Lines 1-7, column 5: The product of column 2, lines 1-7 and column 2, lines 8-14 (or summation for lines 5 and 7). Lines 8-14, columns 4-6: From P. V. Sukhatme, W. Schulte, Z. M. Ahmad, and G. T. Jones, "Demographic Factors Affecting Food Supplies and Agricultural Development," background paper, United Nations World Population Conference, 1965, Table 1, p. 40. We assumed that the absolute totals for 1957-59 were those shown in lines 1-7, columns 1-3. The indexes for year 2000 are given in the source for Group I regions and the world; those for Group II were implicit and calculated by us. Columns 3 and 6: The product, divided by 100, of columns 1 and 2, and 4 and 5, respectively.

TABLE 2   TRENDS IN FOOD PRODUCTION, TOTAL AND PER CAPITA INDEXES, 1925-29 TO 1962-64
(1934-38 = 100)

	1925-29 (1)	1948-52 (2)	1957-59 (3)	1962-64 (4)	1934-38 Percentage Shares in World Total and Relatives of Per Capita Food Production (to World Average) (5)
World incl. Mainland China					
Total Food Production					
1. Low-calorie regions	92	109	142	161	43
2. High-calorie regions	93	117	149	167	57 (67)
3. World	93	113	146	164	100
Population					
4. Low-calorie regions	90	120	143	163	68
5. High-calorie regions	92	105	118	126	32 (42)
6. World	91	115	135	150	100
Per Capita Food Production					
7. Low-calorie regions	102	91	99	99	63
8. High-calorie regions	101	111	126	133	178 (160)
9. World	102	98	108	109	100
World excl. Mainland China					
Total Food Production					
10. Low-calorie regions	n.a.	115	148	167	33
11. World	n.a.	116	148	167	100
Population					
12. Low-calorie regions	n.a.	124	147	165	58
13. World	n.a.	116	135	149	100
Per Capita Food Production					
14. Low-calorie regions	n.a.	93	101	101	57
15. World	n.a.	100	110	112	100
Ratio of Per Capita Food Production, High- to Low-Calorie Regions					
16. Incl. Mainland China ..	2.8	3.5	3.6	3.8	2.8 (1934-38)
17. Excl. Mainland China ..	n.a.	3.4	3.5	3.7	2.8 (1934-38)

(Continued)

TABLE 2, Continued

Rates of Growth per Decade (%)

	1925-29 to 1948-52	1934-38 to 1948-52	1948-52 to 1962-64	1925-29 to 1962-64	1934-38 to 1962-64
	(1)	(2)	(3)	(4)	(5)

World incl. Mainland China

Total Food Production

18. Low-calorie regions	7.7	6.4	35.0	16.8	19.3
19. High-calorie regions	10.5	11.9	31.5	17.7	20.9
20. World	8.8	9.1	33.2	17.1	20.1

Population

21. Low-calorie regions	13.3	13.9	26.6	17.9	19.8
22. High-calorie regions	5.9	3.5	15.1	9.1	8.9
23. World	10.7	11.3	20.9	14.9	16.2

Per Capita Food Production

24. Low-calorie regions	−5.0	−6.6	6.7	−0.9	−0.5
25. High-calorie regions	4.3	8.0	14.3	7.8	11.0
26. World	−1.7	−2.0	10.2	1.9	3.4

World excl. Mainland China

Total Food Production

27. Low-calorie regions	n.a.	10.5	33.2	n.a.	20.9
28. World	n.a.	11.2	32.4	n.a.	20.9

Population

29. Low-calorie regions	n.a.	16.6	24.6	n.a.	20.4
30. World	n.a.	11.2	21.2	n.a.	15.9

Per Capita Food Production

31. Low-calorie regions	n.a.	−5.2	7.0	n.a.	0.4
32. World	n.a.	0	9.2	n.a.	4.3

SOURCE: The estimates for 1934-38 and later years are from P. V. Sukhatme, "The World Food Supplies," *Journal of the Royal Statistical Society*, CXXIX (Series A, General, Part 2, 1966), Table 6A, p. 234. The note to the table indicates that "these index numbers have been calculated by applying regional weights based on 1952-56 farm price relationships to regional production figures adjusted to allow for quantities used for feed and seed." The table shows indexes for total and per capita food production, and the population indexes were calculated from these. For the composition of the low, and high-calorie groups see notes to Table 1. It is assumed that "pre-war" means averages for 1934-38, as is indicated by the use of 1936 as the central year (see "The World Food Supplies," Table 6B, p. 234).

The indexes of total food production were extrapolated back to 1925-29 by means of the League of Nations estimates in *World Production and Prices, 1938-39* (Geneva: League of Nations, 1939), Appendix I, Table 1, p. 87; Table 3, pp. 90-92; Table 5, pp. 97-100. The low-calorie regions here were Asia, Africa, and Latin America; the high-calorie regions were Europe (including the U.S.S.R.), North America, and Oceania. Population figures for these continents (disregarding the minor adjustment for the

River Plate countries here and in the case of food production) were interpolated for 1927 and 1936 between the UN estimates for 1920, 1930, and 1940—the latter two from the *Demographic Yearbook, 1965*, Table 1, p. 103, and the first from *World Population Prospects as Assessed in 1963* (New York: United Nations, 1966), Table A3.1, p. 133—along a straight logarithmic line. The rates of growth thus obtained for total food production, population, and per capital food production were applied to the indexes for 1934-38 to estimate the level in 1925-29.

The shares in column 5 for food production are from *Third World Food Survey*, Basic Study No. 11, Appendix 2B, p. 85; and for population from the UN data indicated in the paragraph above. The entries in parentheses in lines 2, 5, and 8 are the shares and relatives for the high-calorie group in the world excluding Mainland China. Per capita food production for Mainland China in 1934-38 (which was deducted from the total for low calorie regions) was assumed to equal that in the low-calorie regions as a whole, excluding China.

TABLE 3 TRENDS IN FOOD PRODUCTION AND FOOD SUPPLIES, TOTAL AND PER CAPITA, 1934-38 TO 1962-64

(*World and low-calorie regions excl. Mainland China*)

	Far East (1)	Near East (2)	Africa (3)	Latin America (4)	Low-Calorie Regions (5)	High-Calorie Regions (6)	World (7)
Net Balance of Food Exports (—) and Imports (+), % of Domestic Production							
1. 1934-38	−2	−1	−14	−25	−10	+7	0
2. 1948-52	+3	+3	−10	−11	−3	+2	0
3. 1962-64	+5	+6	−11	−10	0	0	0
A. Indexes (1934-38 = 100)							
Total Food Production							
4. 1948-52	105	122	127	129	115	117	116
5. 1962-64	151	192	181	185	167	167	167
Total Food Supplies							
6. 1948-52	112	128	133	154	124	112	116
7. 1962-64	165	211	191	227	185	157	167
Population							
8. 1948-52	121	122	121	135	124	105	116
9. 1962-64	155	166	161	187	165	126	149
Per Capita Food Production							
10. 1948-52	87	100	105	96	93	111	100
11. 1962-64	97	116	112	99	101	133	112
Per Capita Food Supplies							
12. 1948-52	93	105	110	114	100	107	100
13. 1962-64	106	127	119	121	112	125	112
B. Rates of Growth per Decade (%)							
Total Food Production							
14. 1934-38 to 1948-52	3.5	15.3	18.6	19.9	10.5	11.9	11.2
15. 1948-52 to 1962-64	32.2	41.7	31.3	32.0	33.2	31.5	32.4
16. 1934-38 to 1962-64	16.5	27.3	24.6	25.6	20.9	20.9	20.9

(*Continued*)

TABLE 3, Continued

	Far East (1)	Near East (2)	Africa (3)	Latin America (4)	Low-Calorie Regions (5)	High-Calorie Regions (6)	World (7)
Total Food Supplies							
17. 1934-38 to 1948-52	8.4	19.3	22.6	36.1	16.6	8.4	11.2
18. 1948-52 to 1962-64	34.7	46.9	32.1	34.8	36.0	29.7	32.4
19. 1934-38 to 1962-64	20.4	31.9	27.1	35.5	25.6	18.2	20.9
Population							
20. 1934-38 to 1948-52	14.6	15.3	14.6	23.9	16.6	3.5	11.2
21. 1948-52 to 1962-64	21.0	26.7	24.6	28.5	24.6	15.1	21.2
22. 1934-38 to 1962-64	17.6	20.6	19.3	26.1	20.4	8.9	15.9
Per Capita Food Production							
23. 1934-38 to 1948-52	−9.6	0	3.5	−3.2	−5.2	8.0	0
24. 1948-52 to 1962-64	9.3	11.8	5.4	2.7	7.0	14.3	9.2
25. 1934-38 to 1962-64	−1.0	5.5	4.4	−0.4	0.4	11.0	4.3
Per Capita Food Supplies							
26. 1934-38 to 1948-52	−5.4	3.5	7.0	9.9	0	4.7	0
27. 1948-52 to 1962-64	11.4	15.9	6.0	4.9	9.2	12.7	9.2
28. 1934-38 to 1962-64	2.3	9.3	6.5	7.4	4.3	8.5	4.3

SOURCE: Lines 1-3: From P. V. Sukhatme, "The World Food Supplies," Table 11, p. 238. The net balance percentages are given for the three dates for each low-calorie region and for Western Europe, North America, and Oceania among the high-calorie regions. We calculated the net balance for the total low-calorie group (column 5) by using the 1934-38 production weights in *Third World Food Survey*, Basic Study No. 11, Appendix 2B; we did likewise for the high-calorie regions, after eliminating the U.S.S.R., the weights for which were derived from *World Production and Prices, 1938-39*. Minor adjustments were made to the algebraic total of the net balances for the regions in order to have the net balance for the world excluding Mainland China equal zero.

Lines 4-5, 8-9, and 10-11: The indexes in columns 5-7 are identical with those in Table 2 and were kept so by design. Consequently, the weighted averages of the indexes for the several regions (the four low-calorie and the three high-calorie—the latter, in fact, did not account fully for the total since the U.S.S.R. and Eastern

Europe and the River Plate countries were omitted) had to be adjusted to the over-all indexes used in Table 2 to assure identity.

The regional production indexes were taken from *State of Food and Agriculture, 1966* (Rome: Food and Agriculture Organization, 1966), Annex Tables 2A and 2B, pp. 195-98; and linked with the 1934-38 base by the indexes in the FAO *Production Yearbook, 1958*, Tables 6 and 7, pp. 27-28 (the overlap was for 1954-55 through 1956-57). The FAO indexes are for crop years beginning in the years indicated in the stubs. Indexes are given for both total and per capita food production and those for population were derived from these.

Lines 6-7 and 12-13: Indexes of supplies were calculated by applying the net balances of food exports and imports to the adjusted regional indexes of output, and then further adjusted so that the balance added out to zero for the world on each of the three dates.

All adjustments referred to above, made to reconcile weighted regional indexes with given broader and world totals, are minor and do not affect the results significantly.

Lines 14-28: Calculated directly from lines 4-13.

TABLE 4   RATES OF GROWTH IMPLICIT IN FOOD REQUIREMENTS 1958 TO 2000 AND 1958 TO 1975, AND OBSERVED RATES, 1957-59 TO 1962-64

	Rates of Growth per Decade (%)				
	Implicit in Requirements				Fulfillment Ratio, Col. 4 ÷ Col. 3 (5)
	1958-2000, early estimate (1)	1958-2000, later estimate (2)	1958-1975, later estimate (3)	Observed, 1957-59 to 1962-64 (4)	
Total Food Requirements and Production					
1. Far East	39.6	40.5	42.7	34.7*	0.81
2. Near East	30.6	33.3	35.2	27.9	0.79
3. Africa	25.4	33.5	33.8	32.4	0.96
4. Latin America	33.6	35.6	39.5	27.7†	0.70
5. Low-calorie regions	36.6	38.5	40.9	28.6*†	0.67
6. High-calorie regions	11.0	16.7	16.7	25.6	1.53
7. World	24.0	27.1	27.4	27.3*	1.00
Population					
8. Far East	23.5	23.8	21.9	24.8*	1.13
9. Near East	25.8	25.2	23.4	28.6	1.22
10. Africa	18.2	21.0	18.3	26.3	1.44
11. Latin America	32.1	31.4	29.4	31.0†	1.05
12. Low-calorie regions	24.0	24.4	22.4	27.3*†	1.22
13. High-calorie regions	11.0	11.8	13.5	12.7	0.94
14. World	20.5	21.0	19.8	22.8*	1.15
Per Capita Food Requirements and Production					
15. Far East	13.0	13.5	17.1	7.9*	0.46
16. Near East	3.8	6.4	9.6	−0.6	−0.06
17. Africa	6.1	10.3	13.1	4.9	0.37
18. Latin America	1.2	3.2	7.8	−2.5†	−0.32
19. Low-calorie regions	10.2	11.4	15.1	0*†	0
20. High-calorie regions	0	4.3	2.8	11.4	4.07
21. World	2.9	5.0	6.3	3.7*	0.59

* Excludes Mainland China.
† Includes the River Plate countries.

SOURCE: Columns 1-2: Calculated from the indexes in Table 1, lines 8-14. Column 3: From P. V. Sukhatme and others, "Demographic Factors Affecting Food Supplies and Agricultural Development," p. 40. The source shows projected population and requirements for both 1975 and 2000 (as indexes to the base 1957-59 = 100), for the four low-calorie regions, the total for them, and the world. Those for high-calorie regions were calculated using the weights for 1957-59 given in *Third World Food Survey*, Basic Study No. 11, Table 9, p. 20.
Column 4: Based on total and per capita indexes in *The State of Food and Agriculture, 1966*, Annex Tables 2A and 2B, pp. 195-98, for each low-calorie region; on the indexes in Table 2 for the low- and high-calorie regions and the world. Population indexes were derived from those for total and per capita production.

TABLE 5 RATES OF GROWTH AND MEASURES OF VARIABILITY, PER CAPITA FOOD PRODUCTION, INDIVIDUAL LOW-CALORIE COUNTRIES, POSTWAR YEARS

	Rates of Growth per Decade (%)		Measures of Variability (countries showing rise over period in col. 2)	
	1952-54 to 1962-64 (1)	1952-58 to 1958-64 (2)	Absolute Average Dev. from trend (3)	Number of Years of Decline (4)
Far East				
1. *Region*	9.2	10.2	1.7	3
2. Burma	5.3	8.1	3.7	7
3. Ceylon	9.7	9.9	4.8	2
4. China (Taiwan)	7.1	4.7	2.9	4
5. India	4.0	6.5	2.4	4
6. Indonesia	−8.9	−7.5	..	..
7. Japan	27.4	21.1	3.8	4
8. South Korea	8.3	6.8	7.8	6
9. Malaya	35.9	36.2	4.5	5
10. Pakistan	0.6	2.9	3.8	6
11. Philippines	−2.0	−3.1	..	..
12. Thailand	20.1	17.8	7.5	4
Near East				
13. *Region*	7.1	6.9	2.3	4
14. Iran	6.8	6.5	4.8	4
15. Iraq	−9.0	−12.0	..	..
16. Israel	68.8	67.6	3.3	1
17. Syria	−6.5	−22.0	..	..
18. Turkey	4.3	9.0	6.5	5
19. U. A. R.	18.1	10.5	3.8	3
Latin America				
20. *Region* (including River Plate countries)	3.0	1.9	1.6	5
21. Brazil	11.5	12.9	1.8	2
22. Chile	−2.9	−3.8	..	..
23. Colombia	−0.7	−3.1	..	..
24. Cuba	−13.1	−8.7	..	..
25. Guatemala	−2.0	−1.0	..	..
26. Honduras	−6.8	−3.3	..	..
27. Mexico	39.0	39.0	3.3	2
28. Panama	4.8	2.1	2.9	4
29. Peru	−11.0	−6.2	..	..
30. Venezuela	21.1	19.2	5.3	4
River Plate Countries				
31. Argentina	1.0	−4.7	..	..
32. Uruguay	−27.2	−33.8	..	..

Source: The calculations are based on the indexes in *The State of Food and Agriculture, 1966*, Annex Tables 2A and 2B, pp. 195-98.

The deviations in column 3 are from a straight line fitted to the averages for 1952-58 and 1958-64. The underlying series are indexes with 1952-56 = 100; the averages, for series with upward trends, range from about 100 to less than 125. The average deviations would therefore be roughly the same if taken as percentages of the average level.

Column 4 shows the number of years in which the per capita index of food production declines absolutely (the number of annual changes in the entire period is 12).

Comments on Kuznets

Gustav Ranis

Assistant Administrator for Program and Policy
Agency for International Development,
Department of State

THE PAPER before us is a tight, well-documented and well-balanced presentation on a subject of the greatest importance. The data are weighed judiciously; few "quick and dirty" generalizations are made. It provides relief on the one hand, from the purple language to which neo-Malthusians have recently been exposing us, and, on the other, from the general complacency of the "establishment" (both operators and academicians) on the subject of world food requirements and productive capacity. In other words, the paper is in the best Kuznetsian tradition.

Turning first to the estimate of requirements, Kuznets does a thorough job of examining the statistical evidence on population and food output for high calorie and low calorie regions from 1925 to the present. He immediately puts his finger on the central problem—the fact that per capita food output in low calorie regions in recent years is just slightly ahead of 1934-38, while per capita food supplies elsewhere are 12 per cent larger. This demonstrates the need for growing imports from the high calorie to the low calorie regions.

Projecting into the future (year 2000) on the basis of minimum caloric requirements and reasonable population growth estimates (largely based on estimates of the Food and Agricultural Organization), he comes up with a 3.5 per cent required growth rate of food production for the years 1965-2000. The same methodology applied to the same problem has led the President's panel of scientific advisors to similar results. Taking India, Pakistan, and Brazil as test cases, which are then "blown up" to global proportions, this group, projecting population by age distribution and adjusting for body weight, derived nutrient and caloric requirements leading to a 4 per cent annual growth of food requirements to satisfy the minimum nutritional needs. These are very close to Kuznets' results. Coupled with a 0.6 per capita elasticity of demand for food—and working backwards—this yields an approximate 5½ per cent needed annual growth rate of income.

In assessing the potential for meeting these requirements between now and 2000, Kuznets looks at the actual experience over the recent past (1948-52 to 1962-64), and feels somewhat disturbed for a number of reasons.

1 The requirements are already going up faster than projected by the FAO. They are perhaps closer to the 4 per cent annual level of the President's Science Advisory Council.

2 The base period may be misleading. This, I think, was borne out by the recent twenty-seven country study of the U.S. Department of Agriculture, which indicates that the 1960-65 period was not as good as the entire postwar period taken as a whole. This could be attributed to the unusually good performance of the 1950's when, as Raymond Goldsmith would say, "The world was growing back into its skin."

3 The possibility of trade and aid between the high and low calorie regions can help relatively little in the future. It is not as clear to me why this need be true in the future, since it has not been true in the recent past—as Table 3 indicates. The enactment of Public Law 480 in 1954 made a substantial difference, and future food shipments, both commercial and concessional, from many of the developed to the less-developed countries should by no means be given as short shrift as they are by Kuznets. During 1962-64, for instance, net food imports into the Near and Far East amounted to 5-6 per cent of domestic production in that area. U.S. wheat acreage was increased by 30 per cent in the summer of 1966 to make further increases of such shipments possible. The 1965-67 failure of the monsoons in South Asia led to a sharp increase in food flows which, while hopefully temporary, indicates their potential importance.

4 In the past in the low calorie regions, growth was dependent on area expansion, which is no longer feasible in the future. Here I am not so sure that history is a really reliable guide. As Professor Kuznets well knows, we have had experience in a number of countries, including Japan, and more recently Taiwan, Pakistan, and Korea, with dramatic and sustained increases in agricultural yields. This experience can be duplicated elsewhere *if* the proper policy and resources input mix is applied to the agricultural sector and to the relationships among sectors. As we grow more sophisticated about what it takes to activate the peasant on the intensive margin through a combination of physical inputs, adaptive research, incentive price levels, and visible (to the farmer) investment opportunities and financial intermediaries, such admittedly episodal historical experience provides me with room for considerable confidence as to what is possible.

The historical evidence cited by Kuznets on the importance of new land (only 30 per cent of the increase in less-developed countries' food production was on the intensive margin) can be read optimistically in terms of the huge remaining productivity reserves potentially available. We could cite as further evidence large yield differences between developed countries and less-developed countries, and, even more relevant, among less-developed countries; perhaps most important—and not mentioned by Kuznets—are the differences among different regions of the *same* less-developed country. In this connection, as a recent study by Heston of the University of Pennsylvania shows, high-yielding pockets exist even in the slowest-growing agricultural sector, for example in South India. The need for disaggregation is clearly established.

We know that two processes are going forward worldwide all the time, and that we can influence the speed with which these processes are moving. The first is the improvement of best practice as a function of a combination of conventional and nonconventional inputs (whether in developed countries, underdeveloped countries, or at such research centers as the International Rice Research Institute at Baguio). The second is the reduction of the average practice/best practice gap as a function of both technical assistance across national boundaries and of education, extension, market liberalization, and other methods of diffusion within a country.

PROFESSOR KUZNETS probably does not disagree with any of this but feels that caution is the better part of valor (or wisdom) and thus prefers not to assign weight to technological change "as yet unborn." If there were no costs involved in exercising such caution on the possibilities of both trade and technological changes, one could readily agree to "play it safe," especially in an area where there is no comfortable margin for error. But I think there are costs in playing it too safe, just as there are costs in ignoring the problem or simply trusting the gods of exogenous technological change.

I will not spell out these costs here, but, as always when the pendulum swings too far (in this case, from neglect of agriculture to food self-sufficiency for every less-developed country), neglect of these potentialities could lead us to rather uneconomic less-developed country investment patterns, including attempting capital-intensive rollbacks of the extensive margin and unduly autarkic foreign trade and exchange policies. I would rather study the experience of those countries that have been able to activate their agricultural sectors successfully at the intensive margin with the help of the "right" mix of resource allocation and institutional change. Anyone who has closely watched the sharp reversal in the performance of Pakistan's agriculture between 1961-65 is bound to be less skeptical about the possibilities of such successes being repeated elsewhere. Moreover, while the additional food requirements must admittedly be met by action within the less-developed countries, the possibilities of using the reserve capacity of some of the wealthier countries for trade and/or aid (phenomena not taken into account in the basic projections) should not be discounted.

But these are largely differences in emphasis, and Professor Kuznets is fully aware of the potential of such major structural changes; he simply wants to avoid the complacency inherent in an appeal to the simple analogy that neo-Malthusians will be proven just as wrong as Malthus was. Where I do perhaps have a substantive problem with this otherwise excellent paper is with respect to the discussion on the "technological" versus the "economic" aspects of the capacity to produce. If I understand it correctly, I do not find this separation especially meaningful or helpful. Professor Kuznets himself agrees that it does not really make sense in a "properly defined technologically feasible situation," but that does not really help me either. For, according to Kuznets, a "properly defined technologically feasible situation" on the food front converges with one that is "economically feasible" if its appetite for economic resources does not prevent "needed and desirable" growth elsewhere.

Now NO one would deny that certain technological or engineering choices are relevant in some economic contexts and irrelevant in others, depending on the objective natural resource or factor endowment situation. But the notion that technological and economic feasibility coincide only when resources are not withdrawn unduly from application to other desirable ends is not clear. If it is technically feasible to produce more food—and there is excess demand for food—the relative price of food will go up and the technological choice previously irrelevant becomes economic. Just as the extra production of more cars does not starve the economy for more shirts (any more than it wants to be starved), the extra production of food will not starve the economy for more housing than it wants to be starved. It is certainly true that growth in particular societies may be hampered unless trade takes place between those that can expand food production economically and those that cannot. If this trade does not take place, the need for a country to put a large share of the total investment fund into food production may be a very uneconomic thing to do if other countries are better at producing food.

But this is different from saying that under such circumstances a wedge is driven between technological and economic feasibility. If, in a closed economy, people have a choice between growing wheat in the desert or drilling for oil, they will plant the wheat and it will be an economic thing for them to do since the scarcity price of wheat will far exceed that of oil. In the open economy, it is true that countries will hate to give up the "indispensable raw material imports" Kuznets refers to for the sake of food imports, but food imports may be more indispensable under the conditions stated; therefore, this becomes an economic thing to do. In other words, I do not know why food should not be treated like any other commodity with due regard for its superior Engel-Curve strength at low levels of per capita income.

The important question of social feasibility that Kuznets discusses in the last part of the paper is, of course, closely related to the general problem. If the necessary institutional and technological changes that he writes about so eloquently fail us, we will certainly first have to give up growth and ultimately starve to death. But, while Kuznets does not really want to "count his technological change before it hatches," he has a strong underlying faith in the potential of institutional and technological change. Perhaps I am even less worried than he is, but not because I believe that somehow the new technological breakthroughs will occur autonomously at just the right time while we sit back and relax. I believe, rather, that it will happen because we know a lot more than we used to and because we can work on it; we can increase the flow of ideas and energies not previously tapped in the tightly controlled less-developed country society. We sometimes get carried away by the big new "food from the sea"-type of ideas; useful as these may be, I think we can do much better by working consistently toward the stimulation of indigenous nonspectacular technological change among the large number of agricultural decision makers, via the application of relevant policy changes and resource inputs.

Effective central government, as Kuznets points out, may have an important role to play in ensuring that such changes are made; but I would contend that sometimes the greatest contribution such governments can make is to help perfect the markets and then step aside and let local bodies and lots of little people innovate in a relatively free, more price-determined environment. I think it is within our grasp to help create the environment in which domestic innovation and diffusion juices can be turned on so that those forgotten people who know how to build a slightly better mouse trap or adapt a slightly better seed can go to work and bring agricultural yields slightly closer to their potential.

Agricultural Development Is Not Enough

Joseph J. Spengler

*James B. Duke Professor of Economics,
Duke University*

> "*Causes and effects in social systems interweave in a concatenation of reciprocal and cumulative interaction.*"
>
> K. W. Kapp in T. K. N. Unithan, ed.,
> *Towards a Sociology of Culture in India*

A THERAPIST must identify the disease he is appointed to cure. Otherwise, he is unlikely to fulfill his mission—unless the disease in question is one that yields to improvement in the body's general health, which in turn is fortified by the therapist's treatment. Given a specific disease calling for, say, specific chemotherapy, however, general ministration is bound to fail.

My assignment resembles that of a therapist—the assessment of a proposed cure for a disease, albeit a cure not very sharply defined for a disease essentially implied. I shall, therefore, take some liberties with both cure and disease. My discussion is presented under eight heads: the problem, the geographical locus of the problem and its theoretical aspects, the nature of modernization, capital and its role in modernization, the positive role of agriculture, the impact of modernization upon fertility, the empirical aspects of contemporary agriculture and population trends, and the upshot of all this for the theme of the conference.

I

Let me turn first to the disease—"population calamity." Here we must resolve two issues. Is our concern psychic well-being? Or is it the maintenance of an economic indicator at some level? If it be the latter, it is essential that we settle upon an indicator.

If our concern be psychic well-being, then we must allow for the possibility that real income beyond a certain level contributes little to human happiness. Given health and a life expectancy of around 70, men do not need much to live reasonably happy lives. So-called civilization brings in its wake nearly as many afflictions as it supposedly removes. Freud was not mistaken when he linked civilization and discontent, nor is Dubos mistaken when he points to the utopian character of man's hope to escape diseases of his own making.[1] Even accessible space and discretionary time, of increasing importance in the budgets of the educated well-to-do, may not be so significant in underdeveloped lands. All this is probably to the good. It could countervail political instability in countries whose average income is unlikely ever to approximate American levels.[2] We need to ask, therefore, and political leaders in low-income countries need to ask, should policy therein be dominated by the pursuit of happiness or by the pursuit of unattainable objectives? Needless to say, the latter will probably be chosen.

Suppose, however, that we set aside the issue of psychic well-being and focus attention upon indicators of performance. Abstracting from difficulties of measurement and comparison, we then have three types of indicators in terms of which to define population calamity and its aversion or solution. First, we may use some measure of food consumption—calories, for example, coupled with essential nutrients. This indicator is favored by what I call inverted Malthusians, individuals who conceive of the state of the population problem almost entirely in terms of whether numbers or

---

[1] René Dubos, *Man Adapting* (New Haven: Yale University Press, 1965), Chaps. 9, 13.

[2] Even if an underdeveloped country's average income grew, say, 3 per cent per year for a century while that in advanced countries grew only 1 per cent per year, income in the former would still be only about seven-tenths as high as that in the latter, given that today incomes in advanced countries are ten times those in developed countries.

calories are growing faster. This is a primitive approach. It ignores two facts: that man does not live by bread alone, and that, as will be explained later, agricultural skill is highly correlated with other kinds of skills.

Second, we may use an indicator of actual consumption per capita, by country. The monetary cost of a given pattern of consumption tends to be lowest, of course, in the country where the pattern is found, since a particular country's population tends to concentrate consumption upon products whose prices in that country are relatively low.[3] This index provides a reasonably good impression of how a population is living, and of changes in its level of living, but not of its average productivity as reflected in gross or net national product per capita. Thus in 1960 the ratio of GNP to private consumption per head ranged from 1.275 in Turkey to 1.995 in Norway. Even so, the order of countries based upon average private consumption did not differ greatly from that based upon a third possible indicator, namely, average GNP.[4] In my discussion, I shall make use both of indicators of the food supply and of measures of actual or potential productivity expressed in terms of average GNP.

II

While the Third World, consisting of non-Communist underdeveloped countries, constitutes a distinct component of the Whole World, or homosphere, it interacts with the so-called Free and Communist Worlds. This interaction is far more intense today than in the nineteenth century. Verbal and visual communication can be almost instantaneous; transport of most objects can be accomplished in a few hours if necessary; and one country's misery may become another country's concern within a month.

It follows that the Third World can draw upon the capital, technology, skilled personnel, and pool of nonobsolete scientific

---

[3] A. H. Hansen, *Economic Stabilization in an Unbalanced World* (New York: Harcourt, Brace & World, 1932), p. 253; Adam Smith, *The Wealth of Nations* (New York: Modern Library, Inc., 1937), p. 187.

[4] Wilfred Beckerman, *International Comparisons of Incomes* (Paris: Development Center of OECD, 1966), p. 42.

knowledge of the developed Free World—mainly Northern America, Free Europe, English-speaking Oceania, Japan, Israel, and the Republic of South Africa—and in some measure upon the resources of the Soviet Union and its East European satellites. The capacity of the developed Free World to be of assistance to the underdeveloped world turns upon (among other things) the rate of population growth in both the former and the latter worlds.

We are carried back in time, therefore, to a choice point identified by John Stuart Mill in the year of Marx's *Communist Manifesto,* only to be disregarded by European man and his imperialist, military, and trade-oriented rulers. Mill indicated in essence that European man could bring his population growth to a halt and, should he do so, generate more savings than could be offset at home, invest the same in the New World, and there develop supplies of produce and raw materials for Britain and Europe as well as markets for their products. A comparable choice point has been identified by J. R. Hicks.[5]

Population in the developed Free World may continue to grow about as rapidly in this century as in 1920-60. It could, however, come to a stop, should knowledge of contraception continue to increase and incentive to practice it grow. After all, population growth must cease sometime—it cannot continue indefinitely in a finite world—and it had best cease now before too many future options are lost.

Should population growth persist in the developed world, economic life will go on more or less as in the past. Aggregate income will rise, and the demand for the products of underdeveloped countries, especially primary commodities, will rise, provided synthetic production of these commodities is not undertaken. The terms of trade of the underdeveloped countries will benefit, and they will have access to loans, financial aid, and other assistance from the developed countries.

But, should population growth cease, a different set of conditions

---

[5] J. R. Hicks, "Growth and Anti-Growth," *Oxford Economic Papers,* XVIII (November, 1966), pp. 257-69; J. S. Mills in William James Ashley, ed., *Principles of Political Economy* (New York: Longmans, Green & Co., 1921), Bk. IV, Chaps. 3, 4; Joseph J. Spengler, "John Stuart Mill on Economic Development," in B. F. Hoselitz, ed., *Theories of Economic Growth* (Glencoe, Ill.: Free Press, 1960), pp. 130-36.

will come into being. It may be, as Professor Hicks states (though I am more optimistic), that in the absence of appropriate organizational change, "there will then be more danger of Keynesian stagnation; it will be harder to maintain a high level of employment," and more savings may be wasted upon armaments, space-doggling, and ordinary legislative prodigality. Moreover, underdeveloped countries will enjoy less favorable terms of trade. But, in contrast, one may list the advantages. First, since savings will no longer be needed to finance the population increase in developed countries, they will have more to spare for the modernization and industrialization of underdeveloped countries. The increase in savings available could range at a minimum between 2½ and 5 per cent of the national incomes of the developed countries. Second, the resulting changes in the economic structure of underdeveloped countries will ease the pressure upon the prices of their exports and thus countervail the tendency toward a worsening of the terms of trade.[6]

The upshot of what I have said is that the future of the underdeveloped world depends in part upon the course of fertility in the developed world. It appears, as Mill argued and as Hicks seems to be arguing, that not only the developed Free World (except those countries with suboptimum populations, mainly Canada, Australia, and New Zealand) but also the Third World would stand to benefit from a cessation of population growth in developed countries. This possibility must, therefore, be included within the conspectus of approaches contributing to the solution of the population problem in the Third World.

III

What I have just said may be put in more general theoretical terms before I turn to the empirical side. Consider first the standard of life S in effect in a country. This is really a kind of weighted average of the standards of consumption of the diverse groups composing a country's population. It is subject to continuous variation and tends to rise as productive capacity and income rise. This standard represents the demand of a representative citizen

---

[6] "Growth and Anti-Growth," pp. 267-69.

for inputs which are produced in a country or imported from abroad, usually in exchange for other inputs exported abroad.

The aggregate demand of a country's population for inputs at any point in time has three sources. First, the major source is the product of a country's population P and its standard S, namely PS. Second, should the replacement of a country's population and capital absorb inputs beyond those required to satisfy demand PS, an added category arises; call this R. *Finally,* of considerable importance is the set of inputs required for the addition of increments of population and capital to a country's current population P and its stock of equipment; let us call this A. The aggregate requirement of inputs in a given year, then, is $PS + R + A$, and it grows as this sum grows. S is made up, as R and A, of components $s_1, s_2, \ldots s_n$, some of which are variously substitutable for others and some of which are not replaceable. These components may be viewed as inputs, or, when necessary, reduced to terms of more primary inputs. Among these components, time itself must be included, since no one is willing to work beyond a certain amount, and since time is one of the costs involved in consumption activities.[7]

Population P pursues its standard S in a relatively self-contained environment E. This environment in turn is reducible to components susceptible to varying rates of sustained growth, ranging from the relatively high to the relatively low. It is the more slowly growing of these components that in the end will govern the rate of growth of $PS + R + A$. For, as linear programming shows, "the needed component of slowest growth will set the pace for the whole."[8] If some of the components can grow only at a very low rate, the rate of growth of these components will determine the rate of growth of the whole unless the components in question can be replaced or eliminated from the standard of living S. Accordingly, if we would solve the problem of agricultural development, we must identify the slowly growing components and assess their future growth.

[7] See, for example, Jacob Mincer, "Market Prices, Opportunity Costs, and Income Effects," in Carl F. Christ, and others, *Measurement in Economics* (Stanford: Stanford University Press, 1963), pp. 67 ff.

[8] R. Dorfman, P. A. Samuelson, and R. Solow, *Linear Programming and Economic Analysis* (New York: McGraw-Hill Book Company, 1958), p. 281.

Even without such assessment, one conclusion is clear. We live in a finite world. There is, therefore, a limit to the total supply of each component of S and to the rate of growth of each component. Accordingly, if technology is stationary, the ultimate outcome is a stationary state, though probably one robbed of the terrors of the Smithian stationary state. If, on the contrary, technology is dynamic, a country's production possibility curve is pushed outward, and conditions of transformation are changed. This process is subject, however, to the kind of limitations we have already been discussing, namely, that the rates of flow of the quantities of some ingredients of S are limited. The limitations may lie in environment E as noted. They may even lie in the population itself. For, just as in a low-income population the amount of work time that can be put forth is physiologically limited, so in a high-income population the amount of work time that a population will supply is limited by the essentiality of that time to the enjoyment of a high S.

IV

I return now to an implication stated in the prospectus of this conference. There it is said that one obvious method of beating the population problem is to increase agricultural outputs. In a sense this statement is correct. Produce is an important component of the standard of life, especially in low-income countries. Moreover, as I shall indicate, yields per acre are susceptible to great increase. If, however, this statement implies that yields can be greatly increased in the absence of modernization of the whole economy and perhaps also of the polity, then the statement is not valid. Modernization of agriculture is a necessary condition; on this students of the problem seem agreed. Schultz writes: "In traditional agriculture the factors of production on which a community depends are expensive sources of economic growth."[9] He thus implies that these factors are scarce and in inelastic supply.

Modernization of agriculture is not, however, a sufficient condition, for this form of modernization cannot proceed independently of the modernization of the economy. This does not mean that a

[9] T. W. Schultz, *Transforming Traditional Agriculture* (New Haven: Yale University Press, 1964), p. 97.

very high average income is essential to modernization, or that an economy may not remain dualistic, though in diminishing measure. Of this we have evidence in Japan. Japan's economy has not yet entirely shed its dualism; indeed, its high rate of growth has been facilitated by this shedding process and the resources thereby made available to the modern sector. Japan's real GNP per head in 1960 was only about one-third that of the United States, but its agricultural yields per acre compared favorably with those in the United States and often exceeded them by large margins, though yield per labor input was much smaller.

What I have just said comes to this: modernization is a holistic process, of which modernization of agriculture is a part, but not an independent part. The student of modernization must, as Marion Levy points out, be sensitive to the complete society of interrelated elements, to the interaction of a society's members "in terms of their society rather than in terms of their governments, their business forms, their class positions, etc., considered as things apart from one another."[10] The student of agricultural modernization must be sensitive to the context in which agriculture is carried out, to the fact that the best results are often gotten by investment, not in traditional factors, but in nontraditional factors.[11]

Each system of agriculture utilizes both inputs common to all systems and inputs common only to some systems or peculiar to itself. If a new system of agriculture is to be introduced into a country, the inputs essential to it must be brought into existence just as must the inputs essential to a new type of industrial system. The changeover will entail certain additional private costs as well, among them loss of the rents enjoyed by the beneficiaries of any existing system, that is, by individuals who may therefore resist change. A system of agriculture such as that developed in Japan places primary emphasis upon increasing output per acre, and lesser emphasis upon increasing yield per manpower input. A system such as that developed in the United States, on the contrary, stresses output per manpower input, though seldom if ever to the neglect of input per unit of land.[12] In the long run, of course, the behavior of output per agricultural worker is important,

---

[10] Marion J. Levy, *Modernization and the Structure of Societies*, I (Princeton: Princeton University Press, 1966), p. 4.

[11] *Transforming Traditional Agriculture*, p. 93.

inasmuch as it conditions how many persons can be released from agriculture if and when enough capital is formed to permit their employment elsewhere. The principal point I wish to make is that many of the inputs required for a new and modern system of agriculture must be drawn from outside agriculture. Their supply is thus conditioned in fact by what takes place outside agriculture.

An examination of the inventory of yield-increasing practices discloses the dependence of agricultural progress upon progress elsewhere in an economy. Lester Brown lists these practices under the following heads: multiple cropping, fallowing, irrigation and drainage, agricultural chemicals (that is, fertilizers and pesticides), improved varieties, mechanization, careful use (as in Japan) of labor in labor-long countries, and so on.[13] Pursuit of these practices depends upon the degree of support agriculture receives from the nonagricultural sector, which must provide agriculture with most of the goods and services essential to its modernization; these cannot be brought in from the outside in adequate measure. Hence "a country lacking a well developed, nonagricultural supporting sector would find it extremely difficult, if not impossible, to generate a yield takeoff."[14] It is not surprising, therefore, that the rate of adoption and/or perfection of yield-increasing practices is roughly correlated with elevation of the level of literacy, so essential to the diffusion of information, and with the progress of per capita income, perhaps the best single indicator of the degree of modernization of an economy. Moreover, where average income is relatively high, agriculture becomes market-oriented, a condition essential to its progress and to providing farmers with incentive, given that they derive the major benefit from profitable prices.[15] In sum, argiculture cannot progress *in vacuo;* it is a subsystem within both the economy and the larger societal system; it

[12] See, for example, Lester R. Brown, *Increasing World Food Output*, U.S. Department of Agriculture (Foreign Agricultural Economic Report No. 25; Washington: U.S. Gov't Printing Office, April, 1965), Chaps. 7, 8.

[13] *Increasing World Food Output*, Chap. 9. Also W. H. Pawley, *Possibilities of Increasing World Food Production* (Rome: UN Food and Agriculture Organization, 1963).

[14] *Increasing World Food Output*, pp. 56-57.

[15] The preceding facts from *Increasing World Food Output*.

is an industry in the modern industrial world, not a way of life as in the more traditional past.[16]

V

Having argued that the development and modernization of agriculture depend upon the modernization of the economy as a whole, it is in order to identify the main prerequisite to economic development and modernization. This is capital. Not capital defined in terms of "hardware," but capital conceived of in a broader sense. We must, as Harry Johnson suggests, continue in the theoretical tradition of Irving Fisher and Frank Knight and regard " 'capital' as including anything that yields a stream of income over time, and income as the product of capital."[17] Economic growth may then be conceived of "as a process of accumulating capital, in all [its] manifold forms."

> The growth of income that defines economic development is necessarily the result of the accumulation of capital, or of 'investment'; but 'investment' in this context must be defined to include such diverse activities as adding to material capital, increasing the health, discipline, skill and education of the human population, moving labour into more productive occupations and locations, and applying existing knowledge or discovering and applying new knowledge to increase the efficiency of productive processes.[18]

Capital, viewed as a set of productive instruments, yields a flow of goods, not a flow of services as does consumption capital. The capitalistic productive process consists of the use of inputs or resources, in such ways as will make tomorrow's income stream greater than it otherwise would be, and, in particular, tomorrow's income stream per capita. It follows that any expenditure made today and having that effect tomorrow is capital. Capital therefore includes the devotion of inputs to productive education and training and retraining, to the accumulation of scientific knowledge, to the conversion of that knowledge into applied science, invention, and innovation, to buildings and equipment, to so-called public capital, household capital, improvement and preservation of health, and so on. Capital thus includes what is embodied in human beings as well as what is embodied in nonhuman material forms or in a

---

[16] R. W. Lindholm, "The Farm: the Misused Income Expansion Base of Emerging Nations," *Journal of Farm Economics*, XLIII (May, 1961), pp. 236-46.
[17] Harry G. Johnson, *The Canadian Quandary* (Toronto: McGraw-Hill Book Company, 1963), p. 230.
[18] *The Canadian Quandary*, p. 230.

society's disembodied culture and arts. It includes not only manmade capital but also natural resources or capital which is non-renewable and subject to depletion and exhaustion.

Defining capital in this broad fashion enables us to avoid errors implicit in a "hardware" as well as in the old "wage-goods" approach. This definition does not, however, overlook the problem of investment allocation; rather, it accentuates it by stressing the quality of a society's population, its disembodied capital, its assembly of science, invention, innovation, and management, as well as other potential inputs neglected by the hardware approach. This definition therefore emphasizes the importance of accumulating those forms of capital in which the relevant marginal rate of return is relatively high.

It must be kept in mind that I have defined capital broadly enough to permit its formation to entail transformation of the entire social, economic, and legal structures of the underdeveloped world. At the close of the war, when there was much oratorical mouthing about so-called freedom, it was believed, so it seems, that merely augmenting physical capital would disenthrall backward peoples from their misery-ridden cultural traps. After all, such had been the preachment of Marx and Ricardo. It was, moreover, as Harry Johnson observes, a doctrine palatable to the underdeveloped countries since it attributed their backwardness to lack of hard capital instead of to the backwardness of their cultures, thoughtways, and so forth, and since it rationalized various wasteful manifestations of nationalism highly inimical to economic development.[19]

VI

Given my broad definition of capital, the forward movement of average output is essentially a concomitant of the rate of increase in capital per head. It thus depends upon two sets of actions, those making for the formation and correct allocation of capital, and those making for control of births and reduction in the rate of population growth. In general, modernization can proceed most effectively and average income can rise most rapidly when *ceteris paribus* the rate of population growth is very low—say below 1 per

---

[19] Harry G. Johnson, *The World Economy at the Crossroads* (New York: Oxford University Press, Inc., 1965), pp. 72-82.

cent, and generally in the neighborhood of zero per cent in countries that stand to derive no net advantage from further population growth. (We must, after all, never lose sight of a fact I mentioned earlier, namely, that in a finite world or region the rate of population growth must inevitably descend to zero, either because men will it so, or because finitude compels it.) It is even possible—indeed often likely—that GNP or national income will grow more rapidly when the rate of population growth is low than when it is high. The Coale-Hoover study led to this conclusion for both India and Mexico and hence, by implication, for other countries in similar circumstances.[20]

Several partial objections have been raised to the type of argument I have just put forward. It has been shown, on the basis of certain assumptions, that "faster growth of the labour force leads to faster technical progress, and faster growth of output per worker."[21] This argument overlooks the fact that technical progress depends not merely upon research and replacement investment but on the whole set of forces that result in technical progress, some of which are inversely related to the rate of population growth. My counterargument is somewhat weakened, of course, by a fact which Veblen observed in respect to Germany and Japan, namely, that an underdeveloped country need not develop an advanced state of the arts but could borrow it from abroad almost as if it were a free good. Even then, the borrowing country would have to supply the inputs required to implement the borrowed technology.

It is also argued that a higher rate of population growth changes the composition of both the labor force and its physical capital faster than does a slower rate and thus accelerates the rate of modernization. Such an outcome is improbable, however. When the rate of population growth is high, relatively large amounts of the gross capital newly formed must be diverted to widening instead of deepening investment, and to relatively unproductive purposes such as those served by household and public capital. It is true, of course, that the ratio of relatively young to relatively old members

---

[20] A. J. Coale and E. M. Hoover, *Population Growth and Economic Development in Low-Income Countries* (Princeton: Princeton University Press, 1958), p. 173.

[21] W. A. Eltis, *Economic Growth* (London: Hillary House Publishers, Ltd., 1966), p. 19 note.

of the labor force will be comparatively high.[22] But it is also true that when a population's fertility and natural increase are relatively high, its capacity both to educate and transform its increasing numbers and to renew the training of its older members is greatly restricted. The ratio of persons of productive age to those of school and college age is relatively low, and the relative requirement of educational equipment is much higher.[23]

It is not easy to translate the relevant information into terms of capital formation. We may suppose that the material capital required to equip a 1-per-cent-per-year rate of population growth absorbs savings equal to 4 per cent of national income. Add perhaps 2 per cent to cover other forms of capital, and make allowance for the adverse effect of population growth upon a nation's age composition.[24] Or one may estimate the average cost of equipping a person with industrial, household, and public capital or equipment, together with, say, a high school or a college education, and use this average to estimate the cost of the current rate of population growth in particular countries. If, now, we suppose that the total cost of maintaining a rate of population growth of 1 per cent per year approximates 6-8 per cent of the national income, and if we also suppose that the marginal yield on new investment is 15 per cent, then reducing the rate of population growth by 1 per cent will elevate the rate of growth of per capita income by about one percentage point. Whence, if income per capita had been rising 1 per cent per year, it could now rise 2 per cent per year, and double income in thirty-five years instead of in seventy years as formerly. Of course, were the rate of population growth reduced by more than one percentage point, the potential gain in capital formation and output per head would be greater.

We indicated earlier that, even under the most favorable circumstances, many decades must pass before average income in most

---

[22] For example, Frank Lorimer, "Dynamics of Age Structure in a Population with Initially High Fertility and Mortality," *Population Bulletin*, No. 1 (New York: United Nations, December, 1951), p. 32.

[23] For example, suppose that population *A* is growing 2 per cent per year and population *B* zero per cent. In *A* the ratio of persons of productive age to those of school and college age will be only about half as high as in *B*.

[24] When a population is growing 2 per cent per year, the ratio of those aged 20-64 to the total population will be 15 or more per cent lower than when it is growing only around zero per cent. This means that *ceteris paribus* potential productivity per capita will be correspondingly lower.

underdeveloped countries moves within the neighborhood of average income in advanced countries. The hypothetical data I have presented indicate that reduction in the rate of population growth can play a notable part in accelerating the rate of growth of average income in underdeveloped countries. Indeed, in the absence of curtailment of the high rates of population growth now current in the underdeveloped world, it will be impossible for them appreciably to narrow the gap between themselves and the developed world; the gap could even widen as it seems to have done in the past 100-150 years.[25]

I have described the alternatives in quite general terms, on the basis of an implied assumption that the populations compared are stable. This is not empirically valid. Some decades must pass before a population, whether or not initially stable in form, can generate a new stable form in keeping with a new gross reproduction rate and/or a new set of age-specific death rates.

Suppose, for example, that gross reproduction in a population is reduced from a level permitting an increase of 2 per cent per year in what has been a stable population to a level allowing just over zero long-run growth. Suppose also that young people generally enter the labor force at around age 20. For about two decades, the population of working age and hence the labor force will continue to grow 2 per cent per year and GNP will grow initially at least as fast as formerly, about 4 per cent if output per member of the labor force grows 2 per cent per year. Average income will rise faster than 2 per cent because the total population will be growing less than 2 per cent per year since the total number of births per year has been reduced to close to the replacement level. Because of the higher rate of investment now possible, however, output per worker will grow faster than 2 per cent. During these two decades, therefore, all or most of the output that would otherwise have been invested in maintaining and equipping those who have not been born can be invested in increasing capital per head of all sorts and in all sectors of the economy. At the close of two decades, the rate of growth of the labor force will begin to fall below 2 per cent per year because of the earlier decline in fertility

---

[25] L. J. Zimmerman, *Poor Lands, Rich Lands, The Widening Gap* (New York: Random House, Inc., 1965), Chaps. 2, 7; Simon Kuznets, *Modern Economic Growth* (New Haven: Yale University Press, 1966), Chap. 7.

to a level that in the long run will little more than replace the existing labor force.

Eventually, if the rate of growth of the labor force should descend to one-half of 1 per cent, the growth of GNP could fall somewhat. But it would not fall much. We postulated that at the outset GNP was growing about 4 per cent per year because both the labor force and output per member of the labor force were growing 2 per cent per year. Now we have (by supposition) a labor force growing only about 0.5 per cent per year. Nonetheless, because of the increase in capital formation per head made possible by diverting thereto inputs formerly invested in mere population growth, the rate of increase of output per member of the labor force will have risen. Perhaps it will have risen to 3 per cent per year, perhaps to a higher level, with the result that GNP will grow 3.5-4.0 per cent per year. Of primary importance, however, is the fact that the diversion of inputs from equipping additional population increments to augmenting capital per head, that is, from widening to deepening investment, can greatly increase output per worker and income per capita. The degree to which this outcome is realized, however, turns on the degree to which increase in potential productivity assumes the form of output and capital instead of leisure and consumables.

VII

The forward movement of output per head associated with growth of capital per head must become characteristic of agriculture also. The growth of agriculture is not only interrelated with that of the rest of the economy, but is also essential to it. This is particularly true of underdeveloped countries where close to three-quarters of the population may be engaged in agriculture and rural activities and hence must contribute notably to the development of a country's nonagricultural sectors. In the early stage of a country's development it lacks the exchange wherewith to import food and raw materials, support nonagricultural development, and supply nutrient minima. It must, therefore, draw on agriculture,[26] both

---

[26] The capacity of the human organism to perform in the short and the long run depends upon the adequacy of its diet. See, for example, A. Keys and others, *The Biology of Human Starvation* (Minneapolis: University of Minnesota Press, 1950).

to develop nonagricultural sectors and to avert nonagricultural wage inflation[27] and concomitant economic disorder and political instability. As Joan Robinson remarks, "The secret of non-inflationary development is to allocate the right amount of quick-yielding, capital-saving investments to the consumption-goods sector (especially agriculture) to generate a sufficient surplus to support the necessary large schemes."[28] In densely populated underdeveloped countries, increase in output per agriculturist serves to release agricultural labor for employment in nonagricultural activities, given a sufficiency of nonagricultural capital. Foreign aid in the form of food stuffs may have a similar effect,[29] though the beneficial result may be partly offset by the depressive influence of this aid upon the incentive of agriculturists in recipient countries.[30] Agricultural improvements in a less densely populated country may augment its agricultural export and exchange-earning potential and thereby contribute indirectly to industrial development.[31] The

[27] See, for example, B. F. Johnston and J. W. Mellor, "The Role of Agriculture in Economic Development," *American Economic Review*, LI (September, 1961), pp. 566-93; W. H. Nicholls, "An 'Agricultural' Surplus As a Factor in Economic Development," *Journal of Political Economy*, LXXI (February, 1963), pp. 1-29.

[28] Joan Robinson, *Economic Philosophy* (Chicago: Aldine Publishing Company, 1962), p. 120. W. A. Lewis writes, "In practice the overall rate of growth achievable in an underdeveloped economy depends primarily on what happens to its agriculture." A. Waterston, *Development Planning* (Baltimore: The Johns Hopkins Press, 1966), p. 154.

[29] *Economic Philosophy*, p. 121; J. H. Richter, "Agricultural Surpluses for Economic Development," *Journal of Political Economy*, LXIV (February, 1956), pp. 69-73; "The Farm: The Misused Income Expansion Base of Emerging Nations"; M. V. Khambadkone, "Real Costs, Population Transfer Mechanism and Economic Development," *Indian Economic Journal*, XI (1964), pp. 311-36.

[30] See comments of C. Beringer and W. P. Falcon upon D. R. Khatkhate, "Some Notes on the Real Effects of Foreign Surplus Disposal in Underdeveloped Economies," *Quarterly Journal of Economics*, LXXVI (May, 1962), pp. 186-96. The comments are in *Quarterly Journal of Economics*, LXXVII (May, 1963), pp. 317-26. See also Raj Krishna, "Farm Supply Response in India-Pakistan: a Case Study of the Punjab Region," *Economic Journal*, LXXIII (September, 1963), pp. 477-87; F. M. Fisher, "A Theoretical Analysis of the Impact of Food Surplus Disposal of Agricultural Production in Recipient Countries," *Journal of Farm Economics*, XLV (November, 1963), pp. 863-75.

[31] For example, B. F. Johnston and J. W. Mellor, "The Nature of Agriculture's Contributions to Economic Development," *Food and Research Institute Studies*, I (November, 1960), pp. 335-56; Stephen Enke, "Industrialization Through Greater Productivity in Agriculture," *Review of Economics and Statistics*, XLIV (February, 1962), pp. 88-91.

contribution of agriculture to economic development, whatever its form, thus remains very important.

In the long run, of course, the contribution of agriculture to economic development diminishes in relative though not necessarily in absolute importance. Within an economy, a falling income elasticity of demand may slow the growth of agricultural requirements.[32] The augmentation of agricultural production may also decline, though the limit to the increase of crop yields may be far from attained.[33]

VIII

Supposing that a low level of fertility is desired, with what conditions is it most likely to be associated? The answer is almost unequivocal: with the conditions constituting modern life. In the past, when rate of population growth was low, this lowness, when not the result of high mortality, was traceable almost invariably either to infanticide and abortion, as in Japan, or, as in Western Europe, to institutional restraints restricting and deferring marriage, which lengthened the period separating generations.[34] Of course, with life expectancies of 25 to 40 years, gross reproduction rates of between close to 1.5 and 2.5 were required merely to balance deaths. Hence, with the decline of mortality over the past 100 years, pressure to limit fertility increased and fertility fell, albeit very slowly and only in Europe and Europe overseas. As late as 1960, in fact, crude natality exceeded 40 per 1,000 in Africa, most of Asia, and Latin America. It is below 25 only in nations with modernized societies.[35]

While it is not part of my assignment to discuss the determinants of fertility in detail, it is relevant for me to support the view that

---

[32] U.S. Department of Agriculture, *Elasticity of Food Consumption Associated with Changes in Income in Developing Countries* (Foreign Agricultural Economic Report No. 23; Washington: U.S. Gov't Printing Office, March, 1965).

[33] Lester R. Brown, *Man, Land & Food* (Foreign Agricultural Economic Report No. 11; Washington: U.S. Gov't Printing Office, 1963); James Bonner, "The Upper Limit of Crop Yield," *Science*, CXXXVII (July 6, 1962), pp. 11-15.

[34] Irene Taeuber, *The Population of Japan* (Princeton: Princeton University Press, 1958), pp. 31-34; D. V. Glass and D. E. C. Eversley, eds., *Population in History* (Chicago: Aldine Publishing Company), Chaps. 18-20.

[35] United Nations, *Population Bulletin*, No. 7 (New York: United Nations, 1963), p. 1.

the same modernization which is essential to the development of economies and their agriculture is essential also, except under as yet unusual circumstances, to the lowering of gross reproduction to levels commensurate with life expectancies of 50 to 60 years, that is, to rates of 1.5 or less. It has been found that not until indicators of modernization, most of which are highly intercorrelated, rise above certain threshold levels does a shift from high to low fertility begin to take place. The threshold zones are not easy to bound, since the apparent perimeters are variously situated.

It is suggested, however, that the reduced threshold zone for income is $230-339 per head; for energy consumption 360-1,012 kg.; for urbanization, 16-33 per cent; nonagricultural activities, 45-61 per cent; life expectancy, 62-63 years; infant mortality, 44-78 per 1,000 births; early marriage, 11-15 per cent of all marriages; female literacy, 62-75 per cent; newspaper circulation, 80-89 per 1,000 inhabitants; and so on. It is reported, however, that "the launching of new countries upon the transition from high to low fertility seems to have been temporarily halted." Furthermore, such decline in fertility as has taken place has been largely offset by decline in mortality. "It is approximately correct to state as a rough rule of thumb that the populations in which a decline of fertility has occurred, now tend to reproduce at about the same rates which prevailed previously."[36]

What of the future? In his summary comment on the International Conference on Family Planning held in 1965, Friedman found present in at least four populations—those of Korea, Taiwan, Singapore, and Hong Kong—conditions indicative of imminent declines in fertility, though "really major induced fertility declines" are "in the future." He referred also to certain manifestations of fertility control in several other countries (Pakistan, India, Turkey, Tunisia, Egypt, Thailand), though less pronounced than in the previous four. His optimism is highly qualified,[37] therefore, and less pronounced than that of another distinguished student of the problem.[38] It is quite likely that the slowness with which modernization is proceeding will slow the adoption of contraception.

In view of the difficulties that stand in the way of a rapid decline

---

[36] References in this paragraph are from *Population Bulletin,* No. 7, Chap. 9.
[37] Bernard Berelson, ed., *Family Planning and Population Programs* (Chicago: University of Chicago Press, 1966), pp. 811-27.

in fertility, two conclusions are warranted. First, not agricultural development as such but over-all modernization is absolutely essential to the establishment of control over fertility and the rate of population growth. Second, in view of the great rate of return realizable on investment in birth control, heavy investment must be made for this purpose if fertility is to be reduced rapidly.[39] Third, as H. Leibenstein and W. Galenson have pointed out, an important criterion of investment must be its capacity to increase not only aggregate output but output per head.[40]

IX

While my major concern has not been to provide an empirical account of the prospect, its magnitudes may be noted. According to the "medium" estimates of the United Nations secretariat, the population of the less developed regions will grow about 132 per cent in 1960-2000, or nearly twice the 70 per cent increase in 1920-60. By the year 2000 it will number nearly 4.7 billion and comprise about three-quarters of the world's population instead of around two-thirds as in 1960 or in 1920. Moreover, the rate of increase will remain as high as ever in Africa (about 31 per cent per decade), and nearly as high in Latin America outside the temperate zone, namely around 30 per cent per decade. In Asia, outside Japan and possibly Mainland China, the over-all rate of increase will be close to 20 per cent per decade. Should the population of the underdeveloped world increase 2 per cent per year between 2000 and 2100, it would number about 34 billions by the latter date. In contrast, the population of the currently developed

---

[38] In her review of Berelson's book Dr. Irene Taeuber declares its findings already are historic, rendered so by man's reaction to the magnitude of the population problem. *Science* (June 17, 1966), pp. 1,612-13.

[39] In a country with a per capita income of $100, the prevention of each birth is worth $125-250 or more. Paul Demeny, "Investment Allocation and Population Growth," *Demography*, II (1965), pp. 203-32; Stephen Enke, *Economics for Development* (New York: Prentice-Hall, Inc., 1963), Chap. 20; and "The Economic Aspects of Slowing Population Growth," *Economic Journal*, LXXVI (March, 1966), pp. 46-56.

[40] H. Leibenstein and W. Galenson, "Investment Criteria, Productivity, and Economic Development," *Quarterly Journal of Economics*, LXIX (August, 1955), pp. 343-70.

world may number only about 3.5 billion, less than one-tenth of the world's population instead of one-third as at present. For it is now expected that by 1990 the rate of population growth in the industrialized world will range from about 5 per cent per decade in Europe and Japan to 16 per cent in North America, Australia, and New Zealand.

The demand for food grows faster than population, especially in the low-income underdeveloped world where the income elasticity of demand usually falls within a range of 0.5-0.8. Let us put it at 0.5, however, and suppose average income rises 2 per cent per year. Then if population grows about as fast in 2000-2050 as in 1966-2000, perhaps 2 to $2\frac{1}{4}$ per cent per year, the aggregate demand for food will rise at least 3 per cent per year. By 2050 it will be 14 times what it was in 1960, and by 2100, about 63 times.

How fast the world's food supply, or a country's food supply, can grow depends mainly on how much both food acreage and yield per acre can be increased; it depends in a minor degree upon how freely produce can move from surplus areas to deficit areas. This freedom is somewhat limited by barriers to trade and by dearth of purchasing power in food-short countries, for ours is not one world but a divided world; most countries will have to supply nearly all of the food which they consume.[41] In the long run, however, it makes little difference whether the world is one or divided. Continuing growth is impossible in a finite environment, and man's environment is finite, since both cultivable acres and yield per acre are limited. Even if the food supply could be increased 12-15 times, it would be outstripped in about 125-150 years by a population growing 2 per cent per year, and in double that time by a population growing 1 per cent per year.

With the problem stated in the abstract, we may look at the rate of growth of farm output in recent years. Between 1958 and 1966, world agricultural production increased about $2\frac{1}{2}$ per cent per year in both the developed world and the underdeveloped world, exclusive of China where output fell. A study of twenty-six coun-

---

[41] In 1959-61 about one-eleventh of the world's output of food entered international trade. Calculated from U.S. Department of Agriculture, *The World Food Budget, 1970* (Foreign Agricultural Economic Report No. 19; Washington: U.S. Gov't Printing Office, October, 1964), pp. 45, 52.

tries with relatively underdeveloped economies reports an annual increase in crop output of 5.5 per cent in thirteen countries and 2.3 per cent in the remaining thirteen. In Japan, crop output increased 5.5 per cent per year in 1948-63, though at a rate of only 1.3 per cent per year in 1955-63. In the United States, crop output grew 2.2 per cent per year in 1935-60.[42] In the underdeveloped world as a whole, with the exception of Communist Asia, crop output has just about kept pace with population growth.

While in many countries there is considerable land for conversion to crops, it is upon increase in yield per acre that most countries will soon have to depend for increase in crop output. Of the twenty-six countries referred to above, fifteen depended upon increase in crop land for at least one-fifth of their increase in output; among these were India and Pakistan but not Japan, 97 per cent of whose growth of crop output was due to increase in yield per acre or to change in crop pattern that augmented return per acre.[43] Lester Brown reports changes in cereal yield per acre per year for a large number of countries between 1935-39 and 1960-62: rice, 0.3 to 1.9 per cent; wheat, 0 to 3.3 per cent; and corn, 0 to 3.7 per cent.[44] Between 1934-38 and 1960-67, grain yield per acre harvested increased 8 per cent in the underdeveloped regions and 51 per cent in the developed world.[45] In the United States, crop yield per acre increased 1.7 per cent per year between 1935-60.[46] How long increase in yield per acre can continue at rates adequate to match the growth of demand for foodstuffs remains to be seen.

Brown believes that countries containing about two-thirds of the world's population "will find it very difficult to raise yields as much as 1 per cent per year over a sustained period"; he finds long-term prospects better, since in a decade or two literacy and other conditions should improve "enough to permit a sustained upsurge in

---

[42] The preceding statistics are from U. S. Department of Agriculture publications: *The World Agricultural Situation* (Washington: U.S. Gov't Printing Office, 1967), p. 2; *Changes in Agriculture in 26 Developing Nations, 1948 to 1963* (Foreign Agricultural Economic Report No. 27; Washington: U.S. Gov't Printing Office, 1965), p. 6; *How the United States Improved Its Agriculture* (Foreign Agricultural Economic Report No. 76; Washington: U.S. Gov't Printing Office, 1964), p. 3.
[43] *Changes in Agriculture* . . . , Chaps. 2, 3.
[44] *Increasing World Food Output*, pp. 43, 45, 47, 107.
[45] *Man, Land & Food*, p. 56.
[46] *How the United States Improved Its Agriculture*, p. 3.

yields."[47] This upsurge, of course, presupposes adequate use of fertilizer, together with the other relevant conditions. It cannot continue, however, if population growth persists.

X

Four inferences may be drawn from what has been said. First, solution of the population problem requires the transformation of the entire economy, not merely modernization of the agricultural sector. Second, even in land-rich countries with populations of less than optimum size, modernization can proceed nicely only if the rate of population growth remains at or below 1 per cent, and capital per head can increase markedly. Third, it is possible that fertility can be brought down in underdeveloped countries through two types of action: (a) increasing the dissemination of population controls by offering rewards to those who prevent births—say $5-10 per married couple of reproductive age each year they avoid having offspring; (b) imposing tax and other economic burdens upon those producing more than three live births, though in ways that will not penalize the children. Fourth, countries which supply aid to underdeveloped countries might deny aid to countries that failed to cut fertility by specified amounts, unless experience proved this approach relatively infeasible.

I am not arguing against aid as such, or for trade instead of aid. Trade transforms an underdeveloped country's relatively abundant internal resources and manpower into generalized resources, or foreign exchange. It should, therefore, be allowed maximum freedom by advanced countries. But international trade is not enough, even though it brings skills into a country and alleviates population pressure, especially when exports and imports can move freely. Aid is required to supplement trade, to provide external resources in addition to those realizable through trade. Aid cannot produce much if any persisting beneficial results, however, if population growth is not being brought under control in recipient countries.

Given action along the lines I have suggested, the population calamity can be averted, for the present at least. In the long run, however, population growth must be halted everywhere, since this

[47] *Increasing World Food Output*, p. 106, pp. 108-09.

is a finite world subject to economic as well as physical entropy. Delay in halting population growth destroys men's options for the proximate as well as for the immediate future.

Essential to recognition of the long-run problem is rejection of the inverted Malthusianism now common among worshippers of something called technical progress and situated in a providential Aladdin's lamp. In its older version, this view consisted in equating solution of the population problem with adequacy of the food supply, a solution rejected already in the Old Testament. In a newer version, this view consists in equating solution of the problem with man's ability to extricate himself from demographic traps of his own making. In neither case is attention devoted to the purpose of life, to man's aspirations, to what are the proper concerns of the elite upon whom in the end technological progress depends. A skeptic may find warning in the fate of Henry Adams' prophecy that by 1938 man would find himself in a world transformed by the "law of acceleration" into one that "sensitive and timid natures could regard without a shudder."[48]

[48] Henry Adams, *The Education of Henry Adams* (New York: Houghton Mifflin Company, 1931), p. 505.

Comments on Spengler

RAYMOND EWELL

Vice-President for Research,
  Professor of Chemistry and Chemical Engineering
State University of New York at Buffalo

ALLOW ME to preface my critique of Professor Spengler's most interesting and provocative paper with a brief statement of my own background and qualifications. I am basically a chemical engineer with particular expertise in the technology and economics of fertilizer production. However, I have developed a quasi-professional interest during the past fifteen years in agriculture, birth control, and economic development generally.

I have been actively associated with industrial development in India and the Philippines and, to a lesser extent, in Egypt and Peru. I have studied the agricultures of India, Pakistan, the Philippines, Taiwan, Egypt, Peru, and Chile. I have observed developments in organized birth control in India, Pakistan, Peru, Chile, and Costa Rica. My approach to these problems is primarily that of a physical scientist and engineer rather than that of an economist.

Professor Spengler's paper is certainly far-ranging, stimulating, and provocative. His paper is full of ideas for us to chew on. Professor Spengler's most basic conclusion seems to be that birth rates and population growth rates must come down—down to a 1 per cent per year population growth rate in all countries as a first objective and ultimately to virtually zero population growth in view of the finite size and resources of the earth. This appraisal of Professor Spengler's primary conclusion is borne out by the fact that all four of his summary points refer to the importance of reducing population growth.

Professor Spengler argues (1) that agricultural development is not enough since man does not live by bread alone, (2) that agricultural development is not possible anyway unless there is general economic development (or modernization or industrialization), (3) that adequate general economic development (or modernization or industrialization) is not going to be realized, on a per capita basis at least, unless population growth rates are reduced.

I am in substantial agreement, but not complete agreement, with these three arguments, if I read Professor Spengler correctly, particularly in the long term of, say, twenty or more years. But I believe Professor Spengler has underestimated the importance and urgency of the food situation in the less-developed countries in the shorter term of the next twenty years—in fact of the next five years in the case of several of the more vulnerable countries such as India.

My disagreement with Professor Spengler may be summarized by these conclusions based on my observations of the past few years:

Food (plus air and water, of course) is more necessary than the other so-called necessities of life.

Several of the more vulnerable countries will need substantially increased food supplies within the next five years if violent political upheavals are to be avoided or even postponed.

Increased food supplies in these countries cannot wait for general economic development, desirable and necessary as this may be in the long run.

Food deficits in Asia, Africa, and Latin America will, within five to ten years, outrun the capacity of the food-surplus countries to supply the needs of these countries.

Increasing food production on a massive basis is a slow process, since it involves education, research, capital formation, and social change—all slow processes.

Most of the less-developed countries cannot increase food production enough on their own resources because of a shortage of capital and trained people.

Increased food production in the less-developed countries can be achieved in the critical next five to ten years only if the rich countries give them much more help in the form of capital and technical manpower—much more than they are now doing.

Thus my disagreement with Professor Spengler is entirely in what I believe is his inadequate consideration of the potential for disaster in the next five to ten years. I agree with his approach for the long term, but in the long run all of us will be dead anyway. (See accompanying chart for description of areas of understanding needed in appraising the food-population outlook.)

Areas of Understanding Basic to a Realistic Appraisal of the Food/Population Outlook in a Country or Region

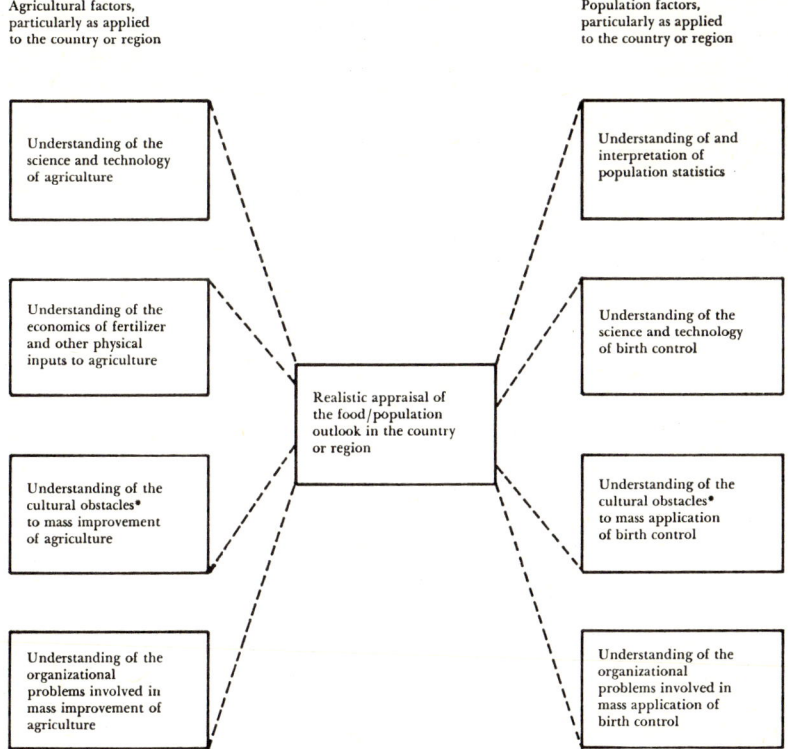

* "Cultural obstacles" include a variety of social, political, educational, and religious factors.

Let me go back to my first conclusion. There are many necessities of life—food, clothing, shelter, transportation, education, medical care, and others—but some are more necessary than others. The relative degree of necessity of these amenities varies from country to country. In the United States we consider many other things as "necessities," such as color television, two cars in every family (and perhaps a motor boat), $400 wigs, 4-way-stretch panty girdles, computerized backyard barbecues, heated swimming pools, fluorescent bathing suits, electronically matched golf clubs, and other wonders of modern science. But most of these things are not considered as necessities in the less-developed world. While Americans may consider an electric meat slicer as a necessity in every home, in most of India they have neither meat nor electricity, so they do not consider an electric meat slicer as a necessity.

But food is an ultimate necessity. People can and do get along without most of the other so-called necessities, but they must have food to survive. When people are hungry, they become irritable and dissatisfied, and eventually become desperate and resort to violent, irrational actions—overthrowing governments, killing people, sacking U.S. embassies, burning cities, and so forth. People may be unhappy because they have ragged, dirty clothes or because they live in a shack with a leaky roof and no running water, as in the slums of Calcutta or the *favelas* of Rio de Janeiro, but they do not usually become desperate and resort to violence. If they do not have at least a minimum amount of food to eat, they are ripe for violent revolution, as history has demonstrated many times in the past.

India is standing on the brink of disaster now, with food shortages in Bihar and Uttar Pradesh with which it cannot cope. Anything could happen in India during the coming months. The Congress party suffered a stunning upset—virtually a defeat—in the February, 1967 election; eight states now have non-Congress governments, and the central government is in a very unstable situation. The deteriorating food situation was the major factor in the February elections, and it will probably be an even more important factor in the next general election in 1972.

As you know, India has had two of the worst droughts in the country's history in the last two crop years—the monsoons of 1965 and 1966. The 1965 drought was quite general, hitting most parts of India. The 1966 drought was more extreme but was localized in Bihar and neighboring areas of Uttar Pradesh, Madhya Pradesh, and West Bengal. The area of the 1966 drought includes nearly 100 million people, and they literally have no food left right now. Some officials of the Indian government have expressed the Pollyanna opinion (or hope) that the 1967 monsoon is certain to be a good one—after two bad monsoons—but there is no scientific basis for such a belief. The 1967 monsoon could be just as bad as the last two, or even worse.

The seriousness of India's deteriorating food situation is illustrated by the following data on population and food grain production during the past seven years.

	Population, July 1, at End of Split Year (in millions)	Food Grain Production (in millions of tons)
1960-61	441	80
1961-62	451	80
1962-63	462	80
1963-64	473	80
1964-65	485	88
1965-66	497	72
1966-67	510	76

The United States has given India enormous help in this emergency by sending 10 million tons of grain, worth about $750 million, during 1966—all virtually as a gift—and the United States will send probably 7 or 8 million tons of grain during 1967. In 1966 this was largely wheat, but now we are running short of wheat so that much of the 1967 shipments will have to be sorghum. But the U.S. government, generous as we have been in sending food aid, has not given India much help in improving her agriculture. The Ford and Rockefeller Foundations, with their relatively limited resources, have done more to improve India's agriculture than our government has.

It is true that the U.S. government financed two large fertilizer factories in India in 1961, but India needs at least fifty such factories. Since 1961 the U.S. government has persistently refused to lend India money to build fertilizer factories in the public sector on the grounds that U.S. and European private firms would build plenty of them if India would only open wide the doors to foreign private capital. This is an ideological debate, of course, but in my opinion a major part of India's present food emergency can be laid at the doorstep of the U.S. government for its rigid, uncompromising stand on public sector fertilizer factories during the past ten years.

You may feel the foregoing overemphasizes the importance of fertilizer in India's agriculture. Other inputs such as seeds, water, pesticides, and machinery are also important, but in the present stage of development of India's agriculture, fertilizer is the limiting factor. It will give more agricultural production even if no other factor is changed. The improved seed varieties now being introduced into India by the Rockefeller and Ford Foundations will yield little additional production unless more fertilizer is used at the same time. There is enough water in India to increase agricultural output, especially if more fertilizer and improved seed varieties were used together. In other words, water is not the limiting factor in the improvement of India's agriculture at this time. More dams and irrigation canals and more pump-wells would be fine, but they are not as important as more fertilizer and better seeds right now.

One aspect of Indian agriculture not generally recognized is the large fluctuations in crop production resulting from the annual variations in the monsoon rains. The difference in crop production between a good monsoon and a poor monsoon is at least 20 per cent, that is, 10 per cent above or 10 per cent below the crop for a "normal" monsoon. For example, the crop for a normal monsoon in the forthcoming 1967-68 crop year might be around 85 million tons of food grains, but the actual crop might be anything between 75 and 95 million tons, for a very poor monsoon or a very good monsoon, respectively. What India must do is increase her basic capacity for crop production so that in years of poor monsoons there will still be enough food for minimum needs. The most important key to this goal is more fertilizer, although improved seed varieties and more irrigation water will help too.

India has enough good agricultural land and enough water to support many more people if she would use these resources effectively. India has some of the best farm land in the world. In fact, that is the basic reason there are so many people in India. India has 350 million acres under cultivation, almost exactly the same as the United States, and yet we produce over twice as much food and other agricultural products as India does. Japan does even better; Japan produces three to four times as much per acre as India does in almost all major crops. Taiwan, Korea, and Egypt are doing almost as well as Japan. (See accompanying table for wheat and rice yields by countries.)

India's resources could easily support twice her present population, but India does not need to double food production in order to eliminate the specter of famine—at least for a few years. Even a 20 per cent increase in agricultural production in the next four or

Average Yields of Wheat and Rice, 1964-65*

(Wheat, including all countries producing over 1 million tons; kg./hectare)

United Kingdom	4,140	Australia	1,380
West Germany	3,600	Canada	1,360
France	3,150	CHILE	1,360
East Germany	3,110	Rumania	1,290
EGYPT	2,760	Soviet Union	1,090
MEXICO	2,550	TURKEY	1,060
JAPAN	2,450	Spain	950
Czechoslovakia	2,220	AFGHANISTAN	950
Italy	1,950	IRAN†	900
Poland	1,870	PAKISTAN	830
ARGENTINA	1,860	ALGERIA†	780
Hungary	1,850	MOROCCO	780
Greece	1,790	SYRIA	750
United States	1,770	SOUTH AFRICA	730
Bulgaria	1,770	INDIA	730
Yugoslavia	1,760	CHINA, MAINLAND†	690

(Rice (paddy), including all countries producing over 500,000 tons; kg./hectare; milled rice = 0.65 × paddy)

Italy	5,160	COLOMBIA	1,990
JAPAN	5,150	NEPAL	1,960
EGYPT	5,040	NORTH VIETNAM	1,860
United States	4,590	MADAGASCAR	1,770
TAIWAN	3,650	INDONESIA§	1,740
SOUTH KOREA	3,330	PAKISTAN	1,680
NORTH KOREA‡	2,940	BURMA	1,640
MALAYA	2,630	INDIA	1,610
IRAN	2,360	THAILAND	1,600
CHINA, MAINLAND†	2,170	BRAZIL§	1,520
SOUTH VIETNAM	2,020	PHILIPPINES	1,250
CEYLON	2,000	CAMBODIA	1,100

* Capitals indicate countries in Asia, Africa, and **Latin America**.
† For five-year period 1948-49 to 1952-53.
§ For 1963-64.
‡ For 1949-50.

Source: United Nations, *Production Yearbook* (Rome: Food and Agriculture Organization, 1965).

five years would put India comfortably ahead of the prospective population growth.

However, the facts of political and economic life in India are such that it is my estimate that India's food deficit in 1971 is likely to be as large or even larger than the deficit in 1967. India's population will grow by at least 50 million between 1967 and 1971—an increase equal to the population of France—and I do not see programs of agricultural improvement in motion in India that will provide the food for that many more people within four years. The quality of the monsoon in the summer/fall of 1970 will, of course, be a determining factor.

India is in this terrible plight because in 1955 Prime Minister Nehru and other members of the cabinet at that time plumped for general economic development rather than giving top priority to agricultural development—in fact, doing just what Professor Spengler advocates in his paper. Because of this decision the second five-year plan (1956-61) and the third plan (1961-66) spread their limited resources on general economic development, and agriculture was neglected. Many economists and advisers, including this speaker, argued with Prime Minister Nehru and other officials of the government that this was a basic strategic mistake, but to no avail. And today India is nearly past the point of no return. In the forthcoming book, *Famine 1975,* William and Paul Paddock classify India, Egypt, and Haiti as three countries that can't be saved, no matter what resources are thrown into the breach.

Personally, I do not think India is quite that far gone. I believe an increase of foreign aid from the rich countries to India of only $1 billion per year more than the present level could reverse the tide. However, money alone will not do it. More important than money are equipment of many types and technical manpower in large quantities from the developed countries. For example, India today has probably only 200 agriculture experts from all the developed countries helping India improve her agriculture, whereas India needs and could effectively use at least 2,000 agricultural experts of many types.

As another example, India needs about $1 billion worth of Western fertilizer plant equipment during the next few years and some Western engineers to help the Indians erect it. If present policies continue, the U.S. government will not be willing to help provide India with this equipment. And Esso and Texaco are not going to do it either, for reasons that are too complex to go into here. As another example, India needs thousands of bulldozers, steam shovels, draglines, and other earth-moving equipment to build dams and irrigation canals faster.

Members of Congress frequently ask why, with all the money and food we have poured into India, India is in worse condition now than ten years ago. The answer is perfectly simple—our aid has not been enough in relation to the magnitude of India's problems. The United States has put some $3 billion foreign aid into Taiwan in the past fifteen or twenty years. Since the population of India is forty times the population of Taiwan, a proportional amount in India would be $120 billion. But our total foreign aid to India has been only $8 billion, including the heavy food aid of the past two years. This $8 billion foreign aid to India has been like sending a troop of Boy Scouts to fight the Vietnam war and then wondering why they were not successful. Many members of Congress have not yet grasped the overriding fact that India has 500 million people and is adding 12 to 14 million more each year.

However, no amount of aid is going to save India from disaster unless India can reduce the population growth rate—and the sooner the better. It is very uncertain how fast India can make a significant reduction in the birth rate. Effective methods of regulating conception are now available, and there are no religious roadblocks in India. However, there are formidable social and cultural obstacles, and success will require a more effective organization than has ever been achieved thus far by the government in India. The government of India has stated in the press recently that its target is to reduce the birth rate from forty per thousand to twenty-five per thousand by the mid-1970's. In view of the poor progress in organized birth control so far this seems unlikely to be attained, and even if it were attained it probably would not be enough of a reduction to permit India to establish a reasonable balance between food and people.

India is the nation closest to mass starvation, but many other countries are not far behind, including Pakistan, Indonesia, Egypt, Peru, and Colombia, to mention only a few. All these countries have population growth rates of 2.5 per cent to 3.5 per cent per year, and their agricultures are not keeping pace with their population growths. Some other countries seem to be in better shape foodwise—Burma, Thailand, the Philippines, Malaysia, Turkey, Brazil, and most of the Central African countries. But these countries all have high population growth rates of 2.5 per cent to 3.5 per cent per year, and these countries, too, will have serious food shortages in ten to fifteen years unless they can reduce their population growth rates. Even Mexico, with a growth rate of 3.5 per cent, may be in trouble by 1980 despite the outstanding record Mexico has made in agriculture production during the past twenty years.

All of these countries could potentially support many more people than they are now supporting, but it takes time. Time is needed for development of agriculture, industry, transportation, and education. Time is the crucial factor. India probably could support 700 million people by the year 2000, maybe even by 1990, but certainly not by 1980, when India will almost certainly have 700 million people. If organized birth control had started a decade sooner, the developing countries would have had the time they needed, but now it is almost too late. Even now only a few of the developing countries have made a serious beginning on organized birth control, and most are still doing virtually nothing along this line.

Personally, I do not think organized birth control is going to make a significant impact in most of the vulnerable countries within the next ten years, and I do not think agriculture is going to increase production enough either. Therefore, I believe that there are going to be very severe food shortages in many of the more vulnerable countries, with India number one, and that these food shortages will be persistent, will feed on themselves, and get steadily worse. Further, I believe this will lead to widespread violent political upheavals in many countries, and that we will therefore see the most turbulent period in the world's history. This is not in the year 2000, but between now and 1980. Clearly, this will be a new situation in the history of the world with mass starvation involving many hundreds of millions of people.

There are four reasons why I do not believe agriculture will make the grade in most of the developing countries:

> Improvement of agriculture is a basic social change, and social changes occur slowly.
> Improvement of agriculture will require vast new programs of educa-

tion of farmers themselves and of agricultural specialists of many types—and education is a slow process.

Improvement of agriculture will require much larger programs of research, particularly in tropical agriculture—and research is a slow process.

Improvement of agriculture will require vast capital investments in fertilizer plants, pesticides plants, seed processing plants, farm machinery of many types, irrigation systems, transportation systems, electric power production, and other economic inputs. Various estimates of the amounts of capital needed have been made—Roger Revelle's estimate is $5 billion per year for the indefinite future—over and above present levels of investment.

And the countries that need these things the most do not have any money—India, for example. Most of the developing countries are flat broke.

The only countries that have the resources to provide the large amounts of money, equipment, and technical manpower needed are the United States and the Soviet Union. The European countries are too small individually and are not inclined to act as a group in such matters. The United States is so involved in Vietnam, pursuit of the Great Society, internal conflicts such as civil rights, and so forth, that we are probably not going to take the steps needed to make a significant impact on this great problem. The Soviet Union is occupied with similar problems—Vietnam, China, and internal problems. Moreover, the Soviet Union has never been much interested in helping the developing countries improve their agriculture. The United States ought to be doing more because we are the richest country in the world, and so we have the most to lose by political upheaval in the developing countries. On the other hand, the Soviet Union has little to lose as a result of political change in these countries—and might, as a matter of fact, welcome it.

Population Growth and the Potential of Technology

HANS H. LANDSBERG

*Director, Resource Appraisal Program,
Resources for the Future, Inc.*

WE LIVE in the age of explosions—population, information, knowledge, expectations. Rapid acceleration is their common characteristic. With it has come an explosion of writings about these explosions, including a special branch of literature that deals with the shape of the future. New phrases such as "inventing the future" and new expressions such as "futuribles" have turned up. There is an abundance of books and articles in which the terms "future," "technology," "prediction," and "forecasting" appear in varying combinations, often with the addition of a specific year—1975, 1980, or 2000.

The most recent bibliography on technological forecasting that has crossed my desk boasts 413 entries, several of which are, in turn, bibliographies with hundreds of citations of their own. Efforts range from the "Commission on the Year 2000," called into existence by the American Academy of Arts and Sciences, to Walter Cronkite's TV series that this year has been upgraded from the twentieth to the twenty-first century. Speculation in the futures market has moved, it seems, from the commodity exchange to the conference room, the TV screen, and the learned journal.

One consequence of this trend is the diminishing thrill some of us get out of dwelling upon, imagining, or merely enumerating the possible changes in future living. Such familiarity is apt to breed creeping apathy, if not contempt. With the growing scope of science and technology, the number and variety of things that are, as the phrase goes, "technically feasible" are legion: from sex and genetic control in unborn children to weather control over unborn storms; from synthetic foods to synthetic kidneys and artificial hearts; and from moving sidewalks to orbiting laboratories. You name it, we've got it.

There is little point, therefore, in repeating or adding to the inventory. For one, I am no better than the next man at imagining breakthroughs. Perhaps worse. For the ones that occur to me as desirable, and that usually are introduced by some such phrase as "Why hasn't someone thought of . . .," are along quite pedestrian lines. I should gladly trade off a leak-proof toilet or a set of sidewise moving car wheels for easier parking, or self-guiding venetian blind replacement cords for the next 100 miles per hour added to a jet plane's speed. Second, and more important, there are extensive lists that have in recent years been compiled by competent scholars. And last, while even frequent repetition may not rob such catalogs of all fascination, they leave one without much orientation about what is more or less imminent, more or less desirable, and how we are going to get there from here.

Of these three areas of uncertainty, I shall leave the first largely untouched. Having in the past twenty years witnessed the ups and downs in both public and private attempts at timing the commercial coming of age of nuclear power generation and—over a much longer period—of the opening to exploitation of the Western oil shale lands, I am impressed by the margin of error that must afflict setting the estimated time of arrival of innovations, such as intercity passenger transportation by rocket-propelled vehicles, or genetic controls, or even the seemingly less revolutionary electric automobile. These face a host of not only technical and institutional complexities but also require each of us to react to them individually, and, in large part, depend on that reaction.

I shall instead concentrate on the degree of desirability of certain technological changes and attempt some evaluation of the chances and speed of achievement. In making such an assessment, it will be convenient to take as a starting point, whenever that is feasible, the area I know best—the degree of adequacy of natural resources. This does not imply that adequacy of natural resources is the only precondition of a satisfactory life, not even when adequacy is defined with broad scope, that is, taking into account qualitative as well as quantitative attributes. I would assert merely that, while resource adequacy may not be a sufficient condition for ease of mind, it surely is a necessary, if not basic, one.

Other contributors to this symposium have dealt with the population side of the equation. I, therefore, limit myself to commenting that, in any meaningful forward look, a successful effort to slow down the rate of population growth seems to me as basic an assumption as avoidance of nuclear war. It is basic in the sense that the arithmetic of runaway population growth, no less than that of runaway nuclear war, makes hash of any resource adequacy balance that one's assumptions and arithmetic may yield. What difference exists is between instant and gradual hash.

It makes good sense, therefore, to take as axiomatic that unchecked population growth at the postwar pace is incompatible with resource adequacy, no matter what portion of the technological potential is eventually translated into what was once called "brick and mortar."

The arithmetic of compound interest makes fascinating reading, to be sure. Who would not be startled by a calculation that a 3 per cent population growth in the United States—the rate that prevailed from 1790 to 1860—would, if unchecked, give each American only 4 square feet by the year 2314; or that the world's population would equal the weight of the globe by the year 4000;[1] or that 100 to 200 billion people could theoretically be supported, given floating islands with algae farms, minimum levels of physical activity, no luxuries, and so on?[2] In such speculations, one is neither right nor wrong; nor, lacking information about likely levels of productivity at so remote a date, can one get into a good argument, except to remark that people do not resemble flies in a closed bottle and that the whole exercise heavily discounts the second term in "homo sapiens."

Calculations resting on the assumption that population growth will continue unchecked for decades to come may have a salutary scare value; but pushing a major variable that hard is not, on the whole, helpful. Above all, the overpopulation specter can be confronted by equally impressive, and equally unconstructive,

---

[1] Henry Jarrett, ed., *Perspectives on Conservation: Essays on America's Natural Resources* (Baltimore: The Johns Hopkins Press, 1958), p. 178.

[2] Harrison Brown, *The Challenge of Man's Future* (New York: Viking Press, 1954), p. 221. Most recently (in an address to the American Society of Newspaper Editors, April 21, 1967), Brown speculated that it may not be possible to stabilize world population at less than 15 billion people.

apparitions on the supply side—such as that a cubic mile of representative rock contains 1 billion tons of aluminum, 625 million tons of iron, 260 million tons of magnesium, and so on and so forth, down to 60 tons of gold.[3]

In the same class are endeavors aimed at calculating the total amount of organic matter produced in the world and relating it to the amount that eventually comes to represent food for humans. One such calculation starts with 150 billion tons per year of "organic matter" resulting from photosynthesis and ends up with 360 million tons of food.[4] The comparisons are interesting but—and their authors usually would not claim differently—not of near-term relevance. At best they create perspective, something to reach for, or something to guard against. At worst they are taken at face value and foster dangerous illusions. The point I wish to make is a simple one: if we choose to be plagued by big nightmares, we are surely entitled to offset them with equally big daydreams, but the combination is not to be recommended.

Moreover, as Professor Mason put it at the 1958 Forum of RFF, ". . . to undertake a serious discussion of conservation the period of time under consideration has to be limited to that within which one can perceive, at least dimly, the approximate magnitude of the relevant variables."[5]

It is, therefore, more rewarding to contemplate tendencies and trends rather than to focus on ultimate results. It is more useful, for example, to know that world requirements for energy are likely to triple in the last third of this century, than to know that, on the assumption of unchecked population growth, they will grow, say, tenfold or twentyfold in the next hundred years. (Development of a successful commercial fusion process would knock out all long-term speculations on energy adequacy, and the odds on this happening within a generation or two are reasonably attractive.)

In a preface to a recent RFF study of unconventional sources of future manganese supply, the forecaster's discomfort is phrased

---

[3] James F. McDivitt, *Minerals and Men* (Baltimore: The Johns Hopkins Press, 1965), p. 11.

[4] Howard W. Mattson, "Food for the World," *International Science and Technology* (December, 1965).

[5] *Perspectives on Conservation* . . ., p. 178.

this way: "To let the limitations of the present cramp his vision makes the analyst feel narrowminded. But he feels no more comfortable being carried away on the wave of the future. More often than not, he compromises by adopting a suitably qualified optimistic view in which the burden of short-run constraints is eased with general references to the conquests of nature yet to come."

This incremental approach, especially when improved by making the "general references" as specific as possible, is quite appropriate when one contemplates the developments that are *most likely to occur* within a given and relatively close time span; but it is less so when one looks for even a vague ordering of priorities in terms of what is *most needed and desirable*. In the latter framework, it is quite useful to think about the "potential of technology" without immediate regard for implementation.

One further introductory comment. It makes all the difference whether we look at the population/resources equation in the economically advanced nations or in the world as a whole. Most of my work in recent years has had the United States as its object of analysis. Here the calamity, to use the leitmotif of this conference, that is besetting us is one of deteriorating quality of the environment, brought on by steeply increased demand on the waste-assimilative characteristics of water and air, and by the consequences of disregard for the esthetic, moral, recreational, and other non-commodity-oriented features of the landscape. This disregard is made more visible and acute by greater density of population, greater mobility, more profound interference with natural phenomena, and mounting awareness of the adverse consequences. When we turn our attention to the countries of rapid population growth and low income—which our addiction to euphemisms has led us to advance from "underdeveloped," to "less developed," to "developing" countries, which by any standard are the poor countries of the world—it is quantity rather than quality that is the core of the calamity.

The focus is thus different. One might argue that since, in terms of commodities, the United States is one of the world's most productive nations, whatever is potentially in short supply there (subject to rising costs, in this country and elsewhere in industrialized nations) is a scarcity candidate to an even greater degree elsewhere. Thus a look at the U.S. position might serve as a useful point of departure. Unfortunately, this approach does not take us very far.

For one thing, the bills of material of the less-developed countries are very different from those of the advanced areas of the world— so much so that tendencies toward scarcity in Europe or the United States may not even have a useful preview function. Second, in agriculture and, particularly, food production, the area most critical to the poorer countries, the United States will for a long time to come encounter no resource problem.

Indeed, were it not for large exports under various government-sponsored programs, the United States would be faced with a crop and surplus problem almost to the end of the century, notwithstanding the growing tendency to favor meat over the less acreage-demanding food grains. Though it can be, and has been, argued that the rising yield curve that has characterized U.S. agriculture since World War II will before long flatten out, there still exists a great amount of slack before the majority of farmers will have caught up with the technological and managerial potential which the best of them have exploited more fully. The spectacle of entire states—Illinois, Indiana, and Iowa, to name only three—approaching an average corn yield of 100 bushels per acre is certainly instructive in this respect. So are the calculations of the Department of Agriculture that in the early 1960's farmers received a return of about $2.50 per dollar spent for fertilizer.

Large-scale substitution of fertilizer for land, if this should become important, could result, the estimates suggest, in raising needed crops by 1980 on a little over 200 million acres by augmenting fertilizer consumption, in terms of nutrients, to about 35 million tons (or about 3 times current practice). I am mentioning these calculations only to indicate the size of the production reservoir in the United States, a country in which commercial fertilizer application on any substantial scale began only in World War II, a fact we are prone to forget.

However, the position that the United States finds itself in does not furnish useful clues to current needs and coming events in Asia, Latin America, or Africa. Though one can quarrel over the exact dimensions of the population-food dilemma, there is not much room for dispute regarding the direction: advance, if any, will be slow, and retreat in the food sufficiency battle cannot be excluded, not only in qualitative but also even in quantitative terms.

True, there are some bright spots. *First,* while it is too soon to judge with assurance, agricultural production in the Soviet Union, and in eastern European countries generally, may be on the eve of a sustained upswing. The attention now being paid to Soviet agriculture seems to have a more workmanlike look about it than has been true in the past.[6] Above all, it does not rely on single panaceas, be these tractor stations, virgin land, or simply a spirit of competition with the United States, but rather it concerns itself with a balanced supply of satisfactory inputs and with production incentives. Rising output would not only eliminate eastern Europeans as claimants on surplus countries, but could before long cast them in the role of badly needed additional exporters.

Second, the recently inaugurated U.S. policy turn towards making food supplies less easily available, with the eventual goal of putting them on a competitive basis with other goods and services that developing countries want, is likely to lead these countries to a reappraisal of alternative paths toward adequate diets. *Third,* growing awareness on their part that even the most attractive industrialization plans are liable to founder on the shoals of recurring food crises is bound to shift emphasis to promoting agricultural growth. *Fourth,* "lessons learned" cannot be easily generalized, yet there do now exist a handful of success stories. Each has its special elements, but each provides proof that progress is possible.

Nonetheless, because the ingredients that go into enhancement of agricultural development are numerous and the participants dispersed and diverse, there is little likelihood of early success, massive in either depth or breadth. Thus inquiring into the role of technology in food production rates high priority. And it is of special urgency during the "interregnum" of the next decade or two, before penetration of birth control techniques can have made much of a dent in the volume of population growth.

---

[6] See the 1966 round of studies on the Soviet economy by the Joint Economic Committee, *New Directions in the Soviet Economy,* especially Parts I and II-B.

The Food Picture

I find it convenient to discuss the food picture under four headings: (1) yields in surplus countries, (2) yields in deficit countries, (3) acreage, and (4) new sources of food. In each instance, it will be useful to look into (a) what advances are most desirable and (b) what their chances are of timely emergence.

Yields in Surplus Countries In the United States (the principal current and prospective source of food surpluses) we have come to live with substantially rising grain yields—and let us concentrate on grains as the crucial element—as a matter of course. But it is well to remember how short that history is and how it has gained momentum only quite recently. In the case of corn, for example, yields fluctuated, without a trend, between 20 and 30 bushels per acre through 1940. The threshold of 30 had been topped a few times before—three, to be exact, since the Civil War—but only when it was passed for the fourth time, in 1941, did it stay passed. Forty was exceeded in 1948, and 50, ten years later. But it took only three more years to break the 60 per bushel acre barrier, and four more to exceed 70. Thus, in twenty-five years the yield has doubled, but the bulk of the rise was bunched in the past decade.

The case is similar, only more so, for sorghum: the yield fluctuated between 10 and 20 bushels per acre through 1948, broke 20 in 1949, and went above 30 for the first time in 1958. Then in quick succession, yield was about 40 in 1961 and above 50 in 1965, an increase of 150 per cent in a decade and a half.

There is nothing to match this performance in wheat. Rather, there is trendless fluctuation between 15 and 20 bushels per acre up to 1957. Then there was a quick rise to about 25 in 1958, and little sustained progress since. Nor are there significant disparities between states. True, there are states that raise 40-bushel-wheat, but they are not the large contributors, like Kansas, the Dakotas, Oklahoma, and Texas—all of which generally remain below the national average. Indeed, it is commonly the Corn Belt states and the northwest states that top the yield list.

Does this mean that a technological advance comparable in impact to hybrid corn and sorghum is required to push U.S. wheat yield into substantially higher ground? Many western European countries achieve wheat yields of 50, 60, and even 70 bushels per harvested acre; Japan achieves 30 to 40; and eastern Europe now harvests in the range of 30 bushels and better; these facts suggest that there is lots of mileage left in wheat yields short of a major breakthrough such as hybridization.

On the other hand, intercountry comparisons and intercontinental comparisons, even more so, must be interpreted with caution. Conditions of soil, moisture supply, hours of daylight, and other environmental factors must be taken into account before conclusions can be drawn. Price relations between crops and inputs, such as (above all) fertilizer, and consequent degrees of incentive toward the achievement of higher yields can be equally important.

Nonetheless, one suspects that U.S. wheat yields are not near their physical limit, though given currently available varieties they may be approaching their economic limit. That is, despite the fact that under ideal physical conditions U.S. yields might be much higher, it is quite possible that—short of raising the economic incentive—only a steep technological advance would lift yields in this country. It is above all the lackluster performance in the areas of major production that points that way. Increased funding of genetic research might thus be desirable, unless one wants to rely on breakthroughs resulting from normal, patient research, such as might be present in the wheat-rye cross *Triticale* that has recently received a good deal of attention.

In the case of feed grains, it is probably less a matter of new technology than of "catching up," in terms of improved practices, closer planting, and better plant protection. A national 100-bushel yield might thus be reached without any innovations and quite possibly within less than two decades. Recent supply projections made in the U.S. Department of Agriculture are, in fact, predicated upon a 100-bushel corn yield as early as 1980.[7]

But even if a 100-bushel corn yield, a 35-bushel wheat yield, and comparable, basically modest, advances in other crop yields were not to be expected until the end of the century they would translate into a U.S. demand at that time for about 475 million acres

---

[7] R. F. Daly and A. C. Egbert, "A Look Ahead for Food and Agriculture," *Agriculture Economics Research*, XVIII (U.S. Department of Agriculture; Washington: U.S. Gov't Printing Office, January, 1966).

of cropland. This is a magnitude that is only barely in excess of the area used, in fact, before the decline in cropland use in recent years. This assumes (one must add quickly) only moderate export demand—that is, excluding a situation in which whole countries and subcontinents would habitually look to U.S. grain fields to fill their deficits, largely on noncommercial terms of trade.

From the strictly domestic point of view, there is thus no pressure to seek new technology on the farms, especially as innovations would further hasten the need for changes in farm size and structure, and therefore impart new urgency to the absorption outside the farm economy of 1 or 2 million farm families. Rather, it is the role of the United States in world affairs that has of late led to questioning the adequacy of the U.S. agricultural establishment.

Yields in Deficit Countries What about technology's contribution to raising yields in the less-developed, food-deficit countries—the regions of the world that reap 10-15 bushel wheat, 15-25 bushel corn, and 1,200-1,500 pound rice (compared to rice yields three times that high and better in the United States, Japan, and Europe)?

Since the arithmetic of urgency is so simple, it need not be performed here. The role that technology has to play is not so simple, for technology is only a part of a bigger package, and there is no agreement over how large a part. In fact, progress sometimes seems as much impeded by the difficulty of diagnosing the illness and prescribing the most effective medicine—within the limitations of resources and time—as by the low level of production. There are those who stress social and political factors; those who indict the absence of attractive markets for selling outputs and of stable markets for buying inputs; those who point to the general low esteem in which agriculture and agricultural pursuits are held; those who deem the absence of roads and satisfactory transportation generally responsible; those who believe no progress to be feasible without rural credit facilities; those who see the principal obstacle in archaic and counterproductive land tenure patterns; those who blame the absence of an effective extension service; those who chase after yet other culprits; and **those who** believe that all elements must move forward together, lest the laggards frustrate what progress the others might bring.

What can be said in assessing the potential of technology in this environment, without unfolding the entire panorama of "how to get agriculture going"? Generally speaking, efficient raising of plants and livestock, in a context of mixed farming, has progressed above all in the temperate zone, under conditions of moderate temperatures and rainfall.

Consequently, much of our knowledge and many of our skills are not directly applicable to large parts of Asia, Africa, and Latin America. There, research has been heavily export oriented, stressing plantation crops and tailored to central control by small groups of experts, usually foreign. At the same time, traditional practices were allowed to prevail in those branches that supplied the domestic market and, above all, in subsistence farming.[8] Nor did the end of colonialism spell a great surge of research activity. On the contrary, if anything, a hiatus of considerable duration seems to have followed in the wake of the achievement of independence, with precious time wasted, and continuity lost. The fact that only in the last few years have there been systematic efforts to set up first-rate institutes of tropical agriculture—one for Latin America to be sponsored by the National Academy of Sciences (but after several years of planning still not past the drawing board) and one, perhaps closer to fruition, in Colombia or Nigeria —is in itself symptomatic of the lag in research.

One of the most urgent tasks of research outside the temperate zone is probably the development and diffusion of varieties adapted to local conditions. The injection into the Pakistan and Indian economies of high-yielding wheat strains, developed in Mexico under the auspices of the Rockefeller Foundation, is a case in point. According to J. George Harrar, president of the Foundation and "father" of the Mexican program, ". . . in Pakistan 350 tons of Mexican wheat have now been multiplied and successfully grown

---

[8] The magnitude of subsistence farming is suggested in an informative article by K. C. Abercrombie in Food and Agriculture Organization, *Monthly Bulletin of Agricultural Economics and Statistics* (May, 1965). It ranges from 1 per cent in the United Kingdom and 3 per cent in the United States to 25 per cent in Japan, 45 per cent in Thailand, and 82 per cent in Ethiopia, where the percentages relate to the value of subsistence production compared to the value of total agricultural production.

As elsewhere in this paper, treatment of the less-developed countries as though they were a homogeneous group should not convey any judgment that they are.

and the seed has been used to plant up to one-half million acres. In India, 250 tons of wheat sent from Mexico last year have now been harvested, and 18,000 tons of certified seed wheat have just been purchased from Mexico for a vast extension of this program."[9] The work of the International Rice Research Institute at Los Baños in the Philippines, jointly sponsored by the Rockefeller and Ford Foundations, is another instance. The new rice varieties developed by the institute, engineered to yield multiples of yields obtained from traditional varieties, are now being planted in a number of Asian countries.

Early failures to raise yields by heavy applications of fertilizer, following well-established Western practices, have opened the way for investigating the joint impact of variety, water, other environmental factors, and nutrients. The potential of technology undoubtedly is large along this road, and the provision in the 1966 Food for Peace legislation for financing "adaptive research" is a step in the right direction. When one realizes that only 3 per cent of India's food consumption in recent normal years has been imported, it becomes obvious how crucial yield increases are.

Four years from now we should be a good deal wiser in this respect. By then the Indian government hopes to have boosted its grain output by one-third or more above what it assumes would have been the production in 1965-66 had not drought conditions disastrously reduced it. The hopes not only of the Indian government, but also of the United States and of the international lending agencies, ride precariously on the payoff from what is called "the new strategy" in Indian planning. This consists basically of emphasis on new, high-yielding varieties, greatly increased fertilizer application, and an altogether much larger allocation of funds to agriculture in India's budget. Moreover, these inputs are to be concentrated on those favored areas that, because of assured rainfall or water from irrigation projects, are least subject to water shortages.

Provided the needed amounts of fertilizer can be procured, provided it is efficiently applied in the right places to the right crops at the right time, provided the new seeds are prepared with the

---

[9] J. George Harrar, "Principles for Progress in World Agriculture," presented at the 33rd annual meeting of the National Agricultural Chemicals Association, White Sulphur Springs, W. Va., 1966.

proper care and combined with the necessary supplementary inputs, and provided India is spared repetition of the last two years of drought, achievement of the target production would reduce the need for imports to zero, while at the same time establishing a reasonably satisfactory per capita level of consumption.

All rides on the provisos. In this connection, it is useful to call attention to a timely word of caution that recently emanated from the International Rice Research Institute: ". . . the same limitation on environmental control which prevents farmers from achieving the yield potentials inherent in existing varieties will represent an equally severe limitation on achievement of the yield potentials inherent in the new varieties that will be introduced in the future. They are being designed to be ever more sensitive to effective environmental control, technical inputs, and management than existing varieties. Thus the same public investment and institutional innovations required to narrow the gap between typical and potential yields under present circumstances will represent a necessary condition if introduction of the new varieties is to be reflected in higher yields."[10]

A far more remote, but in the long run—probably very long run—perhaps even more significant technological task, is the utilization for food of the lush foliage growth in the globe's humid tropical areas. There is growing questioning of the degree to which the standard crops and standard farming patterns of the temperate and subtropical zones are efficiently adaptable to tropical conditions. Native flora and fauna may simply prove to provide too much competition. The thought has arisen, therefore, that to utilize what exists (luxuriant foliage) and render this product edible may offer a better solution.

A breakthrough in this direction would open up a new dimension in food supplies. When we talk of adaptive research these days, we commonly have in mind starting with Western knowledge and practices and adapting them to other environments. Here, adaptation would begin with the native, unused growth and would be chemically transformed into a useful commodity. Despite its remoteness I would put this high on the basic research agenda and

---

[10] V. W. Ruttan, A. Soothipan, and E. C. Venegas, "Technological and Environmental Factors in the Growth of Rice Production in the Philippines and Thailand," *Rural Economic Problems*, III (May, 1966).

would mention in this connection that a somewhat similar thought —the organized and controlled use of certain wildlife in parts of Africa as food—is advancing beyond the "brainstorm" stage.

But in allocating funds for quick results, I would give priority to factors that do not fall into the breakthrough category. Even with currently available varieties, for example, greater use of fertilizer would generally pay off handsomely.[11] Recent statistics suggest that Indian farmers use about 3 pounds of plant nutrients and harvest less than 100 pounds of cereals per acre. At the other end of the scale, Japan, with Taiwan not far behind, spreads out over 250 pounds of nutrients and reaps close to 4,000 pounds of cereals. An interesting associated statistic is that in Japan it takes a little over 1 pound of rice to buy 1 pound of fertilizer; in India, until very recently, more than 5 were required. While there are many other elements mixed up in the results, obviously fertilizer has a high positive correlation with yields, and the relation of fertilizer to product prices plays a crucial part in setting the level of application.[12]

If the less-developed countries used as much fertilizer per person as the developed ones, it has been estimated that the resulting 50 million tons per year (compared to less than 4 million at present), if used on grain alone, would lead to a doubling of grain production, assuming the entirely reasonable equation of 1 pound of fertilizer to 10 pounds of grain.[13] Such a perspective would allow us all to relax.

While one could easily secure agreement on these calculations, consensus is much harder to obtain on how one gets there. Though here, too, a few priorities are beginning to emerge. Ranking high, for instance, are price relationships that are attractive, as already noted, and that, in addition, hold out the promise of continuity. Even in the United States, farmers as a whole go by no means to

---

[11] Again, "development arithmetic" is very seductive. If India's rice yield could be doubled, at which point it would still remain one-third or more below Japan's, the added output would not only remove all need for imports, but permit substantial increases in per capita consumption. A change-over to the higher-yielding japonica variety, higher fertilization, and more secure water supply are all involved, though experiments show that even current varieties will respond at a 10:1 ratio to nitrogen application.

[12] See, for example, Raymond P. Christensen, "United States Role in Alleviating World Hunger," presented at Arkansas Plant Food Conference, Hot Springs, Ark., Dec. 9, 1966.

the economic limit that the cost and price relationship between farm inputs and outputs would permit.[14] This is even much less so in poor and unstable countries.

Once established, the practical consequences of price incentives can be driven home by demonstration and leadership. Just as in U. S. farming, there are pioneers and laggards in other agricultures. "Show me" activities no doubt have a high payoff, but are difficult to organize and sustain, and the kind that is effective will differ from country to country.

Another element now coming in for attention is "image-building." To channel more talent into agricultural technology, extension work, policy positions, and the like, one needs to build up the status of such work at institutions of learning, in the government budget, in legislative assemblies, and elsewhere. Again, this is not done overnight; it is discouraging to learn that even now Indian civil servants in the government's agricultural activities receive lower salaries than their counterparts elsewhere in government.

I offer no apology for having dwelled at length upon the yield-raising aspects of agriculture, and on the Indian experience in particular. Unless the eventual decline in the rate of population growth is met halfway by more satisfactory diets, we will have no resources left over to worry about other gaps. Nor do the experiences of Russia and China suggest that radically changed social orders hold the answer to lagging agriculture. On the contrary, for an intermediate period—and it could be an extended one—the more likely outcome might be stagnation or even declining output.

There is one puzzling aspect in this situation. The experience

---

[13] The quality of statistical information on levels of application, as opposed to experimental matters, is incidentally deplorably poor. At best, fertilizer application, and only commercial kinds, on all arable or all agricultural land is estimated. Next to nothing is known on application by type of crops. Thus correlations between rates of application and grain yields, for example as calculated by FAO, throw only a very dim and diffuse light on the matter. Though it must be added that until very recently, even in this country such statistics were very sparse. Now, the gap is being filled by annual sample surveys under the auspices of the Crop Reporting Board. It is only because the inverse correlation is so striking that even the poor statistical foundations make international comparisons useful.

[14] For the case of fertilizer, see D. B. Ibach, *Fertilizer Use in the United States: its Economic Position and Outlook* (Agriculture Economic Report No. 92, Economic Research Service, U.S. Dept. of Agriculture; Washington: U.S. Gov't Printing Office, 1966).

of the postwar years suggests that the food problem has agitated the deficit countries far less than it has the developed countries—above all, the United States. Otherwise, their development plans and their policies would have aimed, above all, at rapid transformation of their traditional agricultural establishment.

Hindsight, it is true, now tells us that by making it relatively inexpensive for deficit countries to muddle through, the availability of U.S. surplus crops has probably been an important factor. In that sense, the drawing down of U.S. food reserves may be a blessing in disguise.

But there are other factors. It is possible, for instance, that food balance statistics, even when compiled and interpreted by competent technicians, do not reflect the real situation. Perhaps supplies from the local equivalent of "garden plots" that largely escape measurement are more important than we think. If this is so, one could appreciate why governments wisely limit their worrying to feeding the vocal and active urban poor. A second explanation would be that there has been a deliberate decision to push industrial development and exploit agriculture, via low prices, taxation, and so on, as a source of savings, always trusting that the developed countries will come to the rescue should food needs go grossly unmet. And it is also imaginable that in countries in which the rural hinterland has always been ill-fed, with little if any reliance on outside resources, a rising degree of hunger will have relatively little impact upon governments in which the hungry are not well represented in the first place. Whatever the explanation, it is difficult not to be impressed—and somewhat puzzled—by the degree to which the main drive toward agricultural development and enlarged food production has come from the rich and well-fed rather than from the poor and badly-fed countries. Additional inquiry, I would think, might disclose important differences in values assigned to the various strands of which development is composed, including human life itself.

While rising yields will have to bear the brunt of the advance, and while truly new technology is not likely to play a featured role here, there are two further avenues to consider: new land and new sources of food.

Acreage New—that is, arable but presently uncultivated—land there is, in Latin America and in Africa below the Sahara above all. But the cost of bringing such land into production is not well known—nor is the rate of success in establishing new agricultural settlements encouraging, nor the degree of relief that such efforts have afforded the rising pressure of population. Moreover, so-called infrastructure expenditures, over long trial-and-error periods, usually following extended periods of investigation and preparation, impinge heavily upon the final costs, even if they commonly show up on the ledgers of agencies or organizations physically and financially removed from the place of settlement.

There are, however, extensive uncultivated areas that have been tested to varying degrees for their suitability as farmland. These could make important contributions. The central highlands of Brazil, long the object of curiosity and the subject of intensive study by one of the Rockefeller-spawned organizations—the IRI Research Institute—form one such area. The investigators have suggested that between 200 and 300 million acres could be made productive with the application of carefully specified amounts of plant nutrients. Others are less sanguine in their appraisal.

But in any event, what is wanted now is not so much technological as social and political inventiveness. To wait for a gradual, spontaneous filling in by new settlers, or to throw the land open to speculation would, in all likelihood, remove it effectively from making a contribution for a long time to come. But, provided cost calculations show beyond a doubt that, initial infrastructure investments apart, cropping and/or grazing would be paying propositions, would it not be a good use of American foreign aid funds, for example, to offer up such land on contract to experienced agriculturists? This could be coupled with an option to purchase the resulting crops for use in foreign aid itself, in order to minimize the chances that such a development would depress local prices. As mixed corporations seem to grow in popularity, why not one in foreign agriculture? These—and better—arrangements for utilizing potential land areas, short of a slow settlement process, might mean that whatever new technology is available could be applied sooner and more easily. From there it could spread. The gap is between what *is being* done and what *can be* done much more than between what *can be* done and what *cannot yet* be done.

New Sources of Food   Finally, what about new sources of food? Apart from such things as tropical foliage, mentioned earlier, two areas come to mind: (1) substitutes and (2) supplements.

Among the first are the simulated foods, in this country now entering the stage of market testing, which are expected to be on a par with meat as protein sources, for example, but which will probably eventually cost the consumer less.

The role of these substitutes in the developed countries could be important. Based currently on soybeans, and in the future perhaps on alfalfa and other grasses that yield more tons per acre, they would be both land- and time-saving as compared with meat. Whether they could make a significant contribution to food in the less-developed countries is more doubtful. The sociology and psychology of the introduction of new foods into traditional societies is complex. Success to date has not been overwhelming. Although imitation meats might be more attractive and more easily marketed than protein supplements in powder form, such as the Latin America Incaparina, the slow progress of the latter in the face of imaginative marketing methods might nonetheless be symptomatic.[15] Would not a similar fate befall other supplements as well as substitutes?

This is an urgent, practical issue, now that fish protein concentrate, or FPC, has been given a qualified green light by the Food and Drug Administration. If it is to prosper, the problems of introducing it into the diets of less-developed countries will have to be faced; this might prove a harder nut to crack than was the technology that has made its emergence possible in the first place. How does one change food habits? How does one gain acceptability? How does one reach desirability? How does one address the diffused rural masses? How does one avoid the image of a health food, a specialty food, something for the poor, and so on? To be unobstrusive but comprehensive is a hard task. Leadership will be important, and so will "image-building." But even if the new product, whether from petroleum, from algae, or from lignin, can be made palatable, one cannot find fault with the judgment that it is ". . . pointless to mount crash programs to develop exotic foods. . . ."[16]

Things look a little more hopeful on the supply side, at least

---

[15] It is not to disparage its moderate success to point out that current production is 215 tons per month, vis-à-vis an estimated market potential in Latin America of 33,000 tons (see "Food for the World").

[16] "Food for the World."

along some lines. FPC does hold promise, especially if combined with some ingenuity (my colleague in RFF, Francis Christy, for example, recently suggested that harvesting of trash fish for processing into FPC might just be the thing to put the ailing United States fishing industry on its feet, or more appropriately, on its keel). But it would be unwise to count on it as a major aid in alleviating hunger and as a near-term means of correcting malnutrition. The Bureau of Fisheries of the U. S. Department of the Interior has pointed out that it is possible with today's technology for the U. S. fishing fleet to harvest 12 billion pounds of trash fish per year and process it into enough protein to supplement the diet of 1 billion people, 300 days a year, at a cost of less than 0.5¢ per day, or $1.5 billion a year. If this is indeed the opportunity, it will take a great deal of organizing to grasp it.

All this holds equally true for research on raising proteins on a diet of petroleum hydrocarbons. Again, appraisal of this technique depends more, I believe, on how one views the chances of successful distribution to people that most need it than on the engineering features which are indeed overwhelming.[17] For unless you can turn amino acids into a tasty dish by itself—and I can find no hints that this is in the offing—you need something to be enriched before you can use enriching supplements.

Even though most of us have become blasé enough to take it for granted that almost anything can be accomplished, we have at the same time and pace become sufficiently skeptical of our ability as social and political engineers to modify age-old customs and habits, overcome inertia and prejudice and, in many instances, vested interests. If we despair of rapid advances in controlling the rate of population growth, as well as in modernizing agriculture, how can we realistically count on more rapid success in radically changing people's eating habits? I find it hard to accept a policy based on "selective despair" or "selective optimism," if you wish. Thus, to summarize reliance on new foods as the way out for

---

[17] Examples are the estimate that the equivalent of the world's current animal protein supply could be produced from 3 per cent of the world's petroleum production ("Food for the World") or that 1,000 pounds of yeast can produce 100,000 tons of protein in 24 hours, as compared with 0.9 pounds of protein produced by a 1,000-pound steer in the same time, cited in Kermit Bird, *An Appraisal of Some Food Processing Methods of the Future* (Economic Research Service, U.S. Dept. of Agriculture; Washington: U.S. Gov't Printing Office, 1966).

shortages in less-developed countries is for the long term; and for the long term there are perhaps alternatives that yield a more rapid return.

THE ENERGY PICTURE

It has been said that in the last resort it is inanimate energy, in the concentrated, controllable, and mobile form of the nineteenth and twentieth centuries, that has made possible all other material progress. One may not want to go *that* far in pinning progress on a single factor, but one can probably go *quite* far. Abundant, low-cost energy greatly facilitates the extraction of materials from the environment, their transformation, and their movement. The fact that energy in most contemporary industrial processes represents only a modest fraction of total costs of production does not contradict the assertion that without it none would be possible, or almost none. The fact that costs of energy are overshadowed by other costs of production merely reflects the low marginal cost of energy and its high productivity in use. Lower energy costs would thus not significantly reduce the cost of final products. Rather, they would open up different avenues of processing. Production of nitrogen and hydrogen, for example, would become far cheaper; the high cost of hydrogen is today a barrier to many new developments—among which, for example, are the fuel cell and coal liquefaction. In the very long perspective, they will keep costs of basic materials from rising, a matter of increasing importance as resources of poorer quality are reached.

The cost of energy also may affect greatly the economic feasibility of water desalinization. Energy represents, on the average, one-third of the cost of the resultant water. It can be argued that even if energy were free, the cost of desalted water would still be too high to be of use where it is most needed, in agriculture. But even this could change when less costly equipment is engineered and energy thus assumes an even greater relative importance in total cost.

Abundant low cost energy qualifies then as a high priority target. This is not so much because in the near future the current price level will significantly impede developments that might alleviate population pressure; rather, it is because in the more distant future energy that is both cheap and not flawed by the perspective of early depletion and rising cost would permit a faster pace and a more diversified pattern of economic growth. In this connection, one is bound to comment that the concentration on the large reactor (300 megawatt and up) has pushed the gains to be derived from nuclear reactors by less-developed countries further into the future. Per capita consumption and user density are both too low to permit efficient use of such reactors. Let us look at this this way: a reactor of 500 megawatt, now almost the lower limit in size, would, to produce low cost power, have to produce not less than 3.5 billion kwh per year. Presently, there is only a handful of countries outside of North America, Europe, and Oceania that consumes that much electric energy per year altogether. And of these, only Argentina, Brazil, Japan, India, North Korea, and the Republic of South Africa consume greatly more. The case for efficient small reactors is contained in these gross statistics. Without such advance, the less-developed countries are merely being misled by the alleged blessings of nuclear technology.

Concern over energy supplies may appear somewhat out of phase in a period that has energy producers worrying more about adequate markets than adequate supplies. But then the reasonable horizon of private producers and marketers is not twenty-five or thirty, let alone fifty years, but ten or fifteen, and in some industries (for instance, chemicals) shorter yet.

TECHNICAL ADVANCE IN OTHER AREAS

I must confess that when I deal with food and energy, I find great difficulty in specifying other areas in which technological advance could relieve population pressure in a major way. The jump into the twentieth, let alone into the twenty-first, century presupposes levels of income, education, adaptability, political stability, legal institutions, and so on that in some parts of the world do not exist at all, and in others only in rudimentary shape or in various degrees of disarray.

Technology in construction, transportation, and communications, to name some major economic activities of daily life, can surely make a contribution, but hardly a crucial one. A small transistor radio in every villager's hut would be of help in advancing agricultural practices and in changing food habits, to name only two applications. One can go further and advocate the use of television-viewing arrangements to teach improved farming methods. One might even think up some additional angles, but the hinge on which progress pivots is more and more the content of what is being conveyed and the willingness of the recipients of the information to apply it than the excellence of the means of conveyance themselves.

I harbor similar feelings of skepticism with regard to transportation. There are surely occasions when improved transportation will be of help, indeed will be vital, in opening up new areas of settlement and productive participation in the national economy. But more often in thinking about new technology in transportation, we are dealing with the spectacular and unique rather than the pedestrian and commonly applicable. I have seen color slides of carcasses loaded onto freight planes to be flown from Peruvian jungle or near-jungle areas to urban markets. No doubt, there are occasions when such innovations can make their mark. But I find it hard to persuade myself that specialty trade is the answer to rapid population growth. Moreover, the technology we are talking about here is not new as such. Only its application is.

The one area that is perhaps more promising, though I fear quite a way into the future, is more efficient and cheaper massive earthmoving for highway construction. But again, while highways and access roads would enable people to spread out, they still would have to obtain and master techniques for conducting useful activities in such areas and have things to bring in and take out. I disagree with views such as those expressed by the Paddock brothers, for example, that where there is no activity there is good and sufficient reason for there not being any, and that one can only lose time and money in trying to develop such areas.[18] But disagreeing does not blind me from the fact that planning for a spreading out of the population can be successful only if these areas are from the very beginning integrated into the regional or national economy. Just as population pressure cannot be eased by specialty trade, so it cannot be solved by creation of what I have heard a Polish planner refer to as "parachute industries," economic activities plopped into the middle of nowhere.

---

[18] William and Paul Paddock, *The Hungry Nations* (Boston: Little, Brown & Co., 1964).

Structural Materials   Even less relevant is that part of technology that affects the range or costs of structural materials, such as (above all) metals, but also plastics, glass, lumber, and others. From time to time, one comes across calculations of global consumption that conjure up impending shortages of this, that, or the other material. These are usually based on the assumption that demand in the less-developed countries will be rising rapidly toward levels now prevailing in industrialized, high-income countries.

Whether these calculations form the basis of a plea for greater attention to domestic sources (if they are not indeed conducted for that very purpose), or whether they are just part of the urge to look ahead and speculate, they rest on shaky assumptions. On the most general level, per capita income in most poor countries is so low that it will not for a long time to come support rising materials consumption of a degree that will seriously eat into the world's resources. On a more specific level, there is little reason to suppose that economic development everywhere must follow the European or North American mold.

Take steel, for example. Unless one pictures vast increases in railroad networks (certainly not a prominent part of any current planning), the emergence of big ship-building industries, the growth of a substantial native automobile industry, construction methods that (for the larger buildings in any event) rely heavily on steel, and the rapid spread of the more substantial consumer durable goods, it is difficult to see enough demand arising to promote and sustain large steel industries in the less-developed countries.

And when in the much longer run some of these demands should arise, why assume that steel will be the preferred material—just because in the nineteenth and first half of the twentieth centuries the Western world had nothing better to work with? Would it not be more reasonable to expect that developing countries will take off from where we *are* rather than where we *have been*? They are likely to be less encumbered by rules and regulations, and investments as well, that impede the utilization of the newer materials.

If technology has anything to offer in the field of materials, it might, on the contrary, be precisely the chance to skip much of the heavy metal age and to orient materials use toward the light metals and, even more so, toward petrochemicals. One must add quickly though that here again technology can alleviate population pressures only to the extent that fewer resources might be needed for the emerging industrial structure; more resources, therefore, can be released to be devoted to activities tending to increase food production. What immediately comes to mind, for instance, is the impetus that would be given to fertilizer and pesticide production in the context of a large and prosperous petrochemicals industry.

Natural Resources   Out of the foregoing remarks there emerges now a central point. The brave new world of exciting technology that provides an unending stream of intriguing stories in the news media and that keeps symposia and conferences going at a fast clip is, for the most part, designed to improve and enrich the conditions of life and leisure enjoyed by those who have the means of opting out of the strains and stresses imposed by the rising density of population. In the life sciences, the prospects are for reducing degenerative diseases, replacing worn-out or defective organs, correcting deviations from mental health, extending the life span itself, controlling the sex of unborn children, and in the last resort upgrading the species and perhaps synthesizing it.

In the physical sciences, extension of man's domain to the subterranean, the subaquatic, and the extraterrestrial environment may help us add to our store of materials, improve our means of communications, and, indirectly, educate us. It may even solve problems of crowding in that much of our less esthetically attractive activities may be put underground or underwater. But again, it is difficult to conceive of this as significantly related to the pressing problems of the poor countries of the world.

Even where some benefits from the more spectacular new technology can be dimly discerned—such as, for example, earth observations made from orbiting sensors or improvements in weather forecasting—the near-term value to the poor countries is problematic. My colleague Orris Herfindahl points out in an unpublished study of investment in natural resources information: (1) much of the type of data that can be gathered by orbiting sensors can also be gathered by less costly and complex methods; (2) much information that is needed beyond "general orientation" can be gathered only on the ground; (3) to be useful, the information gathered must fit into an administrative and managerial system that can both interpret and use it. Particular usefulness would lie in coverage of large areas inaccessible by other means, including airplanes, in rapid coverage of large areas, and in repeated and frequent coverage of specific areas. That these constitute pressing needs of less-developed countries is very doubtful though one must add that we are, of course, just at the threshold of a new era of observatory and investigatory techniques.

On the other hand, we all have a tendency to embrace new technology as panaceas, forgetting that increased knowledge of the physical surroundings is only one step on the long and arduous road of development (for example, investment decisions) and that the road block is in most instances not lack of knowledge but lack of organizing to utilize it.

If I have concentrated on the problems of the poor countries, it has been on the conviction that the calamities facing the rich or reasonably rich countries are both less pressing and of a basically different order of magnitude. This may be an unpopular view, but I am inclined to go a long way with the sentiments expressed back in February, 1967, in an article in the *New York Times Magazine* carrying the self-explanatory title "Not a Bad Crisis to Live in" (by Irving Kristol). At an M.I.T. symposium in October, 1966, Harold Barnett observed that, after all, considerably more than half of the surface of the United States is given over to grazing and forests; that urban areas occupy only some 1 per cent of the country's surface; and that highways, airports, rail tracks, and so on take up more than an additional 1 per cent. We grow all we need to eat and more on an area that has not increased in over half a century, and we do so to produce a diet that is as wasteful of land as can be, since much more cropland is destined for the highly inefficient detour via the animal digestive tract than for the human stomach directly (over 11,000 calories used up to give us our daily 3,000).

The growth of our forests currently exceeds the annual cut we make of them by 60 per cent, and the range of the energy sources that are at our disposal has so widened that our policy issues are, for the most part, children of abundance—nor can one discern any significant shadows of materials scarcities in the reasonably foreseeable future.

True, we have other problems in the resource area, now categorized under the generic heading of "pollution." The literature on the subject, addressed to pollution of water, air, soundwaves, landscape, and so on, has been expanding so rapidly that I feel justified in confining myself to two brief observations.

(1) While it will require substantial financial resources and capacity for accommodation to doing things in ways that minimize pollution (or maximize excellence), the developed world is short of neither. For example, the difficulties that a radical change in methods of surface transportation might entail would be large, given the enormous investment associated with current arrangements, but they are of a fundamentally different kind, order of magnitude, and time horizon than the problems of transition from traditional to modern agriculture. What if the cost of driving a personal vehicle were to increase 20, 30, or 40 per cent? What if the cost of reducing pollution were to raise the price of water by a similar or even greater percentage, or increase the cost of paper, certain chemicals, and other commodities whose production now contributes to pollution? Surely, the economies of the advanced countries have enough fat to yield some of it for coping with environmental problems, acquiring the necessary knowledge, applying it to practical solutions, and making the necessary institutional adjustments (though just as in the case of the less-developed countries, the last-cited phase will, in all likelihood, prove the least tractable, albeit for different reasons).

(2) We have a great deal to learn about the value that society places on the various attributes of the natural environment. While perhaps all of us here, or a majority, may deplore environmental degradation and may be willing to see a certain quantity of resources devoted to preventing, remedying, and combating it (though each of us surely has a threshold beyond which he would rather tolerate rising amounts of degradation), we know very little of the societal judgment. It is commonplace to say these days that "the country has awakened" or "it is up in arms" in matters of pollution. But the depth of that arousal has yet to be tested in terms of the invoices that will begin to collect—from the new or upgraded apartment house incinerators in New York City that will raise rents, to efficient antismog devices on the family car, or to user charges on hitherto free and common resources.

This is a different setting from quantitative inadequacy, especially of food, where rising prices measure the direction and intensity of demand directly and immediately, and where the connection between deficiency of supply and adverse consequences is not a matter of conjecture, limited to demonstration only on the average. Uncertainty about the nature of demand, therefore, is the second reason for which I cannot see technological advance in matters of quality as urgent as in matters of quantity.

ANALYSIS

In closing, I should like to draw attention to a few points that are implicit in what I have said, but to which I should like to make explicit reference in order not to be misunderstood. Most important, I would be unhappy to have left the impression of advocating food self-sufficiency for each and every country in the world. There are, I am afraid, shades of such a tendency in the wording, and perhaps even in the intention, of the Food for Peace Act that was passed by the Congress in late 1966. Both in the House hearings and in the text of the bill the food deficit countries were urged to switch acreage from production of nonfood crops to food crops. Whether or not this is desirable, I would think, depends in each given case on the relative productivity in the alternative uses, on crop rotation patterns, on local price relationships, on the outlook for world prices, and similar factors. It would surely be unwise for a country to give up raising a nonfood crop, in which it has a strong comparative advantage, in order to grow rice, wheat, or corn, which it could more economically obtain by trading. Neither enthusiasm for fighting hunger nor concern for cotton surpluses must lead us into advocating economic illiteracy.

Further, on the subject of local nonfood resources, the less-developed countries will have much to gain from new technology that will advance the utilization of their barely-touched forests. This is especially true in the tropical regions. While there is presently no indication of any forest product shortage in the countries of major consumption, the transition of tropical woods from specialty products to "shelf items" would add greatly to the foreign exchange earning capacity of these countries. Any effort toward economic exploitation of tropical forests deserves high priority.

What goes for forests goes for any other resource, mineral or otherwise, for which the world market has—and is likely to sustain—a demand that makes exploration and exploitation profitable. Here, however, I suspect it is not so much the lack of an appropriate technology but rather an attitude that keeps the less-developed countries from pushing strongly along the line of primary products production and trade. To many of them this smacks of colonialism and exploitation in the pejorative sense. Yet, it would be a pity if natural advantages were to be sacrificed at the altar of outdated images.

The second observation is, in a sense, the reverse of the first. There are certain technological advances that would drastically damage the very basis of existence of a number of developing countries. I am referring to further progress in substitution. Some of this is history and some is in the making. Inroads on cotton, wool, silk, and other natural fibers are past the halfway mark, at least in the United States. Artificial sweeteners are cutting into the sugar market, and natural rubber continues to struggle for a stable share in its domain. How thin the line is that today keeps us from replacing natural with synthetic coffee, cocoa, or tea, I do not know, but it may be thinner than we think. Yet we have no policy for protecting the means of livelihood of parts of the underdeveloped world.

Does this mean imposition of governmental controls on the application of available technology? Should we turn into modern Luddites and be prepared to prohibit the manufacture of synthetic coffee, for example, if General Foods, or General Mills, or any other large or small food manufacturing company should reach the stage of putting it on the grocery shelves at a competitive price? Or should we refrain from restrictive action and instead devise international schemes to skim off the resulting benefits to the consumer to compensate the losers in the supplying countries? My hunch is that the effects would be so drastic that some kind of interference and regulation would become necessary. This is not a new question, but recent advances in food simulation and food substitution, as discussed earlier, suggest a rising degree of urgency.

This leads me to a third issue I want to open up, and that is the declining degree to which technological development has been, and probably can be, left to market forces. In fact, this has been the trend ever since the end of World War II as far as the crucial and revolutionary advances in science and technology are concerned. Beginning with the achievement of controlled nuclear fission, it has been primarily through public funds, under public direction and stimulation, that our horizons have widened. Where the market has been the principal pacesetter of technological progress (as, for example, in residential construction or in clothing manufacture, and in other consumer goods industries), progress has, on the whole, been modest and directed, above all, toward making things more convenient—not basically different—even where wholly new materials or processes have entered the picture. This has developed so much so that there has been rising concern over the "starvation" of these segments in matters of improved technology. Executive and legislative attempts to remedy this situation have made little headway. Nor have the expected pay-offs from new technology in the more glamorous pursuits, such as communications and the various aspects of space activities, materialized to a degree that is commensurate with the expenditures. One combs in vain through the literature put out by NASA's technology utilization program to discover them. A longer-lasting or otherwise improved paint, better alloying or metal-bonding techniques, and a new precision-casting method are typical kinds of innovation. They are by no means to be discounted in their importance to relevant manufacturing processes, but they are many notches below the products toward which government research and development funds have been expended—the rockets, missiles, satellites, and all the associated science fiction equipment.

There is no comparable effort and no comparable expenditure of funds in the less glamorous field of improving the population-food ratio in the poorer parts of the world. In fact, had it not been for the philanthropic foundations that have pioneered both in matters of population control and improved food production know-how and practices, we would not be nearly as far along as we are in some parts of the world today. It should be amply clear that for the same reasons that the development of space technology could not have been left to market forces, so the transfer and, where necessary, development of technology in the more pedestrian fields of requirements for living in the less-developed countries cannot be entrusted to the care of supply and demand.

Not long ago I came across a listing of the major discoveries and innovations during the three decades 1932-62. They were, without any priority implied in the ranking, as follows: radar; wonder drugs; eleven new elements; earth satellites; television; synthetic rubber, gems, and so on; new metals (titanium and so on); solar batteries; jet aircraft; nuclear reactors; computers.

Accepting this listing as it stands—and what listing would ever satisfy everybody?—one is hard put to find much of it relevant to the dominant problems of the poor countries. At least two of the items, wonder drugs and synthetic materials, have caused part of their present plight, and most of the others do not contribute to its solution. Obviously, the push towards innovation from the market side goes toward the "better mouse-trap," the widening of choices, and the creation of new luxuries to be turned in short order into necessities. The main thrust from the government side is toward revolutionary conquests of nature. The needs of the poor countries are in a no-man's land, poorly attended to and lacking the lure of either profit or glamor. Indeed, unless one counts "the pill" among the wonder drugs (the 1962 cutoff eliminates the intrauterine device), the listing itself reflects this bias. For one cannot think of a more "major" discovery of interest to the less-developed countries than birth control devices.

In a speech in January of this year the Secretary of Agriculture took time out to peer into the future of the American farmer. What he saw in the year 2000 were a computer center helping him to decide how much to plant, what crop to plant, what seeds and fertilizers to use, when to harvest, and so on; virus-free plants, carefully bred for high yield, early and simultaneous maturing, with stalks engineered for mechanical harvesting, and new uses for previously discarded portions of the plant; taped programs directing automated machines, supervised by TV scanning towers, to plant, cultivate, harvest, grade, package, and freeze. What vision of farming is there, one asks, to conjure up for the less-developed countries that would not disclose an abysmal gulf?

We have of late fallen into the habit of terming every major effort a "war." Thus we find ourselves engaged in wars on hunger, on poverty, on ignorance, on disease, and on various other enemies of mankind; but these are unusual wars, in that we have as yet given up none of our comforts and conveniences. Perhaps the war we need to wage most is on complacency, both here and abroad. If it is ever declared, we will find that we have an ample arsenal of technology. If it dies aborning, we might as well never have moved beyond the wooden plow.

Food in the Future—
Comments on Landsberg

T. J. GORDON

Director, Advanced Space and Launch Systems
Missile and Space Systems Division
Douglas Aircraft Company

IN HIS PAPER, "Population Growth and the Potential of Technology," Mr. Landsberg vividly illustrates the problems attendant to increasing the world's food production. He portrays our frustrating situation: on one hand, an accelerating population, growing fastest in areas of lowest food production, and, on the other, an inviting menu of technology which at best is difficult to apply to the problems of increasing our food supply. Further, Mr. Landsberg says the innovations required are not only the "glittering mouse traps" of technology; they lie also in the social, political, and psychological domains.

To a large measure I agree with Mr. Landsberg. Both the amount of acreage which can be brought under cultivation and the crop yields per acre can be improved through technology. Difficult sociological issues will precede or accompany the introduction of new foods and the expansion of our productivity. But I differ with him, I think, in assessing the degree to which technology can and will be important in providing adequate food for man. I am not yet willing to sell short the impact of our better mouse traps. There are technological innovations coming which will produce not only new hardware but also new human values as well, and will deeply influence our social, political, and psychological attitudes toward food and its production in the future.

Genesis of the Problem

In one respect we are fortunate; we know that we have a problem. The work of the Food and Agriculture Organization of the United Nations, the World Health Organization, U. S. Department of Agriculture, and demographic and nutrition organizations all over the world have provided insight into the extent of the food problem which would have been impossible before the middle of this century. Not only do we know we have a problem, we know it is likely to get worse. Barring some catastrophe, world population will probably double by the end of the century. In order to provide a continuing level of nutrition for these people, food production also will have to double. To provide adequate nutrition will necessitate a tripling of food production.

The problem is not only one of magnitude of production, it is also one of distribution. In many less-developed nations, population is increasing at a rate almost twice as great as food productivity. While population is also increasing in advanced nations, food production per capita has been increasing, probably as a result of many factors including favorable economic incentives for farmers, mechanization of farming operations, availability of hardy hybrid varieties, and advanced herbicides and pesticides. In the less-developed nations, productivity has not yet "taken off." The near future promises a situation in which industrialized countries will have a per capita abundance while widespread famine will exist elsewhere.

This is a new trend. For example, before World War II, the Latin American nations were exporting 11 million tons of grain to the developed countries.[1] After the war, the trend reversed; in 1964, 25 million tons flowed in the other direction. It has been estimated that U. S. grain fed 1 person out of 20 in Africa, Latin America, and noncommunist Asia last year.[2] This flow, largely paid for by foreign countries in currency not convertible to dollars, has dissipated our farm surpluses and, for the first time in thirty-three years, farmers in the United States have been asked to increase acreage. This flow has led to increasing concern over how to "prime the pump" of food productivity of the less-developed na-

---

[1] Lester R. Brown, "Increasing World Food Output" (Foreign Agricultural Economic Report No. 25, U.S. Department of Agriculture; Washington: U.S. Gov't Printing Office, April, 1965).

[2] "The Struggle to End Hunger," *Time,* LXXXVIII (Aug. 12, 1966), p. 32.

tions in a way which would promote the growth of their domestic yields. President Johnson articulated our policy: the United States will provide help, but the recipient nations must establish self-help measures to raise their agricultural output. He said:

> We know what would happen if increased aid were dispensed without regard to measures of self-help. Economic incentives for higher production would disappear. Local agriculture would decline as dependence on U.S. food increased.
> Such a course would lead to disaster.
> Disaster could be postponed for a decade or even two—but it could not be avoided. It could be postponed if the United States were to produce at full capacity and if we financed the massive shipments needed to fill an ever-growing deficit in the hungry nations.
> ... Candor requires that I warn you the time is not far off when all the combined production, on all the acres, of all the agriculturally productive nations, will not meet the food needs of the developing nations—unless present trends are changed.[3]

That is our challenge—to change the trend.

Why can't the less-developed nations feed their people? Lester R. Brown of the U.S. Department of Agriculture pictures it this way: in countries of lower population density, agricultural output can be increased by expanding the land under cultivation. Today, however, in many of the densely populated less-developed nations, almost all cultivable land is already planted; there is no room left for farm expansion. The application of surplus population to the farms doesn't ameliorate the problem; productivity is area controlled. Brown places nearly half the world's population in these fixed land economies. The major alternative in lands with no additional farming space is to increase the yield per acre, that is, the efficiency of land which is already in production.

We have seen remarkable increases in farm land efficiency in the developed nations; in North America, yields per acre have doubled since the war. In Asia, however, yields have increased only 7 per cent. Furthermore, in the developed nations the rate of increase appears to be accelerating while elsewhere it is remaining constant. What prompts this take-off? The take-off appears to be correlated to several socioeconomic factors: literacy, per capita income, market oriented agriculture, and the vitality of the non-agricultural sector of the nation's economy. In other words, yields

---

[3] John Walsh, "Food: Population Trends Move U.S. to Tie Aid to Self-Help," *Science*, CLII (May 6, 1966), pp. 732-34.

per acre characteristically appear to increase as nations move into the domain of the Western present: educated, industrialized, and a part of what Kenneth Boulding calls the superculture.

Technology also holds the promise of developing new foods, perhaps superior to those found in nature. These products may be of biological origin or completely synthetic; they may augment or perhaps eventually replace the foods we know today. Is this so unreasonable? Everywhere else man is about to control his environment and development. What he eats will come under his control as well. This manufacturing is not a solution for today's problem, but it may well solve tomorrow's.

These then are the facets of the food-technology interface which I will discuss: the role of technology in increasing cultivated acreage and per acre yields; the technology of new foods and the problems of their acceptance; and finally some thoughts on the sociology of technological spread and its relationship to future food production.

INCREASING PRODUCTION

Space Agriculture Perhaps no more than twenty years from now, earth-orbiting space stations will add materially to the earth's agricultural productivity. A hundred miles or so above the earth, space stations will gather data pertaining to agriculture/forestry; geology/hydrology; oceanography/marine technology; and atmospheric science and technology.[4]

In agriculture and forestry, global crop surveys will be conducted to obtain estimates of crop yield and damage losses. Certain types of infrared and multispectral detectors have already demonstrated the feasibility of detecting some types of crop and timber disease from orbit. This information could be used to predict potential famine situations and to aid harvests, disease control, and the determination of future crop planting requirements. Forest fires or potential fire sites might be detected from orbit using infrared detectors. Migration of wildlife can be surveyed, and ecological factors associated with crop and animal productivity will

---

[4] This discussion parallels the results of two study programs conducted for the NASA: Contract NAS W-1215, ORL Experiment Program, conducted by IBM (Rockville, Md., February, 1966); and SRI Project M-5465, Priority Analysis of Manned Orbital Research Applications, conducted by Stanford Research Institute (Menlo Park, Calif., September, 1965).

be assessed. Portions of the earth's land surfaces which could support the expanding agriculture of the twenty-first century could also be identified.

In the area of geology and hydrology, orbit-borne sensors might be used to detect new mineral and fuel deposits. Some scientists believe that incipient volcanic eruptions might be detected; certainly volcanic, earthquake, and flood damage assessment could be accomplished. Soil moisture content and erosion patterns will be determined; most important, water pollution surveys will be rapidly accomplished. Infrared radiometers can be used to detect small differences in soil temperatures from orbit. These measurements can be used to locate underground rivers and fresh water reserves, which promise to be immensely important to the development of new agricultural lands. In effect, space stations may prove to be orbital divining rods.

Measurement of changes in ocean current and bulk temperature will be useful in predicting synoptic and long-term weather changes. In the area of atmospheric science and technology, collection of data required for weather prediction may be a primary function of space stations. Air pollution measurements and contamination warning systems can be operated from orbit. Storms and climatic hazards can be observed and appropriate warnings issued to the earth.

In the next century, weather control may be possible. A special panel of the National Academy of Science has investigated the results of cloud seeding over a period of years. Its report stated in part, "We find some evidence for precipitation increases of as much as 10 or even 20 percent over areas as large as 1000 square miles over periods ranging from weeks to years."[5] Shortly after this report, on Feb. 4, 1966, Senator Clinton Anderson introduced a bill directing the Department of the Interior to "conduct a comprehensive program of scientific and engineering research, experiments, tests, and operations for increasing the yield of water from atmospheric sources." This marked the beginning of government sponsored weather control, including rain-making; snow-making; and hail, hurricane, tornado, fog, and lightning suppression.

[5] National Academy of Science, "Weather and Climate Modification: Problems and Prospects," Publication No. 1350 (Washington: Printing and Publishing Office, National Research Council, 1966).

Many commercial operators are already in the business of cloud seeding, and, judging from the NAS report, are meeting some success. Experiments have also been conducted in which the severity of hurricanes was modified through silver iodide crystal seeding.[6] A French meteorologist has created artificial tornados; Jean Dessens of the University of Clermont has formed twisters by generating heated vertical columns of air using oil burners.

It may be possible to accomplish some of this weather manipulation from orbit. For example, large scale cloud seeding might utilize orbital bombing with silver iodide. An orbiting mirror might be used to heat certain portions of the atmosphere to deflect atmospheric currents and thus divert rain-laden clouds or storms.

Weather manipulation would have three major effects on agriculture: rain could be triggered under the proper circumstances to provide additional irrigation, crop-damaging storms could be diverted, and clouds could perhaps be dissipated or routed over nonagricultural lands so that maximum sunlight would fall on the crops. This latter application might double the per acre output of temperate zone farms. But these manipulations are undoubtedly more than two decades in the future.

The near-term potential aid to agriculture from orbit is not being overlooked by today's developing nations. Dr. Vikram Sarabhai, chairman of the Indian National Committee for Space Research, recently said:

> . . . Agriculture is the most important activity on the sub-continent of India. A majority of the population of 480 million earn their livelihood from this occupation which is largely dependent on rain that occurs during the monsoons. It is hardly necessary . . . to stress the importance to India's economy of a better understanding of the processes by which the monsoon rains occur, processes which commence over the vast Indian Ocean, where there are relatively few observing stations undertaking even the normal observations at the surface or with balloons. What applies to the economy of India applies to the economy of most of the countries in the Indian Ocean region. Space meteorology which permits the acquisition of valuable data from satellites as well as with the use of sounding rockets has therefore a special significance for us. . . .[7]

---

[6] R. H. Simpson and Joanne S. Malkus, "Hurricane Modification," *Scientific American*, CCXI (December, 1964), pp. 27-37.

[7] Vikram Sarabhai, "The Value of Space Activity for Developing Countries," paper presented to the American Astronautical Society (August, 1965).

The earth orbital programs in support of agriculture which I have just described are already beginning. The National Aeronautics and Space Administration and the U.S. Department of Agriculture have signed a contract for the use of remote sensing equipment to make large area surveys of land use, detect forest fires, assist in predicting future crop yields, warn of insect infestations, determine specific locations suitable for growing certain crops, locate potentially reclaimable land, and monitor wildlife migration.[8] The Treasury Department has requested similar assistance in detecting narcotic producing plants such as poppies to aid in controlling illicit narcotics traffic. The U.S. Forestry Service and Department of the Interior are also cooperating with NASA in the development of earth oriented programs.

Space agriculture has already begun.

Education Education, patient teaching, can lead as almost no other innovation to an increase in the world's food production, adoption of appropriate irrigation techniques, and crop rotation and density. Use of hybrid seeds, knowledge of weather conditions, markets, fertilizers, pesticides, herbicides—all of these will bring primitive agriculture into the twentieth century. Education is itself a developing technology, and our knowledge of how to transfer information and influence behavior can and should be applied to the problem of food production. Information transfer satellites can transmit broadcasts which originate on earth to whole continents. From synchronous orbit they can relay instruction, properly perfumed with Madison Avenue exhortations, to rural farmers, hopefully listening with mass-produced, integrated circuit receivers. These receivers might be produced for less than a dollar each; the United States could probably launch a small direct broadcast satellite for less than $10 million, including the launch vehicle. This would be a form of aid, which, in the giving, would stimulate our own economy, give new purpose to our space achievements, and dramatically invite into the present the millions of people who will benefit from learning what today can offer.

The instructors will have to use the best of our behavioral control techniques—for example, saving stamps for achievement, use of local celebrities, the "star" image, sex, youth, fire and brim-

---

[8] "The National Space Program," Staff Study for the Subcommittee on NASA Oversight (Washington: U.S. Gov't Printing Office, 1967).

stone, tribal music, and ultimately the god, Acquisitiveness. Is it worth it? I suspect so. Our experts in behavior control who inhabit the offices of media will have their chance to contribute.

Earth-Bound Technology The programs beamed over this education network might carry as their message the proper uses of fertilizers and agricultural chemicals, pesticides, the practices of multiple cropping and crop rotation, irrigation and drainage, mechanization, hybridization, agronomy, and animal husbandry.

Fertilizers increase yields. There is no doubt of this. Certainly there are local crop, soil, and climate conditions that vary the requirements for nutrients and local economic conditions, which, in turn, vary the incentives for purchasing and utilizing fertilizers; here too, technology can have an effect. Based on FAO field trials in fourteen countries, the average increase in agricultural production for all countries, worldwide, across the spectrum of crops could be 74 per cent. But the economics of fertilizer application tends to inhibit their use in the less-developed countries. For example, the cost of nitrogen fertilizer was 50 per cent higher in India than in the United States, yet the rice produced in India brought the farmer only half as much as his American counterpart. Moral? Economic innovations will be as important as the technological.

New types of fertilizers are possible which will increase nutrient value for a given mass applied with increased accessibility and at lower cost. A significant recent example is the development of a "super-acid," an ammonium polyphosphate which contains 16 per cent N_2 and 60 per cent P_2O_5. Research into new manufacturing methods involving high capacity centrifugal compressors promises to lower the costs of ammonia-based fertilizers. But even with these improvements and others likely to follow in the near term, it will probably be uneconomical for a developing country to import fertilizers; therefore, indigenous production must be encouraged. This implies again the need for education, the development of economic and simple manufacturing plants, the use of efficient distribution systems, and the development of economic strategies which encourage the use of fertilizer.

Proper *irrigation and drainage* of agricultural lands could greatly increase per acre productivity and could make millions of new acres suitable for cultivation. However, to achieve an important increase in productivity by this means would seem to be an engineering task of large proportions. Fresh water is being produced from brackish and saline sources at several places in the world, from Kuwait to San Diego, but at a cost two orders of magnitude higher than economic farm irrigation requires. Whether the process used is steam distillation, freezing, or filtering, energy is required and energy costs money. The brightest hopes for lowering costs seems to be in either of two directions, use of by-products or free power.

The possibility of using the by-products of the purification process is intriguing. If, for example, the distillation permits the extraction of valuable metals and minerals from sea water, perhaps the water will be free, or even have negative cost. At Freeport, Tex., the Dow Chemical Corporation is experimenting with such by-product processes using the efflux desalination of the Office of Saline Water Plant next door.[9] Perhaps in this manufacturing of water we will reach the point where we will deliberately permit residual tract minerals to remain in the irrigation water, or even add certain nutrients, to provide fertilization automatically at the time of irrigation.

The second approach is to develop sources of essentially free power. Solar stills have been used in the distillation of sea water, but very large surface areas are required to obtain reasonable quantities of fresh water. A breakthrough not too unreasonable to expect in the next two decades is the production of controlled nuclear power by *fusion processes*. Here plasmas at temperatures approaching that of the sun's surface generate electrical energy directly by magneto hydrodynamic interactions. The major problem has been containment of the plasma since its temperature exceeds the melting point of any materials which might surround it. Progress is being made on the containment problem, however, by using magnetic fields to "bottle" the plasma. If the problem is solved, the cost of large-scale power production could drop by 50 per cent, and desalination might rather suddenly become more economically practical and widespread.

But the availability of cheap fresh water, even free water at the sea coasts, does not solve the total problem because of the costs of water transportation and distribution. The ocean is always disappointingly at sea level and inland farms are at higher altitudes;

---

[9] Lorus and Margery Milne, *Water and Life* (New York: Atheneum, 1964), p. 191.

this requires the expenditure of power or up-hill running water. One might imagine that an organized systems attack on the problem of cheap water pumping and distribution might include such items as: thermal pumps using solar power; magnetic pumping using filterable metal slurries; solar cell-powered pumps; laminar flow, low friction pipes, and canals; covered distribution channels; in situ fiberglass pipe fabricating and laying machines which would wind, coat, cure, and lay in one continuous operation; similar canal digging and coating machines; and unattended nuclear powered jet ejector pumps, gently pushing water through concrete and fiberglass arteries to the new farms of the world's deserts and steppes.

Food preservation techniques are being perfected which could add greatly to food availability. These spoilage-reducing techniques could permit more effective stockpiling in years of abundance and mitigate the impact of droughts or crop failures. *Freeze-drying,* the vacuum dehydration of frozen foods, is still expensive, but it allows long storage without refrigeration and preserves texture and flavor. *Vacuum-drying* is a similar but less costly process which is applicable to certain foods. Dr. Nevin Scrimshaw, a nutrition expert, has found these techniques particularly applicable to the preservation of food in tropical areas.[10] Other experimental techniques which may bear fruit include sterilization by ionizing radiation, antibiotic dips, and new chemical preservatives. All of these techniques are relatively expensive and suffer from logistics problems. They cannot immediately solve the problems of tomatoes rotting in a farmer's wagon, slowed by archaic roads and uncooperative burros, under an intolerant sun. Regional preservation centers, perhaps mobile centers, might give some aid. Certainly central facilities could be used in those rare but, hopefully, more frequent instances of local surpluses.

In 1961 the ESSO Research and Engineering Company conducted a *soil modification* test project in Libya. They sprayed 125 acres with low-grade oil to stabilize the shifting sand dunes. Ordinarily, the sand dunes support the growth of only scrub brush and sparse low-grade vegetation, but the oil-stabilized soil now holds trees, some over 25 feet tall. Eighty per cent of the acacia and euca-

---

[10] Nevin S. Scrimshaw, "Food," *Scientific American,* CCIX (September, 1963), p. 76.

lyptus seedlings survived in the test, and the Libyan government contracted for treatment of 3,000 more acres. *Scientific American* has speculated that this technology could lead to the "creation of a national forest in the treeless desert kingdom."[11]

Clarence Hansen and A. Earl Erikson of the University of Michigan are experimenting with methods of undercoating sandy soils with asphalt. This undercoating greatly increases the soil's ability to hold water, and, for certain crops, can double the yield. In their method, a plow-like blade lifts a cut of soil, and an asphalt coating is sprayed in at a depth of about 2 feet. They have estimated that the yield of crops such as potatoes, cabbages, and cucumbers is so increased that the undercoating can pay for itself within a year.[12]

In another process, black polyethylene strips, twenty inches wide, are laid over soil prepared for planting. The seedlings are inserted into holes in the plastic. The effect of the strip is to absorb heat and trap moisture in the soil while discouraging the growth of nearby weeds. The process has been found to double tomato crops and is being used widely on cotton acreage, now that new farm machinery has made the laying of the strips practical over large fields.[13]

Mechanization may also help improve productivity. In the industrialized countries, farm equipment has been used primarily to supplement human labor which, in many cases, is more desirable than increasing per acre productivity. In the less productive countries these conventional implements will also improve productivity when they can perform operations which cannot be matched by people no matter how large the number. For example, tractors towing steel blades can plow deeper than oxen towing wooden blades. Special seeding and fertilizing equipment is more accurate in placement and dosage than hand application. Mechanization speeds planting and harvesting to take advantage of particular weather conditions.

If we were to ask designers to contemplate machinery which would primarily increase yields, rather than replace labor, however, we might have an entirely new family of equipment. Smudge pots are an example of such implements. We might also find

---

[11] "Science and the Citizen," *Scientific American*, CCXVI (January, 1967), p. 60.
[12] "Science and the Citizen," p. 60.
[13] "Mechanized Plasticulture," *Time*, LXXXI (April 19, 1963), p. 75.

efficient fertilizers, cultivators, and weeders, designed to make the application of large numbers of human operators more productive.

Genetic Control Farmers in many parts of the world can buy seed which has been genetically developed to yield crops with certain predetermined, desirable characteristics. These traits match the crop to local weather, pest, disease, and soil conditions. For example, we have today:

> ... wilt resisting peas and cabbages; mosaic-resisting snap beans, virus-resisting potatoes; mildew resisting cucumbers and lima beans; anthracnose-resisting watermelons and leaf spot resisting strawberries. We have new cereal grains rich in Vitamin A; cotton seed from which the toxic pigment called gossypol has been bred out....[14]

Two strains of rice are being cultivated in Asia: the subspecies japonica and the subspecies indica. Among the physiological differences between the out-species is their responsiveness to fertilization; the japonica subspecies, which is raised in Japan, northern China, Korea, and the Philippines, is much more adaptable to intensive cultivation. As Dr. Landsberg pointed out, high-yield Mexican wheat strains are being cultivated in India and Pakistan; intensive study of rice varieties is being accomplished in the Philippines. What directions might this manipulative selection take?

Brown, Bonner, and Weir have computed the maximum yields that might be obtained through conventional agriculture, assuming a 2 per cent energy conversion of sunlight to plant products—a figure representative of the best cultivated crops, for example sugar cane in the tropics. On this basis northern temperature regions under cloudless skies could be expected to produce 100 to 135 bushels of wheat per acre and 150 to 220 bushels of corn. Assuming a shading figure of 50 per cent, the anticipated yields would be reduced to a figure close to that already attained. In other words, conventional crops in the United States are close to the present theoretical limit of production efficiency.[15] This brief analysis indicates that decreasing cloud cover, as suggested earlier, and genetic research into strains with high carbon conversion efficiencies will be important to future food production.

An increase of only 1 per cent in conversion efficiency would

---

[14] "Food ...," p. 75.
[15] Harrison S. Brown, James Bonner, and John Weir, *The Next Hundred Years* (New York: The Viking Press, 1957), pp. 167-68.

double the world's crop food potential. But whether this efficiency "is fixed by the plant's whim or whether it is already determined by selection at a value which maximizes yields [is a] question which needs to be explored. No ready answer can be given to it at present."[16]

Brown, Bonner, and Weir have also suggested another interesting direction for genetic selection: self-fertilizing plants. While most crops require fertilizer, leguminous plants such as peas and beans have nodules on their roots containing bacteria that act on the molecular nitrogen of the atmosphere to produce ammonia, which then fertilizes these plants. It may be possible, they speculate, to transmit this nodulation characteristic to other crops and thus make their growth "independent of nitrogen fertilization."[17]

As we learn more about cellular genetics, we come closer to direct manipulation of the characteristics of crops. Rather than using eugenic techniques to develop favorable strains we may, in the future, perform genetic surgery on the DNA coding of crop cells to obtain the precise performance we desire. This is a technology of the next century which could give varieties, productivity, and nutritional characteristics unimagined today. A RAND Corporation study, which investigated the opinions of many experts about the patented scientific breakthroughs of the next few decades, forecast that crop characteristics probably will be selectable through genetic engineering by the year 1990.

New Foods   So far I have discussed some technological opportunities for coaxing more food out of the ground by manipulating the environment which surrounds agricultural productivity. Other unconventional opportunities for increasing our available food supply and augmenting its diversity may also become important in the decades ahead of us. Science and technology will play a major role in discovering these new foods and making them palatable (or changing our tastes to allow us to find them palatable). The spectrum starts with the "second generation pills," which contain contraceptives (as well as all of the nutrients to sustain our physiological needs) and augment our bulk filler, much as superfertilizers provide tailored plant nutrients. Within the spectrum one can find reference to telemetered whole farming,

---

[16] *The Next Hundred Years*, p. 168.
[17] *The Next Hundred Years*, p. 80.

multitiered hydroponic gardening, algae culturing, protein manufacturing *in vitro,* mollusk cultivation, and chicken factories.

The diversity of concepts is as wide as the imagination; some of these ideas are already in what might be termed wide scale field trials; others will remain impractical imagination a hundred years from now. I will mention only some, and these briefly, to indicate how wide our breadth of choice really is and how rewarding certain lines of research might prove to be. I will be probing for the unexpected breakthrough in the classes of new biologic and synthetic foods.

New Biologic Foods While animal derived protein is generally regarded as an inefficient method of food production because of the dual conversion from photosynthesis to plant and from plant to animal protein, there are certain situations which must be regarded as potentially valuable. Generally these relate to the breeding of animals which consume plant protein, which would have been otherwise unfit for human consumption.

According to N. W. Pirie of the Rothamsted Experimental Station in England, many wild herbivores yield more protein per pound than domesticated species. This suggests that we seek a group of animals for domestication which can thrive on such unneeded plants as we can provide, and yet produce an optimum protein output. Examples suggested by Dr. Pirie include the eland, an African antelope which can graze on marginal lands not suitable for agriculture; the capybara, a large palatable South American rodent which feeds on aquatic weeds; and the manatee, a herbivorous aquatic mammal.[18] These animals could be developed into the most favorable strains in a relatively short time using current eugenic practices. For example, we now have bred hens that lay more than 200 eggs a year and meat-producing broilers that are market-size in 10 weeks.

Certain fish could be bred in a similar fashion. Domesticated fish have the advantage, of course, of converting algae and plankton, largely unusable and unpalatable, into high-grade protein. Pirie has pointed out that mollusks and crustaceans are particularly adaptable to this kind of cultivation; they feed on suspended organic matter in the ocean and would apparently multiply rapidly

---

[18] N. W. Pirie, "Orthodox and Unorthodox Methods of Meeting World Food Needs," *Scientific American,* CCXVI (February, 1967), p. 31.

if they were grown in protected beds. A prototype of this kind of farming is practiced successfully today with mollusks off the coast of Spain where the shellfish adhere to long ropes suspended from barges (as could oysters and clams around the world). These shellfish are, of course, considered delicacies in many places, and there should be little difficulty in breeding desirable varieties and gaining acceptance of these foods.

There has been extensive investigation into the practicality of whole fish processing in which trash fish are processed into high-protein powder which can be added to wheat or other grains as a protein supplement. There are difficulties here, too, such as preserving the fish before processing and distribution and acceptance of the powder, but technology can offer the prospect of massive trawling and handling equipment, processors, dryers, advanced refrigeration concepts, and so forth, if the economic incentives favor this form of protein production.

Many authors have pointed out that valuable nutrients are currently being wasted by the technique of our food processing. Pirie's estimate is that 20 million tons of protein is left over when the oil is extracted from soya, groundnut, cottonseed, and sunflower seeds; this amount is twice the world's current shortage.[19] In other words, if all of this protein could be made available, we would have no protein shortage. What is required is an economic means of separating and processing the protein to make the residue palatable and digestible. Research into these techniques has begun at several experimental stations. The seed-meal Incaparina (made, distributed, and promoted by the Quaker Oats Company) has been well accepted in some countries; General Mills and Worthington Foods are developing products which have texture and taste like meats.

Synthetic Foods Foods of the future can come from factories as well as the land and oceans. In the factory we can provide idealized environment for biological plant growth, of course, but this is probably impractical because of the large capital investments required. In this category, I include large-scale algae vats, growing on saline surfaces under carbon dioxide-rich atmospheres and illuminated by the sun; and hydroponic farms with plants growing in

---

[19] "Orthodox and Unorthodox Methods of Meeting World Food Needs," p. 32.

artificial nutrient broths and stimulated into photosynthesis with lamps whose emission spectrum is matched to the plant's needs. I might be very wrong in both cases, however, particularly if land becomes extremely scarce and a means is found to build these food factories economically. In that future world we might find such factories covering hundreds of acres in high mountains, in deserts, in bogs, or perhaps even in the Arctic and in the Antarctic regions.

More likely will be the manufacture of the specialized chemicals of nutrition. We are already making synthetic vitamins, some amino acids have been built and proteins can be synthesized or made by fermentation processes. These additives, superimposed on the cheap carbohydrates and starches which all men like to eat, will give man a new freedom, the right to nutrition. The quantities required for many of these additives are very small; manufacturing in the industrializing countries might indeed be practical because large investments would not be required.

As we reach deeper understanding of the DNA replication processes, it may prove feasible to manufacture proteins *in vitro*—that is, to replicate cells directly from natural models or to trigger certain cellular processes to produce proteins directly from amino acid raw materials surrounding the cells. In that far future day, factories would become massive artificial stomachs growing the world's food from inorganic raw materials. We would have broadened our ecological cycle to the limit of our world.

Pertinent questions have been raised about how these new foods or additives will find acceptance in peoples not ready for new taste and texture experiences. The problem is perhaps simplest in the case of the trace additives. Nutritional elements could be legislated in, in much the same way that iodine has been added to table salt to avoid goiter. For the bulk foods, we can attempt to simulate current foods or we can attempt to foster new food mores. The latter approach may well prove more economic. Here too we have models of success: advertising has made Coca Cola accepted all over the world in less than one hundred years; Metrecal and other dietary specialty foods have made the grade through proper promotion and image-building in less than ten years; judging from newspaper reports, smoked banana peels are attaining a special kind of acceptance in our country. One of our skills is promotion, the infant science of behavior control. It is as applicable to the problems of food as increasing yields.

So the list of better mouse traps can be quite impressive. It can increase food supplies and quality in many ways including observational services from orbit, education in advanced farming techniques (which can also benefit from orbital operations), lowering fertilizer costs, improving storage techniques, providing advanced irrigation systems, promoting the development of new foods and food processing systems, and improving plant strains to provide varieties tailored to particular environments.

Dr. Landsberg said, "The brave new world of exciting technology that provides an unending stream of intriguing stories in the news media and keeps symposia and conferences going at a fast clip is designed for the most part to improve and enrich the conditions of life and leisure enjoyed by those who have the means. . . ." There is no doubt that technology, when first developed, is expensive. Ball-point pens used to cost $15; now they cost 10¢, and this reduction of price was also a product of technology. I submit that, where the benefits are high enough, research can produce not only innovations but cheap innovations. The secret to the cost reduction is the systems approach where research and development is tuned to a cost benefit analysis which maximizes benefits for least cost.

The systems approach can go beyond directing development; it can also indicate the best ways of organizing and applying new knowledge in the field. I quite agree with Dr. Landsberg that, "The road block [to the use of new technology] is in most instances not lack of knowledge, but lack of organizing to use it." If this is the problem, I urge that we get organized. Organization implies coordination between the diverse agencies working to increase food; the selection and apportionment of research and development goals; perhaps the pooling of funds, talent, and other resources; the organized interchange of data; and the early testing and application of new innovations. This kind of centralization of effort is being practiced by advanced countries all over the world. It originated with the need for rapid development of weapon systems and is now, for the first time, being haltingly applied to public problems. Why should the development of weapons command better management practices than development of adequate food supplies?

SOCIOLOGICAL ASPECTS
AND QUALITY OF LIFE

Urbanization—Problems of High Density Living

Philip M. Hauser

Director, Population Research and Training Center and Professor of Sociology, University of Chicago

The city or urban agglomeration is a relatively recent phenomenon[1]. Man has inhabited this earth for perhaps 2 million years. But agglomerative living is a product of the Neolithic Age—for neither towns nor villages antedated the domestication of plants and animals and the proliferation of the crafts.[2] Hence it is only some 10,000 years ago that permanent settlement became an important form of human habitation. Moreover, it is only since 3,000 B.C. that permanent human settlements have become large enough to be termed "cities." Cities of 100,000 or more, with the possible exception of those in China, did not emerge until Greco-Roman civilization; whether a city of a million or more may have appeared earlier, certainly the proliferation of cities of a million or more inhabitants had to await the industrial revolution and the beginning of the nineteenth century.

The development of relatively large agglomerations of population required more, however, than an increasingly efficient technology. Relatively large aggregations required more complex social organ-

---

[1] Previous papers by this writer have been heavily drawn upon in the preparation of this paper and especially the chapter, "Urbanization: An Overview," in Philip M. Hauser and Leo F. Schnore, *The Study of Urbanization* (New York: John Wiley & Sons, Inc., 1965).

[2] Ralph Turner, *The Great Cultural Traditions*, I, *The Ancient Cities* (New York and London: McGraw-Hill Book Company, 1941), pp. 51 ff.

ization, including improved communication, and social and political mechanisms permitting some form of exchange among the emergent specialists, agricultural and nonagricultural. Chief among the social organizational requirements was a working arrangement between the population agglomeration and the hinterland, its source of food and raw materials. The history of cities reveals evidence of great variation in forms of organization that integrated and coordinated activities between city and hinterland and within the city. The rise and fall of empires, as recorded in ancient history, may in large measure be read as a chronicle of developments in social organization by means of which the ancient cities acquired a hinterland. The Roman Legion may be interpreted as a form of social organization enabling the city to achieve effective working arrangements with a hinterland.[3] The same function centuries later was performed by emergence of the market mechanism, including money as an instrument of exchange.

It was not until the nineteenth century that mankind had achieved both the level of technological development and social organization that permitted the relatively widespread appearance of very large cities. On the technological side, the developments included techniques which greatly increased productivity in agriculture as well as in nonagricultural commodities. A critical factor in increased productivity was, of course, the utilization of non-human energy in production—the emergence of the machine, powered first by water or wind, then by steam, and now by mineral fuels or electricity derived therefrom, with atomic energy increasingly being utilized. Technological advance proceeded at an exponential rate under the impetus of the "scientific revolution."

Social organizational developments paralleled the technological. Strong central governments were formed, bringing relative peace and tranquility to increasingly large areas and permitting the development of local, regional, national, and international markets. Further divisions of labor and specialization were accompanied by various forms of formal and informal organization, providing essential integration and coordination. New social institutions evolved or were invented to meet the needs of the increasingly complex and interdependent social and economic orders. A full

---

[3] *The Great Cultural Traditions*, II, *The Classical Empires*, pp. 856 ff.

account of the emergence of the large city in the context of its antecedents has yet to be written if, indeed, it ever can be documented. But the available literature certainly provides a basis for at least pointing to the major factors associated with the emergence of the city and of relatively high urbanized nations.

Both the city and problems of urban living, then, are of relatively recent origin. Both the city and problems of urban living are the product of man's culture-building activities. For man not only adapts to environment, he creates environment to which to adapt. And he is still in the process of adapting to urbanism and metropolitanism as a way of life.

Urban Growth

Among the more significant of the great changes which have characterized the three centuries of the modern era are the increases in the size and concentration of world population. Man in all the millenia of his existence on this planet had produced a population of only 500 million persons by mid-seventeenth century. By 1967, however, world population was in excess of 3.3 billion. Within the three centuries of the modern era, world population had increased by an amount five times that generated and simultaneously alive through man's previous habitation of the globe.[4]

It is possible to quickly summarize the effect of the remarkable acceleration which man has experienced in his growth rate. Between 1650 and 1750, at an annual rate of growth of 0.3 per cent, world population would have required 239 years to double. Between 1850 and 1900, the growth rate had risen to 0.6 per cent per year, and the period required to double world population had declined to 109 years. By the decade 1930 to 1940, world growth, at 1.0 per cent per annum, would have doubled the population in 70 years. At the present rate of growth, 2 per cent per annum, world population would double in 35 years.

In consequence, it took most of the millenia of man's habitation of this planet to produce a population as great as 1 billion persons simultaneously alive. This population was not achieved until

---

[4] Based on United Nations, *Determinants and Consequences of Population Trends* (New York: United Nations, 1953), Chap. 2, pp. 5-20.

approximately 1825. To produce a population of 2 billion persons simultaneously alive required only an additional 105 years—for this number was achieved by 1930. To reach a population of 3 billion persons required only an additional 30 years—for this was the total in 1960. Continuation of the trend would produce a fourth billion by 1977, in only 17 years; a fifth billion by 1987, in only 10 years; and a sixth billion in 1995, in only 8 years.

Accelerating world population growth was accompanied by even more rapid increases in urban population since at least the beginning of the nineteenth century. Between 1800 and 1950, world population increased over 2½ times. Population in places of 5,000 and over, however, increased 26 times; population in places of 20,000 and over, 23 times; and population in places of 100,000 and over, more than 20 times. In consequence, by mid-twentieth century almost one-third (30 per cent) of the world's people lived in urban places having 5,000 and over, about 21 per cent were in places of 20,000 and over, and 13 per cent in places of 100,000 and over.[5] By 1960, 30 per cent of the world's people lived in places of 20,000 or more and 20 per cent in places of 100,000 or more.[6]

In the United States both total population growth and urban concentration far exceeded the world rates.[7] During the three centuries of the modern era, the population of the United States increased from perhaps a million Indians and a few shiploads of Europeans to about 180 million persons as reported in the eighteenth decennial census. When the first census of the United States was taken in 1790, 95 per cent of the population lived in rural places, places having fewer than 2,500 persons. There were only twenty-four urban places in the nation, only two of which had populations

---

[5] Kingsley Davis, "The Origin and Growth of Urbanization in the World," *American Journal of Sociology* (special issue on "World Urbanism" edited by Philip M. Hauser), LX (March, 1955), p. 433.

[6] Gerald Breese, *Urbanization in Newly Developing Countries* (Englewood Cliffs, N.J.: Prentice-Hall, Inc., 1966), pp. 16-23.

[7] Statistics relating to the United States are drawn from publications of the U.S. Bureau of the Census unless otherwise indicated. The historical data are drawn largely from: U.S. Bureau of the Census, *Historical Statistics of the United States, Colonial Times to 1957* (Washington: U.S. Gov't Printing Office, 1960); U.S. Bureau of the Census, *Statistical Abstract of the United States* (Washington: U.S. Gov't Printing Office, issued annually). Other data are drawn mainly from decennial census volumes. To save space and repetition, specific references to the census publications are not given.

in excess of 25,000. By 1960, however, there were about 5,400 urban places containing 70 per cent of the entire population. For the first sixty years of the present century, the population of the United States increased from about 75 million to 180 million. The increase in urban population over the same period absorbed 92 per cent of the total increase of the nation. In the last decade of that period, 1950-60, increase in the urban population accounted for more than 100 per cent of the total population growth of the country. That is, for the first time in the history of the nation, rural population actually declined during the intercensal decade.

The extent to which the population of the country is becoming concentrated is even more dramatically indicated by growth of metropolitan and large metropolitan area populations. Over the first sixty years of the century, the increase in metropolitan population absorbed 85 per cent of the total growth of the nation. Although the increase in population of metropolitan areas between 1950 and 1960 (using 1960 boundaries) absorbed about the same proportion of total national growth during the decade, the increase in population classified as metropolitan (boundaries as in 1950 and 1960, respectively) absorbed 97 per cent of the total growth of the nation during the decade.

In 1900, only five metropolitan areas in the United States contained a million or more persons—about 16 per cent of the total population. By 1960, there were twenty-four such places in which over a third of the nation's population resided (34 per cent). Over the first sixty years of the century, the increase in large metropolitan area population absorbed 48 per cent of total national growth. In the decade between 1950 and 1960, population increase in large metropolitan areas accounted for 60 per cent of total national growth.

Over the first sixty years of the century, then, total population increased about two and a half times, urban population increased almost fourfold, metropolitan area population increased more than fourfold, and large metropolitan area population increased fivefold. During this same period, the United States changed from a predominantly rural to a predominantly urban nation. At the turn of the century, about two-fifths of the population was urban. It was not until 1920 that more than half of the inhabitants were urban (51.2 per cent); in 1960, 70 per cent of the population was urban. It will not be until the end of this decade, 1970, that the

United States will have completed its first half-century as an urban nation—which is why there is still evidence that it is still in transition from a preindustrial and preurban order to "urbanism as a way of life."[8]

The process of urbanization in the world and in the United States is still underway. For the world as a whole the "medium variant" of the United Nations' population projections indicates a total population of 6.3 billion by 2000. This would represent an increase of 3.3 billion persons from 1960 to 2000. Of this increment, 2.4 billion (73 per cent) would be urban increase (in places of 2,000 or more); 2.1 billion (64 per cent) would be increase in population in places of 100,000 or more. By 2000, almost 21 per cent of the world's inhabitants would be residing in places of 1 million or more, 42 per cent in places of 100,000 or more, and well over half (55.5 per cent) in places of 2,000 or more.

Similarly, in the United States, even with declining fertility, large total population growth and urban and metropolitan growth are indicated. Between 1960 and 1985, the total population, according to one of the projections of the U.S. Bureau of the Census may increase by some 83 million.[9] Of this number all may be absorbed in urban places, and perhaps 71 million, or 85 per cent, in metropolitan areas. By 1985, 76 per cent of the population of the United States may reside in urban places and 70 per cent in metropolitan areas.

Consequences of Urbanization

That the city makes a difference in the way of life was perceived by the ancients and recorded in the earliest historical records.[10] In the nineteenth century, Maine, Tönnies, and Durkheim, and, in the twentieth century, Sumner, Goldenweiser, Redfield, and Wirth grappled with various aspects of the difference that aggregative living makes.[11]

[8] Louis Wirth, *Community Life and Social Policy* (Chicago: University of Chicago Press, 1956), pp. 110-32.
[9] U.S. Bureau of the Census, "Revised Projections of the Population of the United States," *Current Population Reports: Population Estimates* (Series P 25, No. 329; Washington: U.S. Gov't Printing Office, March 10, 1966), "Series B," p. 5.
[10] Joyce O. Hertzler, *The Social Thought of the Ancient Civilizations* (New York: McGraw-Hill Book Company, 1936), pp. 298 ff., p. 350.

The Size-Density Model A relatively simple size-density model provides a basis for understanding the consequences of urbanization. The theoretical basis for the development and consideration of the model is given by Durkheim. He has stated:

> Social life rests on a substratum whose size as well as its form is determined. This substratum is constituted by the mass of individuals who make up society, the way in which they are distributed on the soil, and the nature and configuration of all sorts of things that affect collective relationships. The social substratum differs according to whether the population is large or small and more or less dense, whether it is concentrated in cities or dispersed over the countryside, how cities and houses are constructed, whether the area occupied by the society is more or less extensive, and according to the kind of boundaries that delimit it.[12]

Let us consider the implications of variation in size and density of population, confining our attention to a fixed land area. For purposes of convenience, consider a circle with a radius of 10 miles. Such a circle would have a total area of approximately 314 square miles. The size of the total population in such a circle under different density conditions is shown as follows:[13]

Population Density (population per square mile)	Number of Persons in Circle of Ten-Mile Radius
1	314
50	15,700
8,000	2,512,000
17,000	5,338,000
25,000	7,850,000
75,000	23,550,000

The population densities shown are not unrealistic ones. The population density of 1 may be taken as an approximation of the density of the United States prior to European occupancy. Actually, the Indian population was approximately one-third as dense as this. The density of 50 is approximately that of the United States in 1960, and also approximately the population density of the

---

[11] For a summary of this literature and bibliography, see *The Study of Urbanization*, "Observations on the Urban-Folk and Urban-Rural Dichotomies as Forms of Western Ethnocentrism," pp. 503-17.

[12] Translated from Emile Durkheim, *L'année sociologique*, II, 1897-98.

[13] Adapted from Amos H. Hawley, *Human Ecology* (New York: The Ronald Press Company, 1950), pp. 100 ff.

world as a whole. The density of 8,000 in round numbers is not too far from the density of the average central city in metropolitan areas of the United States in 1960. The density figure 17,000 is approximately that of Chicago, the figure of 25,000 approximately the density of New York, and the figure 75,000 approximately the density of Manhattan Island.

In aboriginal America, a person moving within the ten-mile circle could potentially make only 313 different contacts with other human beings. In contrast, the density of the United States as a whole today would make possible 15,699 contacts in the same land area. The density of the average central city in the United States would permit over 2.5 million contacts, the density of Chicago over 5.3 million contacts, the density of New York City over 7.8 million contacts, and the density of Manhattan over 23.5 million contacts in the same land area. The potential number of contacts, when considered as a measure of potential human interaction, provides, in a simplistic way to be sure, a basis for understanding the difference that city living makes.

Since Durkheim, in his consideration of the structure of the social order, spoke of "social morphology," the multiplier effect on potential human interaction of increased population density in a fixed land area can appropriately be described as an index of the "social morphological revolution." The size-density model presented may be taken as a quantification of the social morphological revolution and provides at least one theoretical basis for considering the city as an independent variable. More specifically, it may be stated as a hypothesis that the increase in potential human interaction produced by aggregative living has produced in the realm of the social a major transformation that is the equivalent of genetic mutation in the realm of the biological.

Physical Problems Increased population size and densities, of necessity, required a tremendous modification of the physical world in which man lived, once permanent human settlement was achieved. Permanent settlement led to fixed and relatively long-lasting shelters, evidences of which are manifest in the archaeological finds of the Neolithic peasant village. Man with great ingenuity learned to make selective use of his environment. Contemporary primitive peoples provide some indication of the way in which forms of habitation must have evolved. Says Turner,

"Everywhere over the earth habitations are constructed which show fine adaptation of materials to the particular needs for shelter that distinguish different environments."[14]

Mumford describes the evolution of the physical plant of the city as essentially an extension of more complex "containers." He notes that the Neolithic period was characterized by containers: "It is an age of stone and pottery utensils, vases, jars, vats, cisterns, bins, barns, granaries, houses, not least great collective containers like irrigation ditches and villages."[15] A prerequisite to the emergence of aggregative living, as has been noted, was the development of a surplus. "Wherever a surplus must be preserved and stored, containers are important," says Mumford. Increased surplus made possible larger agglomerations of people which, in turn, increased the need for containers of every variety.

Mark how much the city owes technically to the village: out of it came, directly or by elaboration, the granary, the bank, the arsenal, the library, the store. Remember, too, that the irrigation ditch, the canal, the reservoir, the moat, the aqueduct, the drain, the sewer are also containers for automatic transport or storage. The first of these was invented long before the city; and without this whole range of inventions the ancient city could not have taken the form it finally did; for it was nothing less than a container of containers.[16]

The development of the city from the village was characterized by an increase in built-up area and population. Archaeological finds suggests that densities in ancient cities (2000 B.C.) were approximately 76,000 to 128,000 per square mile. High densities under the conditions of life of the times must have been a factor in restricting the size of the agglomeration—by reason of high morbidity and mortality. Mumford also points out that houses dating from about the middle of the third millenium B.C. were about the same size as those built over a period of some 5,000 years thereafter. They were primarily row houses. "Detachment and openness were originally attributes of the palace." The walled city emerged as a means of protection for the ruling group and was "one of the most prominent features of the city, in most countries, right down to the eighteenth century."[17]

---

[14] *The Great Cultural Traditions,* I, p. 73.
[15] Lewis Mumford, *The City In History* (Harcourt, Brace & World, 1961), p. 16.
[16] *The City In History,* p. 16.
[17] *The City In History,* pp. 61 ff.

The interrelation of physical plant and social interaction is suggested in Mumford's observation that "early cities did not grow beyond walking distance or bearing distance." This restriction on the size of the early city also implies restrictions on urban life and possibly contributed to high densities. Mumford's historical treatment of the city, despite shortcomings, permits the tracing of the development of the urban physical plant as the product of human agglomeration, and suggests the way in which the city as a physical entity affected the character and size of the aggregation.

Sjoberg has summarized spatial arrangements of the preindustrial city. Within the typical wall the city tended to be further divided into sections sealed off one from the other by walls, moats, and the like. The central area of the preindustrial city typically contained the prominent government and religious structures and the main market. Clustered close to these major edifices were the relatively luxurious dwellings of the elite, often facing inward and presenting an inhospitable blank wall to the streets. The distribution of the population within the city from the center was directly associated with power and wealth, the poorest living farthest from the center or outside the city walls, excluded from their protection. Within this general framework the city tended to be sectioned off on the basis of ethnic or occupational lines. There was little in the way of contemporary territorial specialization. Place of work was often identical with place of residence. The preindustrial city, with limited means of circulating peoples and goods, was highly congested and lacking in many of the amenities of contemporary urban existence with respect to environmental sanitation and hygiene.[18]

The industrial revolution and concomitant developments greatly transformed the physical preindustrial city. Walls disappeared, changing to arteries of transportation as they lost their defense function and as advancing technology permitted increasingly larger agglomerations of population to expand beyond established boundaries. The industrial city, characterized by the steam engine, the belt and the pulley, and the horse-drawn vehicle, was still influenced in physical pattern by centripetal forces which tended to

---

[18] Gideon Sjoberg, *The Preindustrial City* (Chicago: The Free Press of Glencoe, Illinois, 1960), pp. 91 ff.

crowd population around factory plants. With improvement in transport, however, residential location near the centry city lost much of its attractiveness; the newer outlying edifice, and detachment and openness became increasingly attractive to the elite.

In the older, well-established cities, the new patterns of land use and population distribution generated by industrialization fused with and were superimposed upon the established preindustrial order. In the newer cities, as manifested in the United States, land use patterns and the distribution of population in accordance with socioeconomic status literally turned inside out—that is, the elite tended to move outward with the expansion of the city to newer and more desirable locations. In contrast with the preindustrial city, a direct relationship between status and distance from the center of the city became the dominant pattern.

With industrialization, a combination of technological and social organizational changes was made possible. A much larger agglomeration of people and economic activities emerged than was ever previously possible on an extensive scale. Urban infrastructure investment was tremendously expanded to include not only more elaborate and permanent habitations but also more complex networks of transport and communication and the multiplication of amenities, including piped water, sewerage, lighting, and waste disposal.

Twentieth century developments set new forces in motion affecting the physical structure of the city. Twentieth century technology symbolized by electric power, the automotive complex—the automobile, the truck, and the highway—and the telephone generated centrifugal forces dispersing population and economic activities over the landscape. Moreover, twentieth century technological developments made possible much larger agglomerations of people and economic activities than was possible with nineteenth century or any prior technology. In Mumford's language, twentieth century technology permitted "the removal of limits." The city, as a "container," burst with "urban sprawl and the emergence of megalopolis."[19]

In mid-twentieth century the city, spearheaded by major metropolitan complexes, such as New York, London, Tokyo, Paris, and

[19] *The City In History*, pp. 540 ff.

Chicago, has become a gigantic physical entity both above and below the ground. The physical problems of the twentieth century city have assumed tremendous proportions.

Urban physical plants in the United States, for example—residential, industrial, commercial, and governmental—were constructed hurriedly in response to rapid urbanization. Land-use patterns and infrastructure development were largely the product of market forces, which produced a remarkable physical plant but also permitted rapid obsolescence and decay. They include by prevalent standards relatively large proportions of "substandard housing" and are pockmarked by areas of slum. The United States has only recently begun to face up to these physical problems in a major way through programs of "urban renewal," public housing, and expanded efforts at city planning. In the United States the automobile, which has been a major factor in the development of the twentieth-century metropolis, is now threatening to strangulate it with congestion, and new attention is being focused on problems of circulation within the city. Finally, problems of air and water pollution are also becoming critical in many areas.[20]

In the United States we have demonstrated that we can build an urban plant, and that we can bulldoze it and rebuild it after it deteriorates and decays. We have yet to demonstrate that we can adequately maintain an urban plant. "Urban maintenance" may become the next major program to complement urban renewal.

In the developing regions of the world—in Asia, Latin America, and Africa—the most visible consequence of rapid urbanization is the decadence of the urban environment. The physical city is characterized by a large proportion of shanty towns and tenement slums; inadequate urban services, including housing, water supply, sewerage, utilities, and transport; uncontrolled land use; excessive population densities; deficient education and recreational facilities; and inefficient commercial and marketing services. Rapid urbanization in the underdeveloped areas is accompanied by an urban environment that is not only defective but deteriorating. It is estimated that, in Latin America alone, some 4 or 5 million families

---

[20] Philip M. Hauser, *On the Impact of Population and Community Changes On Local Government*, Seventh Annual Wherrett Lecture on Local Government (Pittsburgh: Institute of Local Government, University of Pittsburgh, 1961), pp. 19 ff.

live in urban shanty towns and slums. The miserable physical conditions of cities create great pressure for "social" instead of "productive" investments. However, many of the public housing and physical improvement programs undertaken in such areas have necessarily tended to benefit families with moderate incomes, rather than meet the needs of the lowest income families—the residents of the shanty towns and slums.

Of course, the underdeveloped nations are very aware of the need for city and regional, as well as national, planning. But the city planner in the underdeveloped country is confronted with insuperable difficulties. These stem largely from low income levels; from rapid population growth, including hordes of immigrants from rural areas who are ill-adapted to urban living; from inadequate urban infrastructure development—all in all, from a bewildering array of needs, each of which seems to have first priority.

Although urban agglomerations of the size of Western cities are to be found, the physical amenities associated with those in the West have not yet developed—at least not for the mass population. The amenities of urban existence are available only to very small fractions of the total urban population. It is in the impact on the already inadequate urban physical plant that the rapid rate of urbanization produces some of its more serious consequences.

This by no means complete overview of the physical problems of the city indicates that, with increasing size and density of population, the urban plant became a more complex, intricate physical entity assuming quite distinct patterns in accordance with the potential of the prevalent technology. New York City as a physical entity, whether considered as a monstrosity or as an elegant illustration of man's ingenuity in creating environment, is certainly a product of the size and density of population in that area and the forces that contributed to them.

There is much about the urban plant that we do not yet understand. In the Western world we have inherited urban physical works which, in predominant measure, are the product of market forces neither fully recorded nor fully understood. The size and density of population producing the physical problems of the contemporary city are forcing an increase in city planning activities. With increased city planning, new forces are in motion reshaping the city as a physical construct with its various intricate layers of historical development. The future of the city as a physical entity, increasingly as a planned phenomenon, can at this stage be only a matter for speculation.[21]

Economic Problems The city owes its origin to the economic advances represented by the domestication of plants and animals and the proliferation of the crafts. It required a combination of increased agricultural productivity, a greater surplus, evolving forms of social organization and, therefore, considerable time before full-time specialists freed from food functions appeared. The foundation for an increased economic surplus was laid with the evolution of the plow from the hoe, the utilization of the ox as a draft animal, improvement in field agriculture, developments in husbandry, increased water control and irrigation, and developments in metallurgy. Once permanent human settlement was attained, however, aggregative living exerted profound influences on economic activity.

The characteristics of the city as an economic mechanism were clearly discernible in the development of the ancient Oriental urban cultures. Larger agglomerations of population made possible both a greater division of labor and a greater number of nonagricultural specialists. A relatively complex division of labor and specialization resulted in increased productivity permitting even greater surplus. In the matrix of ancient urban areas, a number of key economic elements emerged including "work," "property," "power," "luxury," "poverty," and new forms of economic administration such as gang slavery, a state system of cultivation, and an elaboration of the right to private property.[22]

Self-interest as a key economic motivation—incentive not only to secure means of subsistence but to get as much as possible of the surplus—was manifest. Self-interest was bolstered by increasing size and density of population, which tended to devalue personal and

---

[21] Coleman Woodbury, ed., *The Future of Cities and Urban Redevelopment* (Chicago: University of Chicago Press, 1953); *Report of the Committee on Environmental Health Problems*, U.S. Department of Health, Education and Welfare, Public Health Service (Washington: U.S. Gov't Printing Office, 1962); Coleman Woodbury, ed., *Metropolis in Ferment*, Annals of the American Academy of Political and Social Sciences (November, 1957); John C. Bollens, *Exploring the Metropolitan Community* (Berkeley and Los Angeles: University of California Press, 1961).

[22] *The Great Cultural Traditions*, I, pp. 277 ff.

familial relationships founded on close interpersonal interaction and sentiment. Greater size and density of population produced an ever more minute division of labor, specialization, and the shifting of economic relationships from "status" to "contract."

The proliferation of the crafts and growing numbers of artisans led to an important element in the preindustrial city's economic organization—its guild system. This, in turn, influenced the physical pattern of the city, for the guilds—crafts, service, and merchant—tended to become localized into "quarters" along specific streets.[23] Increased division of labor and specialization necessitated heightened exchange activities and generated merchants in growing numbers. The proliferation of specialists led also to specialization in the provision of services—the barber, the sweeper, the scavenger, and the like. Money, credit, the price system, and financial institutions were all consequences of increased division of labor and specialization. They may be regarded as mechanisms for the integration and coordination of economic activity necessitated by the increasing size and density of the population clumping. The urban economy raised the status of the trader and manufacturer over that of the landlord and, with organization, eventually led to a greatly increased power position for workers.

Increased division of labor and specialization also accelerated technological advance. It was easier to devise a machine to do a relatively simple part of a job than to produce an entire product. Technological advance, implying more extensive use of nonhuman energy, produced the industrial plant and the "factory system." Workers were tending to become "operatives" rather than artisans, and employees rather than self-employed.

Broadened markets, partly a function of the emergence of central governments with increased power over broader expanses of territory, encouraged "mass production." The industrial city provided evidence of economies of scale, permitted external economies, operated to minimize frictions of space and communication, and led to more complex forms of economic organization. The joint stock company and corporate organization involving limited liability developed. Capital was amassed, management became professionalized and separated from ownership. Gigantic industrial combines evolved, including "integrated" economic empires. To cope

---

[23] *The Pre-Industrial City*, pp. 187 ff.

with large management, labor unions were organized. "Big labor" evolved to deal with "big management."

With the dissolution of feudalism, the emergence of the industrial city, and the expansion of trade, the market mechanism was largely relied upon to order the economy—to allocate resources and to regulate the production of goods and services. This was achieved largely through the play of competition and the operation of the price mechanism. Greater complexity in economic organization, however, with more specialization and interdependence were accompanied by severe frictions, such as abuses to labor, inequitable distribution of wealth, extreme fluctuations in the level of economic activity, increasing levels of unemployment, monopolistic practices, adulteration of products, bucket shop operations, and outright fraud. Despite Adam Smith's injunction that each man acting in his own interest would act, as "if guided by an invisible hand," in the interests of the larger society, it became necessary for government to intervene in the operation of the economy. Intervention took many forms, including military adventures in relation to international trade and investment, the establishment of various regulatory agencies, provision for more equitable distribution of income (for example, income tax), encouragement of labor organizations, the creation of various forms of social security such as unemployment compensation, old age pensions, and medical care.

Government intervention in more areas tended to provide greater protection for the weak and to broaden enormously the services of government. Thus, the public sector of the economy was greatly expanded, including the local governmental sector, in the provision of more services for education, health, welfare, recreation, protection, transportation, and so on. This development was largely the result of greater population size and density that generated new collective needs. Because these needs were not met through the market mechanism, they became increasingly the province of government. Urbanization together with industrialization, then, by creating greater interdependence and new forms of vulnerability (for example, unemployment, industrial accident, sweat shops, contagious disease, water and air pollution), stimulated the expansion of government functions and personnel. The most extreme form of interventionism, of course, became manifest in the Soviet Union and in the Communist bloc in general.

Thus, developments providing an agricultural surplus, which

made possible aggregative living of nonagriculturalists, set in motion forces which have continued to augment the size and density of population agglomerations and economic activities. The increased size and density of such agglomerations profoundly affect the ways in which man makes a living. They generate the highly complex form of economic organization which characterizes contemporary life. Needless to say, productivity advanced tremendously in the process, producing unprecedented levels of living for mass populations. As an inevitable consequence of the more segmented division of labor and specialization, an interdependent society has necessarily evolved new forms of coordination and integration, including further government interventionism. The city, itself a product of economic advance, also became a major force in economic development—the emergence of our contemporary form of complex economic organization.

In the developing regions, the economic antecedents of contemporary urbanization differ greatly from those in the economically advanced areas. The "primate" cities in South and Southeast Asia, for example, are less the result of indigenous economic development than they are the product of economic development oriented essentially to one or more foreign countries. They developed as links between the colonial and mother country. Today, they usually still have an external orientation, serving as a link between the local elite and the outside world, rather than as an economic outpost of the national economy. In the underdeveloped nations, economic and urban development was largely directed toward external markets in the framework of patterns established under colonial administration. Moreover, the process of urbanization in the underdeveloped areas has been accelerated by the low land-population ratio arising from excessive population growth in relation to agriculture resources; by the disruption and disorganization produced by the last war, which forced refugee populations to choke already swelled populations in cities; by the lure of urban existence, to which large parts of the peasant population were exposed as a result of military service and other wartime dislocations; and by various other forces that pushed population to the city instead of attracting it by economic opportunity of the type experienced in the West.

Thus, the underdeveloped areas of the world are "overurbanized," in that larger proportions of their population live in urban places than their degree of economic development justifies. In the underdeveloped nations, a much smaller proportion of the labor force is engaged in nonagricultural occupations than was the case in the West at comparable levels of urbanization. Furthermore, during the postwar period, the rate of urbanization in the underdeveloped areas has continued proceeding more rapidly than the rate of economic development.

To say that the underdeveloped areas of the world are overurbanized is to pose the major economic problem with which they are confronted, namely, that they do not at the present time have an adequate economic base to support present urban populations by the standards of the Western world. They must find a way of achieving higher levels of economic development to support their present, let alone their prospective, urban population. Continued rapid rates of urbanization are, therefore, likely to aggravate, rather than alleviate, present urban poverty and distress. In general, the outlook for the remainder of this century is a dismal one indeed. It is very doubtful that, over this span of time, the underdeveloped nations can attain economic development of adequate dimensions to meet Western standards of living for their present and future city dwellers. The fundamental economic objective of the underdeveloped areas is that of increasing productivity; the many difficulties they meet in their efforts to attain this objective are likely to be exacerbated rather than ameliorated by present and prospective rapid rates of urban growth.

Human Problems In a small, sparsely settled population, the potential of human interaction is much below that in a large, high-density population. This is illustrated in the size-density model. In the small community, potential and actual contacts are fewer, and, because they are fewer, they tend also to be quite different in character. These differences, as many students have tried to show, help to explain the way in which the city influences human behavior. The classical treatment of the effect of size and density and, also, heterogeneity of population on behavior is that of Louis Wirth.[24] He stated, "On the basis of the three variables, number, density of settlement, and degree of heterogeneity, of the urban population, it appears possible to explain the characteristics of

---

[24] *Community Life and Social Policy,* pp. 117 ff.

urban life and to account for the differences between cities of various sizes and types."

According to this hypothesis, the small community is characterized by "primary group" contacts.[25] They tend to be face-to-face contacts of persons who meet and interact with one another in virtually all spheres of activity. In such a setting, personal relations tend to be based on relatively full knowledge of the other person—on sentiment and emotion. In contrast, in the large, high-density population situation, contacts tend to be "secondary" rather than primary, segmental rather than integral, utilitarian rather than sentimental. Moreover, in the large-size, high-density situation, populations are apt to be more heterogeneous—to include peoples of greater range and diversity in background. The person is, therefore, subjected to a greater variety of ways of thought and action.

The combination of heterogeneous and secondary contacts greatly modifies human behavior. Thus, it is held that thought and action tend to become rational as opposed to traditional, and interpersonal relations become based on utility rather than sentiment. With increased size, density, and heterogeneity of population, the constraints of tradition—the influence of the folkways and mores—diminish. In larger spheres of thought and action, behavior is determined by a willful decision taken by the person, rather than automatically determined by the norms of the group. The sphere of personal decision making is greatly extended, including areas of activity previously determined by tradition, such as kind and degree of education, occupation or profession, residential location, choice of mate, size of family, political affiliation, religiosity or even religion.

It follows, then, that greater size and density of population, especially if accompanied by heterogeneity, diminishes the power of informal social controls. Informal social control, effected largely through the play of folkways and the mores, gives way to increased formal control, the control of law, police, courts, jails, regulations, and orders. The breakdown in informal social controls is in large measure responsible for greater personal disorganization as manifest in juvenile delinquency, crime, prostitution, alcoholism, drug addic-

---

[25] Charles Horton Cooley, *Social Organization* (New York: Scribner & Sons, 1925), pp. 118 ff.

tion, suicide, mental disease, social unrest, and political instability. Formal controls have by no means proved as efficacious as the informal in regulating human behavior.

The effect of the city on the way of life may be observed in the adjustment problems of the in-migrant. The city as a recipient of migrants has played and continues to play a prominent role in the modification of thought and behavior in subjecting people with traditional and rural backgrounds to the conditions of urban living. Most of the severe physical, social, and economic problems of the city are disproportionately manifest among newcomers and are symptomatic of the difficulties of adjustment to urban life. In-migrant populations provide an opportunity for observing the impact of urbanization on the human being. In the accommodation of the rural newcomer to the city, transformations in thought and behavior may be traced.

In the United States, for example, the newest newcomers to urban and metropolitan areas are the Negro, the Puerto Rican, the Mexican, and the American Indian. They are now faced with accommodation to the urban milieu as were earlier immigrant groups. Each of the newcomer groups to the urban and metropolitan areas of the United States followed essentially a similar pattern with respect to location in space, the economy, and society.[26] Each of the in-migrant strains found their port of entry or areas of first settlement in the inner, older, blighted zones of the city. The longer the period of settlement, the farther out was the median location point of the newcomer group and the more dispersed was its residential pattern. The shorter the period of settlement, the closer to the center of the city was its median location and the more concentrated or segregated was its residential pattern. Similarly, the shorter the period of settlement, the lower was the occupational level and income of the newcomers. The longer the period of settlement, the higher the educational and occupational level and income. Finally, with respect to social status, a common pattern was also visible. Each of the newcomer groups was in turn greeted with hostility, suspicion, distrust, prejudice, and discriminatory

---

[26] Philip M. Hauser, *Population Perspectives* (New Brunswick, N.J.: Rutgers University Press, 1960), pp. 120 ff.; Oscar Handlin, *The Uprooted* (Boston: Little, Brown and Company, 1951), and *The Newcomers* (Cambridge: Harvard University Press, 1959); Otis Dudley Duncan and Beverly Duncan, *The Negro Population in Chicago* (Chicago: University of Chicago Press, 1957).

practices. With the passage of time each of the newcomer groups climbed the social as well as the economic ladder to achieve access to the broader social and cultural life of the community, as well as increased general acceptability.

The patterns by which immigrant groups became "Americanized" indicate in general the processes by which the newest newcomers—the Negro and Puerto Rican—will change from traditional behavior in their rural areas of origin to urbanism as a way of life. The process of acculturation will be similar in some respects to the process by which immigrants before them settled in American cities and metropolitan areas. This is not to say that there will not also be differences arising from their greater visibility and significantly different background. The differences have, in fact, precipitated a crisis in the intergroup relations in the United States manifest in the "Negro Revolt."[27]

Transformations in thought and behavior induced by increased size and density of population are, of course, greatly augmented by the heterogeneity of the population. Since increasing size and density of human agglomerations multiply the probabilities of greater heterogeneity, the city may in a fundamental sense be regarded as the source of a whole range of problems arising from intergroup differences, whether based on language, culture, religion, or race. The problem of intergroup relations is essentially an urban problem, or at least reaches its most critical manifestations in the urban area.

It may be that to the extent that size, density, and heterogeneity of population have changed behavior in urban places, they represent necessary, rather than sufficient, conditions for such a transformation. Certainly, behavior in urban places, especially in the economically underdeveloped areas, still tends to be traditional rather than rational, and in certain respects resembles folk rather than urban characteristics. The explanation for this may lie in the difference between potential human interaction in the city as portrayed in the size-density model and that actually achieved. That is, in large population clumpings of high density, which are essentially an agglutination of separate and distinct noninteracting communities, human behavior may still be largely the product of the primary group.

---

[27] Philip M. Hauser, "Demographic Factors in the Migration of the Negro," *Daedalus* (Fall, 1965), especially pp. 862 ff.

Problems of Social Organization Social organization has necessarily been greatly modified by reason of the increasing size and density of human agglomerations. Greater division of labor and specialization in creating a much more complex and interdependent society affected social as well as economic organization. It is held that the basis for social cohesion was altered in that a society became dependent on "organic" rather than "mechanical" solidarity.[28] That is, cohesion is effected in the urban setting through interdependence and the mechanisms of coordination and integration, rather than achieved mechanically through the operation of a homogeneous culture. In the large-size, high-density society, organization is based more on "contract" than on "status." Relationships among persons or groups are made explicit in terms of reciprocal obligations and duties, on the one hand, and rights or powers, on the other. Needless to say, utility rather than sentiment enters into the definition of the relationships.

As a microcosm of the social whole, the family is a convenient unit through which to trace many of the influences of the city on social institutions. The family is in most societies regarded as the primary social unit. The colonial family in early America, predominantly resident in rural areas, was the keystone of social organization. For example, it was a basic and largely self-sufficient economic unit; it had primary responsibility for the socialization and education of the young; it was a focal point for religious training and practices; it provided for the security and protection of its members; and it was the center for the affectional and recreational life.

The family in contemporary urban United States, however, has been transformed. Compared with the colonial family, the urban family today is smaller; it is more often childless and has fewer children, if fertile. The urban family, collectively and individually, is much more mobile; it is not rooted to the soil or even to a home in the manner of its rural counterpart. It possesses comparatively little economic or social unity; it is more frequently broken by separation or divorce and, as William F. Ogburn demonstrated some time ago, has long since lost or shared many of its various

---

[28] Emile Durkheim, *On the Division of Labor in Society* (New York: The Macmillan Company, 1933), Book 1, Chaps. 2, 3.

historic functions with new specialized urban institutions.[29] Examples of these new institutions include, on the one hand, the clothing store, the grocery, and the restaurant, and on the other, the school, the library, and social security system.

Accompanying these changes in the family have been redefinitions in the roles of its members—in the relationships of spouses and in parent-child and sibling interrelationships. Especially important in this regard is the changed role of the woman in the family and in society at large, a phenomenon certainly not unrelated to the changed conditions of urban life.

Finally, in respect to the family, it may be noted that in the urban milieu the "nuclear" family, the two-generation family, tends to replace the "extended," the three-generation family (or more), as the modal household unit.[30] This, however, does not necessarily mean that the larger family unit disappears as a system of interaction and as an important element of social organization. More study is needed on the role of the extended family in the urban area, even when it no longer occupies a single household.

In the city, social institutions tend to be "enacted" rather than "crescive."[31] In the mass society, social institutions are frequently invented, are the product of administrative edict or legislation, rather than the result of slow development representing the crystallization of patterns of thought and of action as a product of group life. New institutions arise in great number partly as the result of the breakdown of traditional ones that do not meet the requirements of urban living, and partly through the need to invent new institutions by reason of unprecedented situations and problems for which tradition has no answers. Examples of the multiplication of new institutions in response to new and unprecedented needs are represented by the proliferation of such institutions associated with urban living as the police and fire departments, the welfare agency, and public housing.

In the city, "bureaucracy" becomes a ubiquitous form of organi-

---

[29] William F. Ogburn, "The Family and Its Functions," *Recent Social Trends*, I (New York: McGraw-Hill Book Company, 1933), pp. 661-708.

[30] William J. Goode, *World Revolution and Family Patterns* (New York: The Free Press, 1963), pp. 128-29.

[31] William G. Sumner, *Folkways* (Boston: Ginn and Company, 1907), p. 54.

zation. It is a rational-formal-legal organization that is an inevitable and indispensable product of all societies of large population, size, density, and high levels of interaction. It is a form of complex organization involving (1) the distribution in a fixed way of regular activities, (2) the distribution in a fixed way of authority in accordance with rules, (3) the methodical provision for fulfillment of duties and execution of rights, and (4) the selection of personnel on the basis of qualifications rather than on birth or status.[32] Bureaucracy in this sense is found not only in government but also in business enterprise, in labor unions, in religious organizations, in educational institutions, in fraternal organizations—in brief, in all aspects of the mass society in which collective activity is required on a continuing basis. Bureaucracy is necessarily impersonal and requires the subordination of the individual to the organization. It produces the "organization man," despite the fact that it also produces greater individual freedom. City life makes man relatively free from the constraints of tradition and opens up wide avenues of choice in many realms, even while it may require conformity in some facets of existence as exemplified in the organization man. This is more an apparent than a real contradiction—for conformity in an organization touches only a single segment of the total human experience. Though conformity in some realms is stifling and may incite rebellion, it is, nonetheless, a necessary aspect of life in a mass society.

The development of the city has altered and produced forms of social stratification, both on a power and a prestige basis. The surplus making cities possible was at first controlled by the king and the priest, or, as in the case of Egypt, the two fused into one. The military, an adjunct to the top administration, was closely associated with the elite and enjoyed the distinction of being part of the upper class. Workers, peasants, craftsmen, or slaves were subordinate and lower classes in ancient societies.

The rise of the commercial city greatly increased the importance of the merchants, who became a powerful group. With the growing size and power of the city, merchants displaced landlords not only in the power structure of the cities but in the power structure of larger entities, including nations as a whole. With the ascen-

[32] Max Weber, *Max Weber: Essays in Sociology* (New York: Oxford University Press, 1946), pp. 196 ff.

dancy of the industrial city the industrialist, the financier, and the manager achieved positions of power arising from wealth and strategic location in the economy. Older sources of social stratification also persisted, and the "upper" social strata, in varying degrees, included persons whose position was based on status, that is, birth or "social" honor as well as on economic power.[33]

The development of urban culture produced a new basis for status based on prestige rather than power. The development of intellectual traditions, bolstered by the scientific revolution, provided high status to persons in intellectual and professional pursuits. Contemporary society tends, therefore, to be stratified on three axes: power as achieved through wealth, status as achieved through birth, and prestige as achieved largely through intellectual and professional pursuits. The tremendous increase in mass levels of living, however, and the emergence of a large middle class which is becoming a predominant proportion of the population tend, of course, to undermine existing systems of social stratification.

Problems of Government An especially significant influence of increasing size and density of population on social organization is manifest in the transformed nature of government. The complex of technological, economic, and social changes which have been both antecedent to, and consequent upon, increasing urbanization profoundly affected the role of government, the nature of representative government, the political party system, the substance of political issues, the character of public administration, and the structure of local government. The growing size, complexity, and interdependence of contemporary agglomerations have also posed new and more difficult problems of intergovernmental relations as manifested within the United States. They have greatly altered and are still modifying relations between state and city government, federal and state government, federal and city government, and intrametropolitan area governments.

We have noted that government in its earliest form in the city performed primarily the function of distributing the agricultural surplus that made aggregative living possible. Early government also embodied defense and police functions, and, in collaboration

---

[33] *Max Weber: Essays in Sociology,* pp. 180 ff.

with the religious hierarchy, played some role in respect to the welfare and spiritual life of the people.

Significant changes in government, dependent upon size and density of population, are apparent in the history of the United States. The Constitution of the United States (which established the framework of the federal government) and, in the main, the constitutions of the individual states (which, in turn, created the local governments) were drawn in a preindustrial, rural setting. The political thought that dominated the minds of early America in the critical period during which the federal government and many of the state and local governments were established was composed of many strains reflecting the transition of the political order from a feudal-autocratic to a liberal-democratic state. The great alterations that have occurred in the original governmental system established by the Founding Fathers, which are still in process, may be interpreted as a consequence of the changes that have occurred in the size, distribution, and composition of the population.

At the risk of oversimplification, it may be said that foremost in the concept of the role of government in the American political heritage, the product of a preurban world, is emphasis on the tenet that "that government is best which governs least." This doctrine, coupled with the liberal tradition in economic thinking, that each man acting in his own interest automatically acts in the interest of the larger whole, constitutes fundamentally the inherited framework of principles on the basis of which the Founding Fathers laid out American government. Yet, despite the dominance of these principles in the political philosophy of the United States, the record, reflecting the power of forces of social change, shows that the functions of American government on all levels have tremendously expanded and multiplied in the course of history; the expansion has been continuous without regard to the complexion of the political party in power.

The increasing size and density of population, the increasing interdependence of the social order, the breakdown of traditional social controls, and the inability of inherited social institutions to cope with the new problems of urban life have led inexorably to the manifold expansion of government functions and powers. This process is by no means yet completed, and, one might add, by no means yet fully understood by many who still long for the simplicity of both nineteenth century life and government. A few concrete examples may serve to clarify this point. There is certainly some relationship between the inability of the family as an inherited social institution to cope with the security problems posed by urban health hazards, industrial accidents, and unemployment, and the development of governmental programs such as the public health services, workmen's compensation laws, unemployment insurance benefits, and Medicare. Similarly, the creation of the Federal Reserve Board, the Federal Trade Commission, the Department of Health, Education and Welfare, the Council of Economic Advisers, and the Department of Housing and Urban Development are but a few additional examples of the expanded functions of government necessitated by increasing urbanization.

The impact of urbanization on the role of government is by no means restricted to the domestic scene. Worldwide urbanization has produced increasing international interdependence, which in turn is modifying the traditional concepts of "sovereignty" and "nationalism." The role of the United States, as a member of the United Nations and its specialized agencies, has certainly profoundly altered inherited concepts of both.

Increasing size and density of population have also brought about great changes in the nature of representative government. Representative government as provided for in the United States was an adaptation of the "democracy" of the Greek city-state. It is one thing, however, for a representative to speak for a small, homogeneous, rural, agricultural constituency, and quite another thing to "represent" a heterogeneous population of a quarter to a half-million persons with diverse and often conflicting interests. The contemporary representative must determine for himself just whom he represents in his votes on specific issues, and he is almost mercilessly subjected to conflicting pressures and influences. The emergence of the public opinion poll may be regarded as an invention in the urban setting for the measurement of "the will" of the people. It may play an increasingly important role in representative government in the years to come.

Urbanization has also greatly altered the character of the two-party system in the United States. The historic differences that led to the formation of political parties are more and more obscured by the problems of the complex urban order. In consequence, the range of interests in political philosophies and policies *within* each of the great political parties is wider than the range *between* them. The increased area of decision making opened to urban residents extends to the choice of political parties. The urban voter is more apt to choose than to inherit his political preferences, to split his ticket, or to change his political party from election to election. The "independent" voter gains more importance in determining the outcome of elections.

Furthermore, increasing urbanization has generated the foremost political issues of the time. First, the role of government itself has become a major political issue. It constitutes undoubtedly the major point of cleavage between the conservatives and liberals at the present time. Then, too, specific issues, especially those involving provision of welfare and security measures, arise from conditions of urban living.

The complex and often technical character of urban problems has changed the requirements of "governing." In the urban setting, governmental problems grow increasingly technical and require professional attention. The "expert" has emerged as a new and powerful element in government, and "public administration" has become a profession. With the proliferation of government functions, government has become increasingly "bureaucratized," and, because of its conspicuous role in mass society, government bureaucracy is frequently misinterpreted as the only form of bureaucracy in the contemporary order. Government bureaucracy, like other forms of bureaucracy, has become an indispensable tool in the function of the mass society.

Expanding urbanization has also greatly affected the structure of government in the United States and intergovernmental relations. The creation and development of the federal, state, and local levels of government were a natural outgrowth of the pre-industrial, rural structure of the United States as a pluralistic nation. In the colonies and in the new nation comprising relatively homogeneous rural communities, it was logical and feasible to delineate arbitrarily bounded units of local government—the township, county, village, town, and city. But clumpings of population and economic activities have ignored the historical state, as well as city and other local jurisdictional lines, and have followed natural and economic rather than political boundaries. In consequence, local government today is by no means that envisaged by the Founding Fathers. It has been necessary to add many governmental units to the original system to deal with the new problems with which the inherited governmental structure could not cope.

This is why inherited local government structure today is supplemented by such governmental overlays as sanitary districts, water districts, drainage districts, port authorities, park districts, metropolitan area planning commissions, and by such instrumentalities as the interstate compact and the Tennessee Valley Authority.

Rapid urban and metropolitan growth in the United States, which has already outmoded local government structure, is further accelerating its obsolescence. At mid-century, the 168 metropolitan areas of the United States had among them something in excess of 16,000 local governmental units—that is, agencies with powers to tax and to spend. These, to be sure, included school districts, but the number is a good quantitative index of the anachronistic character of the inherited local governmental structure. This anachronism is manifested in movements toward consolidation of city and county government, in the creation of metropolitan area-wide agencies to perform specific functions, in the creation of metropolitan area planning agencies, and in the creation of the Toronto metropolitan governmental structure, which may serve as a prototype for other metropolitan areas. Basic deficiencies of present metropolitan governmental organization are becoming more apparent, and proposals for changes in local governmental structure may be expected to increase.[34]

The growing size, complexity, and interdependence of contemporary agglomerations of people and activities have also posed new and difficult problems of intergovernmental relations. State and city governmental relations have become tenser as population has shifted from a rural to an urban majority. "Upstate-downstate" conflicts are reaching the crisis stage in many of the states. In 1960, urban populations outnumbered the rural in some thirty-nine states, but in virtually all of them the dwindling rural population still maintained a vise-like grip on state legislatures by refusing to reapportion legislative representation to reflect the changing population distribution.

In 1960, counties with less than 25,000 inhabitants were 71 per cent overrepresented in state legislatures; at the other extreme, counties with 500,000 or more inhabitants were 24 per cent underrepresented. Of 102 "rural" congressional districts, almost half

---

[34] Luther Gulick, "Metropolitan Organization," in Coleman Woodbury, ed., *Metropolis in Ferment*, pp. 57 ff.

(49 per cent) were overrepresented in the House of Representatives in Congress; in contrast, in the 91 urban districts 19 per cent were underrepresented, and in the 15 suburban districts 52 per cent were underrepresented.[35] It was cognizance of these facts, contrary to constitutional requirements, that led the U.S. Supreme Court to its "one-man, one-vote" decision.

The "rotten borough" situation constituted a source of irritation and pressure that not only modified state-city governmental relationships but also federal-city relationships. The greater extent to which federal government agencies are working directly with municipal governments is the product of the callous disregard of urban problems by rural-dominated, malapportioned state legislatures. The states have increasingly made themselves the fifth wheel of the American system of governance, and this is what has led to federal participation in programs relating to public housing, urban renewal, highways and expressways, civil rights, mass transit, education, and air and water pollution.

The recent Supreme Court decisions forcing more equitable reapportionment may conceivably provide urban and suburban populations with more political power. As the rural population loses its disproportionate control over state legislatures and the House of Representatives in Congress, it is likely that important shifts will occur in the domestic and foreign policy of the United States in the direction of greater "liberalism."

The combined trends of population concentration in metropolitan areas and decentralization within them have greatly altered intrametropolitan area relationships. Population and community changes, along with economic and technological changes, have jurisdictionally separated place of residence and political responsibility, on the one hand, and place of work and economic responsibility, on the other. Moreover, they have also sometimes jurisdictionally separated both place of work and place of residence from place of shopping, place of recreation, or place of schooling. In consequence, great disparities have arisen among local jurisdictions within metropolitan areas between the need for urban services, and the utilization of such services, and the ability to

---

[35] Paul T. David and Ralph Eisenberg, *Devaluation of the Urban and Suburban Vote* (Charlottesville: The University Press of Virginia, 1961), p. 9; Andrew Hacker, *Congressional Districting* (Washington: The Brookings Institution, 1963), p. 84.

adequately plan for, administer and finance them. The common explanation for these afflictions is to be found in the outmoded assumption, valid in preurban America, that the area of local governmental jurisdiction was simultaneously the area of residence, work, consumer expenditure, schooling, religious observance, and living in general. The differentiation of function and urbanism as a way of life exacerbate the frictions produced by the disparity between twentieth century clumpings of people and economic activities and nineteenth century local governmental structure.

One specific and serious source of difficulty arises from the pattern of intrametropolitan area population distribution described above. The tendency for higher socioeconomic elements of the population to move outwards has left central cities with larger proportions of population with relatively low socioeconomic status. Thus, central cities find they are confronted with a shrinking tax base even as their problems—physical, human, and governmental—become more severe and even though they continue to provide indispensable services to the entire metropolitan complex.

As the problems discussed indicate, the system of governance in the United States may be described as still in transition from a rural to an urban society. The increasing size and density of the population may be regarded as a most important factor in the undermining of the structure and processes of government as visualized by its eighteenth and nineteenth century founders.

MANY OF THE problems of the contemporary scene, national and worldwide, may be viewed and better understood as frictions of the transition still underway from agrarianism to urbanism and metropolitanism as a way of life. Man has lived in urban places but a small fraction of the time that he has inhabited this earth. He has been able to proliferate cities of a million or more and approach the possibility of an urbanized world, in the sense that more than half the world's population would reside in urban places, only within the last century. As the only culture-building animal on the face of the earth, man not only adapts to environment but creates environment to which to adapt. He has created an urban and metropolitan environment, and the many problems that accompany urbanism as a way of life bear testimony to the fact that man is still accommodating himself to the new world he has created.

Comments on Hauser

LOWDON WINGO, JR.

Senior Researcher
Resources for the Future, Inc.

PROFESSOR HAUSER's paper for this conference grows out of extensive experience and notable wisdom in the matter of world urbanization. It is the latest in a stream of studies, filled with insight, with which the author has enriched scholarly work on the city. I have read it with interest and, I must confess, with some disappointment.

First, for a short paper, I found its scope excessive. It ranges over the historical antecedents, the global distribution, and all of the social science perspectives of world urbanization within only a few pages, and so lets breadth triumph over depth. Then, its sheer multiplicity dissipates its thrust; in rapid succession, the author puts on the garb of the sociologist, the demographer, the city planner, the political scientist, the historian, and the anthropologist. In the study of a phenomenon so complex as the city, an eclectic viewpoint can be a virtue, but eclecticism of concept is something more than an unsystematic assortment of statements from the various branches of the social sciences. I find that Professor Hauser's observations tend toward the latter. Finally, the paper pursues summarily and uncritically the current state of social science knowledge—and perhaps one should add, speculation —about cities, wherever these strands may lead. It sums up the entirely unsatisfactory state of things without changing them even a little by pointing out useful new directions, or by restructuring what we do know so that it is left more intelligible, or by marking out with danger signs the areas in which our knowledge is simply too fragile to bear the heavy weight of policy or of further theorizing. It is true that I am arguing for a paper that Dr. Hauser did not write, but I am suggesting one that his many valuable contributions to the field of urbanization lead us to expect. At the most general level, a greater intensity of focus, a consistency of perspective, and a more manifest sense of purpose would allay in large part the dissatisfaction with which the paper leaves me.

Particular elements of the paper, however, warrant further discussion. For example, the paper begins with the observation that the modern large city is a recent historical phenomenon made possible only by the achievement of certain levels of technology and degrees of sophistication in social organizations. It might equally well have said that at any recent stage of development the levels of technology and social organization were made possible by the existence of cities, a fact that highlights a recurring ambiguity in the paper about the cause-and-effect relations of the city with many of the social, political, and economic dimensions of historical development. This ambiguity resembles the correlation fallacy: if events A and B can only coexist, it is misleading to say that A causes B, and even more misleading to say that A causes B because they have historically coexisted. Thus, it seems inaccurate to me to imply that some states of technology and social organization "caused" the city, and even more so to imply that the city "caused" in some fashion corporate organization of business, "big" unions, the Federal Reserve Board, and the Council of Economic Advisers. We may have to talk to outsiders about the social sciences that way, but we do not have to believe it ourselves. We have more sophisticated ways of dealing with coexistent historical phenomena and with the complexities of social causation.

Actually, the city in its various states of development is not simply an artifact thrown up at various moments in history by specific historical forces, nor is it fruitfully viewed as an independent social variable responsible for such things as corporate organization and the loosening of traditional social controls. For our purposes, it is better viewed as a dimension of the stage of development of local and even of world society and economy. At each point in history, certain functions could only be performed in the urban environment; the city is no more or less than the sum of these roles. All of society is encompassed by the city and the noncity and their relations; they are parts of the same whole, and from this observation two corollaries follow. First, indispensable in understanding the city is knowledge of its relations with the rest of society, that is, of the functions it performs for its hinterland, its nation, indeed, for the world at large. A second important kind of knowledge is the way in which its parts are organized to perform these functions. As this discussion proceeds, we will perhaps refer more to the second point, since most of the issues associated with density and its problems fall most naturally here.

Dr. Hauser's introduction closes with a recapitulation of the demographic statistics of past, present, and expected urbanization on world and national scenes. It would have been useful to carry out some speculative interpretation of these figures into their policy dimensions. While urban populations will clearly increase both absolutely and relatively, while we are evolving more and bigger cities, can we conclude that cities will get denser, become more unmanageable? Can we conclude that more people will be exposed to the problems of high density living—that such problems will change in scale and character? In short, to what extent are rates of change, as distinguished from sheer volume, significant elements in these problems?

Caracas, Venezuela, will double its population within the next ten years, but its rates of real capital formation and attrition mean that ten years from now as much as three-fourths of the city's physical capital will be less than ten years old; Caracas, in effect, will rebuild itself every generation, even while it is growing at an extraordinary rate. The moral of this story is that the headlong advance of urbanization throughout most of the world does not necessarily carry with it derogation of the quality of life for future urban masses. As a matter of fact, there is evidence that even in developing countries urbanization and the growth of cities is not an unmixed catastrophe. At least in Latin America national *per capita* incomes are directly associated with the per cent of the population residing in urban centers, which is only another way of saying that income levels and degrees of urbanization are dimensions of economic development. Thus, it is difficult to know what to conclude from the author's historical and projective statistics on urbanization.

The title of this session suggests that we should give particular attention to the density aspects of urbanization, which the paper introduces with a size-density model. The model shows how many people are potential contacts within a circle with a radius of 10 miles at several density levels ranging from that of aboriginal America to that of present-day Manhattan. It also follows that the average distance between any two adjacent members of the population of aboriginal America was something greater than a mile, while on Manhattan Island the comparable distance is barely 20 feet. While one member of our pair of average Indians had to travel a mile to make contact with the other, our average Manhattanite barely has to raise his voice.

Please bear in mind that population density is always a slippery concept. Density is not a measure as such; it is the ratio of one measure with respect to another. The meaning of a specific density statement depends on what kinds of information are put into the ratio; for some purposes, we might make better use of the "proximity" measure used above—the square root of the inverse of the density measure.

Thus, density measures have two kinds of difficulty. First, what population and areal units are employed, and how do they relate to the more general assertions made about them? Workers per square foot of factory floor area and farm laborers per acre of cultivated land are gross production function statements, as is the site-floor area ratio of commercial buildings. Persons per room and users per acre of recreational area reflect intensities of use of the housing stock and recreational facilities, and so on. The point can be made with some justification that the city is characterized by a high intercorrelation of density measures simply because of the great concentration of people and activities around the urban center. However, this begs the question, for our concern is with the problems of high density living, and these are associated with individuals playing out quite specific roles in the supercharged environment of the city, so that we need to focus on the functional relationships between various kinds of density characteristics of the city. If the daytime and nighttime population distribution of the city were roughly the same, we could rest assured that our urban transportation problems would be of only local and immediate interest!

A second conceptual problem with population densities arises from the choice of areal scales, for density figures tell us little about how the densities of subareas vary. Thus, for a given problem of discourse it is useful to distinguish *macro* from *microdensities.* Macrodensities suggest a dimension of urban organization, but a highly generalized one that obscures details of internal organization. Since we have little reason to believe that there is more than a weak relation between macrodensities and the scale and composition of urban policy problems, more interesting information relates to the microdensities that reflect urban organization. We can conclude very little from the knowledge that Phoenix, Ariz. and Peoria, Ill. have roughly the same density over-all. While there is probably some correlation between the macrodensities of cities and the microdensities under which the most densely settled 10 per cent of the population live, I would doubt that it is very strong, and hypothesize that it results from much stronger relationships of both variables to size of city and age distribution of the housing stock. Contrast Boston and Houston, for example, cities of roughly the same size. The great contrasts in their densities, apparent to even the most casual visitor, can be explained by the fact that Boston's housing stock in large part antedates World War II, while Houston is an "auto-age" city, where most of the housing stock has been constructed in the last twenty years.

A synthesis of the micro- and macrodensity relationships exists in the urban population density gradient. Considerable literature now exists on urban density gradients to which economists, geographers, and sociologists have made useful contributions. We know a number of useful things about them. First, density gradients are associated in significant ways with the characteristics of urban transportation technology, with independent economic as well as physical characteristics of the urban environment (such as large industrial plants or waterfronts), and with the way in which urban land and housing markets operate. Second, we know that over time there is a tendency for the gradient to flatten out and for the region of maximum density to decline and move outward as the city grows. This is especially true of the United States, but it is likely to become increasingly true of cities in developing countries as they move up the development ladder, adopting along the way urban technologies and organizational characteristics of the cities of economically advanced Western countries. Indeed, it seems to me that the problems of high-density living are related in critical ways to the density gradient (and the manner in which it tends to change with growth), with technological innovation, and with changes in the mechanisms allocating space and overhead services among urban claimants.

At the low end of the gradient we can identify the problems of sprawl, to which Dr. Hauser alludes. The extravagant use of land, the costliness of providing public services to households and establishments scattered thinly over the hinterlands, the income segregation implicit in the factors making for suburbanization—all create a unique bundle of public policy issues that we associate with suburbanization. At the other end of the gradient, we find the old housing stock, the deteriorating infrastructure, congestion, and the concentration of urban poverty with its immense needs for supporting urban services. Thus, the city has two "problem fronts" associated, not so much with size or with density per se, but with the rates of change of crucial urban dimensions—the development front expanding into the hinterlands, and the redevelopment front surrounding the urban core.

I find Dr. Hauser's assessment of both of these problem fronts conventional and unpersuasive. I am not certain that urban sprawl can support any long-range and broadscaled indictment—outside of its inherent untidiness—of being basically inefficient. Indeed, Lessinger has made a very interesting case for scattered development. Others have argued that the consumers of low-density housing do not pay their way, and that sprawl results from a bundle of implicit subsidies to the beneficiaries of sprawl. Muth's studies of land and housing markets, however, suggest that what we call sprawl can be almost totally explained by the growth of demand for new housing operating under extant market conditions. People who move to the suburbs are getting housing and related services that they want, and I'm not at all sure that marginal cost pricing of public services, *where it is feasible,* would make all that much difference in the operation of the land and housing markets on the development front.

On the redevelopment front, the paper scores our inability to maintain an urban plant. However, differential deterioration of the physical plant represents investment responses to the rapid changes imposed by growth and by institutional and technical change. A good part of our problem at the center results from the lack of responsiveness of market institutions to the rapidly changing economic environment, which explains, if it does not justify entirely, the urban renewal program. A good part of so-called urban blight can be explained probably by unrealistic expectations—and the sentimental attachment to sunk capital—of central area property owners. The redevelopment problem is not a problem of "urban maintenance." On the contrary, it is a problem of directing the land-use response to crucial changes in the urban parameters.

On the other hand, I find myself in agreement with the paper in that air and water pollution are becoming increasingly critical problems for the whole of society. Actually, these problems seem to me to be much more menacing than those of sprawl and blight. The prospect of an increasingly hostile physical environment confronts us so squarely that I cannot help wondering at our capability to respond. Each pound of coal and gallon of gasoline that we burn exacts a price from our environment; at present levels of consumption, the price has become intolerable in many places, but however we respond the price is going to go up. While this is a general rather than an urban problem, this price usually comes to rest on the urban dweller. The interface between the immense concentration of people and productive activities and the diminishing supplies of pure air, clean water, and unsullied land will enter more and more into our policy calculations in the future.

Turning now to the relationship of the urban with the nonurban sectors, Dr. Hauser frequently turns to the historical antecedents of the twentieth century to enrich our perspectives about urbanization, speculating particularly about the sizes and densities which characterized the early cities. In a recent paper, Hoselitz added a dimension to these speculations by asking the question in a broader context: how much of an urban superstructure was permitted earlier societies by their resources, technologies, and social organization? He identified the character of the early city with the state of urbanization, which really expressed the interdependence between urban and rural sectors of society. It does not seem likely that before the industrial revolution many cases could have existed in which more than 10 per cent of the population was supported in cities. Implicit in the static model of rural-urban interaction is an equilibrium state. History, of course, abhors equilibria and endures them only for the most transitory of moments; nevertheless, the equilibrium concept is valuable in bringing front and center the factors which disturb the equilibria, or which create new equilibrium conditions toward which rural-urban relations will tend. It is valuable furthermore in describing in dynamic terms the interaction of rural and urban elements.

Rural-urban relations can be largely described by the fact that each sector is a market for the other's products, that there is a high degree of mobility of capital and labor over the rural-urban boundary, and that cities have market linkages among themselves. The evolution of the rural-urban system, then, takes place in large part through continuous changes in these relationships. The historical process of urbanization can be conceived against the background of urban-rural relationships seeking new equilibria as the equilibrium conditions changed. The disturbance of a primitive equilibrium with a rural-urban population ratio of, say, 90:10 would result in rural out-migration at a very low rate, which means that cities would grow much more rapidly than the countryside. As the proportions more and more favor the city, the rate of urban in-migration tends to decline even though rural out-migration rates are continuing to increase, and rural growth rates, while still positive, are declining. Then, rural natural increase is surpassed by rural out-migration, and the rural population begins to decline. Cities are growing slowly, but still more rapidly than the nation as a whole. Finally, a new equilibrium is reached as the rural-urban ratio stabilizes at a new level, say 10:90. Actually, the United States has never reached anything resembling this second equilibrium. At last count, the ratio was 6.7:93.3 and still declining.

Within this context one can examine Dr. Hauser's dictum about "overurbanization" as a problem of developing countries. Harris and others have pointed out that overurbanization is simply the other side of the coin marked "overruralization." In short, they describe a society in which labor is in a chronic state of oversupply. Indeed, several scholars have found substantial underemployment of agricultural labor in developing countries. In India the estimate was 30 per cent, while Currie has estimated that the current output of Colombia's agriculture could be produced with U.S. factor proportions with about one-sixth of Colombia's present agricultural labor force. I simply do not know of any case in which the migrant flows from the rural sectors to the urban areas have reduced total agricultural output; the opportunity costs of labor in the rural sector must be close to zero. Examining Chile's migration experience, Herrick concluded that migratory behavior of the Chilean *campesino* was not inconsistent with rational economic behavior. Indeed, a case can be made that the only people who are left worse off by this process are earlier migrants who have not fared well in the urban labor markets, but even here, we are accumulating evidence in Latin America that the socioeconomic characteristics of migrants converge rapidly with those of earlier migrant and resident populations. The conclusion seems to be that, while there are frequently high rates of underemployment in the principal cities of developing countries, employment gets passed around a lot, and almost everyone shares in some manner in whatever economic tasks do exist. The overurbanization concept seems to me not to contribute a great deal either to our understanding of urbanization during economic development, nor to suggest normative dimensions that might usefully guide policy.

Finally, let me react briefly to the hypothesis that the infrastructure costs of rapid urbanization lead to truly abysmal conditions by Western standards, which Dr. Hauser explicitly applies to the cities of developing countries. In the first place, I think we too frequently are ignorant of the truly appalling state of affairs in the rural countryside, to which we would condemn those fortunate, strong, and ingenious enough to escape if we prevented them from moving. At their very worst the conditions in cities rarely approach those of the countryside in developing countries. More than this, however, conditions in the cities of developing countries are going to be strongly correlated with per capita GNP, and as this rises urban conditions improve. This means, however, that it is unreasonable to expect that the cities of developing countries in early stages of development will approximate Western standards. Indeed, I would expect them to be quite different with respect to their service levels. First, I would expect rationing and discrimination in the provision of overhead services toward users with a high development priority. Second, I would expect some concentration on labor intensive as against capital intensive services. Finally, I think it would be sensible to explore the implications of the low-service-level city and put far behind us prevailing Western standards. The urban middle classes will not let us forget them, but there is no reason why the rate of development need be eroded by such inappropriate concepts. In short, I think it is irrelevant that urbanization in developing countries produces low levels of overhead services; this is done in the interest of development.

I have perhaps been more critical of Professor Hauser's paper than I intended to be. However, it is an important measure of his remarks here that I wish I had more time than circumstances permit to explore some of the issues he has posed.

Life Expectancy and the Life Cycle— Some Interrelations

Harley L. Browning

Director, Population Research Center
Professor of Sociology
The University of Texas

This paper is an effort to show how the demographic concern with life expectancy can be fruitfully joined with the sociological conception of the life cycle. More specifically, I want first to address myself to the question of why there has been so little interchange between two professional groups dealing with the same subject matter, the life cycle. Second, I want to document the astonishing increase in life expectancy of recent times and some of the implications than can be drawn from it. Third is my consideration of the potential and actual consequences of greatly improved life expectancy in altering the timing or spacing of events in the life cycle. Finally, I want to conclude with some comments about the possibilities for planning changes in the life cycle.

My original assignment for this conference was to consider problems of population "quality," but I have chosen not to deal directly with this subject. Nonetheless, I hope to show that some features of my argument have important implications for population quality. Since my purpose is to set forth a perspective for the linking of life expectancy and life cycle, I have not attempted any formal statement of the relationship, nor have I attempted systematically to provide data for all of my generalizations. For the purpose of eliciting discussion I have made my position as unequivocal as possible, eschewing the qualifications and hedges that would otherwise be called for. As a result of the incomplete formulation of the argument, the slender empirical support provided, and the dogmatic manner of presentation, this paper must be considered exploratory and tentative.

Two Kinds of Myopia

Two professional groups have concerned themselves with features of the life cycle in the United States, and it is my contention that there has been surprisingly little interchange of data and ideas between them. This is strange because their approaches are not mutually exclusive; indeed, each is well suited to complement the work of the other. The one group is made up of sociologists, anthropologists, and developmental psychologists, and the other group is made up of demographers.

Why has there been this failure of communication and lack of mutual enrichment? The answer, I believe, is to be found in the ways in which these two groups conceive of their common subject matter. Sociologists, anthropologists, and developmental psychologists take a "normative" approach to the life cycle, whereas demographers see the same subject from a "distributive" standpoint. (One might substitute behavioral for normative, but much of the literature concentrates more on the way the person in a given situation ought to behave rather than on his actual behavior.) Much of the work of the former has been an elaboration of the normative conditions attached to a person's status and role at various stages in his life cycle.[1] The demographer's customary concern is with finding out how the members of a given population "distribute" themselves in certain positions or categories, most commonly by age, sex, labor force participation, educational attainment, marital status, and so on. And, of course, demographers use life tables and other measures of mortality to determine the number of persons removed from the population during some time interval.

Now there is nothing intrinsic about either of these two ways of looking at the life cycle that would make it impossible for the

---

[1] The best general recent review by a sociologist is Leonard D. Cain, Jr., "Life Course and Social Structure," in Robert E. L. Faris, ed., *Handbook of Modern Sociology* (Chicago: Rand McNally & Co., 1964), pp. 272-309.

findings of the one to be used to complement the findings of the other. Yet, historically, such has not been the case. The normative approach virtually ignores the demographic information of how many persons occupy various statuses and how this differs from society to society or even for the same society at different points in time. It would be possible to provide many examples, but one will do. S. N. Eisenstadt uses a Parsonian functionalist framework to determine the significance of age groups and how they differ in a large number of societies, ranging from primitive to modern.[2] His special concern is with the importance of youth groups. Although he must have been aware, for example, of the great variations from society to society in the proportion that youth groups (ages 15-24) represent of the total population, he never introduces this factor nor any other distributive factor into his discussion to help explain why youth groups differ in their importance. In other words, his normative approach assumes demographic factors completely as given rather than as problematic.

The demographers' type of myopia assumes another form. They know all about the number of persons who occupy various categories, but all too often they content themselves with purely descriptive presentations, making little or no effort to at least suggest what their data mean for the normative order. Kingsley Davis as both sociologist and demographer has long been keenly aware of these forms of myopia. About ten years ago he contrasted the normative approach of Parsons to the study of the American family with that of Glick who has made notable demographic contributions to the same field.

It is a melancholy indication of how far we have yet to go that the Parsonian analysis previously cited makes no reference to the relevant demographic materials, and that Glick, in his *American Families,* makes no reference to Parsons. One would not know that these two men are both members of the same professional group and are dealing with the same phenomenon, the American family.[3]

Another important feature of the normative approach to the life cycle is that it tends to ignore the transformation of the life cycle

---

[2] S. N. Eisenstadt, *From Generation to Generation: Age Groups and Social Structure* (Chicago: The Free Press of Glencoe, 1956).

[3] Kingsley Davis, "The Sociology of Demographic Behavior," in Robert K. Merton, Leonard Broom, Leonard S. Cottrell, Jr., eds., *Sociology Today* (New York: Basic Books, Inc., Publishers, 1959), p. 331.

itself over time. The unintended consequence has been to give a sort of static "Ages of Man" tone to such an approach because time is taken only as some fixed interval between events in the life cycle. One reason for this static way of dealing with the life cycle is simply that many anthropologists and sociologists can study their phenomena at only one point in time, and therefore they may be unaware of changes in the life cycle that have taken place prior to their study.

Demographers are more fortunate in this respect, for they often have comparable data available to them for extended time periods, and they can hardly avoid an appreciation of change because of the central place of population dynamics (the interrelation of birth, death, and migration rates) in their field. On the whole, however, demographers have not been notably successful in using their longitudinal data to illumine changes in social structure. Perhaps this is because of excessive caution and unfamiliarity with the literature in the social sciences. Perhaps it is also because of their relatively small numbers and the heavy demands placed upon them to process their mountains of data for such "service" activities as population projections and the like.

Another case in point that demonstrates the lack of mutually beneficial interchange between the normative and distributive approaches is the conduct of family studies dealing with the importance of birth order. Psychologists and sociologists have created an extensive literature linking birth order and size of family with other factors such as achievement and personality formation. Their work, unfortunately, has rarely been linked to the large body of studies made by demographers of family composition, particularly to changes that have occurred through time. A recent exception to this generalization is an article by Kenneth Kammeyer. In this article Kammeyer presents evidence indicating that in American culture first-born children tend to be "conservators" of the traditional culture. What is unusual about his presentation is that he goes on to say that the proportion of the first-born in societies will vary significantly according to fluctuations in completed family size, such as took place in the United States between the 1930's and the present. He then suggests that these changes may have possible implications for social change. While he is well aware of the difficulty of linking birth order to social change, Kammeyer at least displays an *awareness* of the possible interplay between demographic changes and changes in social structure.[4]

One of the few studies encountered in the preparation of this paper that exemplifies the joint approach advocated here is the suggestive article by Jean Fourastie, "De la Vie Traditionelle à la Vie Tertiaire."[5] He calls his work, "recherches sur le calendrier démographique de l'homme moyen," and it is a comparison of the mortality conditions of France at the end of the seventeenth century with those of the present time. He goes on to spell out a number of consequences of social significance that derive from the quite different life expectancies of the two periods.

THE GREAT LEAP FORWARD IN MORTALITY CONTROL

Only quite recently in man's history has he been able to exercise any important and lasting influence on the control of his mortality. In Western Europe and North America, mortality declines have been documented for periods ranging up to several hundred years, but this accomplishment recently has been overshadowed by the spectacular drops in mortality rates for developing countries representing a large share of the world's population.[6] They are now able to accomplish in a few decades what the European countries took many generations to achieve. There also have been concomitant declines in morbidity rates, but because of the lack of data it is difficult to know with any degree of certainty how much of a decline has taken place.

To take one case, Mexico has nearly doubled male life expectancy at birth within the span of a single generation (1930-65). During this time, life expectancy rose from 32 to 62 years.[7] Perhaps equally remarkable, and certainly more surprising, is what has happened to

---

[4] "Birth Order and the Feminine Sex Role Among College Women," *American Sociological Review*, XXXI (August, 1966), pp. 508-15.

[5] *Population*, XIV (July-September, 1959), pp. 417-32.

[6] For a good recent review of the situation in these countries see George J. Stolnitz, "Recent Mortality Trends in Latin America, Asia and Africa: Review and Re-interpretation," *Population Studies*, XIX (November, 1965), pp. 117-38.

[7] These figures are taken from Raul Benitez Zenteno and Gustavo Cabrera Acevedo, *Proyecciones de la Poblacion de Mexico, 1960-1980* (Mexico City: Banco de Mexico-Investigaciones Industriales, Oficina de Recursos Humanos, 1966).

the age structure of Mexico during the same period. Contrary to the common sense notion that when life expectancy improves radically there naturally is a parallel "aging" of the population, very little change in the age structure has occurred. Indeed, there has been a perceptible "younging" of the population as indicated by the per cent distribution given below:[8]

Age Grouping	1930	1965
0-14	44%	47%
15-64	53	50
65+	3	3
	100	100

The explanation for this violation of common sense is to be found in the trend of fertility for it, rather than mortality, is the principal determinant of the age structure of a population.[9] In Mexico fertility throughout the 1930-65 period remained high and relatively constant. It is likely that there actually has been an increase of perhaps up to 10 per cent in fertility during this period.[10] Of course, the fact that Mexican fertility has remained relatively stable for the last generation does not imply that it will continue to do so during the lifetime of persons born in 1965. Probably it will decline somewhat in coming decades, although to an unknown degree, thus bringing about an aging of the population.

Mexico is a striking case but by no means an isolated one. A number of other developing countries will achieve much the same record within a fifty-year period or less. Thus, for a substantial part of the world's population, the mortality experience of succeeding generations will differ markedly and to an extent unparalleled in any other historical period.

Perhaps the best way to appreciate this fact is to use model life

---

[8] The 1930 figure is my adjustment of census figures to correct for the underenumeration of the 0-14 age group. The 1965 figure is an estimate from *Proyecciones de la Poblacion de Mexico, 1960-1980*.

[9] Ansley Coale, perhaps more than any other demographer, has shown how this is possible. See, for example, his article, "How the Age Distribution of a Human Population Is Determined," *Cold Springs Harbor Symposium on Quantitative Biology*, XXII (1957), pp. 83-88.

[10] For a recent appraisal on this point see Alvan O. Zarate, "Fertility in Urban Areas of Mexico: Implications for the Theory of the Demographic Transition," *Demography* (forthcoming).

TABLE 1 SURVIVORS TO CERTAIN AGES FOR FIVE MODEL LIFE TABLES
(MALES)

	Model Life Expectancy at Birth				
	I	II	III	IV	V
	22.851	32.484	47.114	61.228	73.899
Age	Number Surviving				
0	100,000	100,000	100,000	100,000	100,000
5	50,957	64,242	79,961	91,744	98,510
15	46,151	60,000	77,147	90,444	98,273
25	40,254	54,520	73,107	88,240	97,723
35	33,087	47,598	67,851	85,429	97,079
45	25,149	39,332	60,979	81,255	95,876
55	16,955	29,623	51,289	73,412	92,076
65	8,963	18,343	37,047	58,427	81,150
75	2,706	7,232	18,685	34,223	56,701
	Per cent surviving from age 15 to selected age				
25	87.2	90.9	94.8	97.6	99.4
35	71.7	79.3	88.0	94.5	98.8
45	54.5	65.6	79.0	89.8	97.6
55	36.7	49.4	66.5	81.2	93.7
65	19.4	30.6	48.0	64.6	82.6

SOURCE: Adapted from the "West" series of model life tables given in Ansley J. Coale and Paul Demeny, *Regional Model Life Tables and Stable Populations* (Princeton, N.J.: Princeton University Press, 1966).

tables to show the proportion surviving in various ages under very different mortality conditions. In Table 1, five model life tables are presented with life expectancies ranging from 23 to 74 and the number of survivors in various ages from a radix of 100,000.[11] Because they are model life tables no one country will have exactly the same age-specific patterns of mortality, but the model tables were generated on the basis of actual life tables from a large number of countries. They have been selected to show the wide range of life expectancy possible, but they are not unrealistic. As Table 2 indicates, each of the five has been selected because of its correspondence to life expectancies at birth for actual countries, and all are for time periods within this century.

[11] The data are taken from Ansley J. Coale and Paul Demeny, *Regional Model Life Tables and Stable Populations* (Princeton: Princeton University Press, 1966). All are taken from the "Model West" group.

TABLE 2   MODEL LIFE EXPECTANCIES AT BIRTH (BOTH SEXES); ACTUAL LIFE EXPECTANCIES IN THREE COUNTRIES (MALE)

	Model*		Actual
	Female	Male	Male
I	25.000	22.851	22.59 (India, 1901-11)
II	35.000	32.484	32.44 (Mexico, 1930)
III	50.000	47.114	47.92 (Mexico, 1950)
IV	65.000	61.228	62.62 (Mexico, 1965-70)
V	77.500	73.899	73.90 (U.S.A., 1950)

SOURCE: Ansley J. Coale and Paul Demeny, *Regional Model Life Tables and Stable Populations* (Princeton, N.J.: Princeton University Press, 1966); Kingsley Davis, *The Population of India and Pakistan* (Princeton, N.J.: Princeton University Press, 1951), p. 62; Raul Benitez Zenteno and Gustavo Cabrera Acevedo, *Proyecciones de la Poblacion de Mexico, 1960-1980* (Mexico City: Banco de Mexico-Investigaciones Industriales, Oficina de Recursos Humanos, 1966); Paul H. Jacobson, "Cohort Survival for Generations Since 1840," *The Milbank Memorial Fund Quarterly*, XLII (July, 1964), Part 1, p. 48.

The extremes are Models I and V. The first (corresponding to India of 1901-11) is characteristic of mortality conditions in primitive and preindustrial countries with unusually high death rates. Such conditions are now rare in the contemporary world. Model V (approximate to a generational life table from the U.S.A. in 1950) stands for the level many countries in Western Europe and Anglo-America either have already reached or are closely approaching. It may be considered as the lowest realistic mortality under current conditions. The intermediate models II, III, and IV all correspond to the Mexican experience within a generation, and are intended to show how rapidly survivorship can change. In Table 1, the model distributions are given only for males because most of the discussion of the life cycle will concentrate upon this sex. As may be appreciated from Table 2, female life expectancies invariably are higher, ranging from about two years in Model I to over three and a half years in Models IV and V.

The differences among the five model life tables for survivors to various ages are indeed striking. Model I, as has been noted, presents the conditions of extremely high mortality under which mankind lived during most of his time on earth. But it is a common mistake, often seen in popular writing, to assume that if the life expectancy at birth is very low, in this case age 23, then there can be few survivors beyond that age. This simply is not true! Even under the frightful conditions of mortality represented by

Model I, one-quarter of the original population still is alive by age 45. Eric Hoffer has a well-deserved reputation as a shrewd observer of society, but in his most recent book he makes some bizarre statements on length of life.

> Until relatively recent times man's span of life was short. Throughout most of history the truly old were a rarity. . . . Thus it seems plausible that the momentous discoveries and inventions of the Neolithic Age—the domestication of animals and plants; the invention of the wheel, sail and plow; the discovery of irrigation, fermentation, and metallurgy—were the work of an almost childlike population, and were perhaps made in the course of play. Nor is it likely that the ancient myths and legends, with their fairy tale pattern and erotic symbolism, were elaborated by burnt-out old men.[12]

Model II is probably close to the pattern of Europe from late medieval times until well into the industrial revolution. It is worthy of note that even the elites of society in these times were not exempt from the risk of early death. For example, Peller (in his analysis of the mortality of 2,888 male members of European ruling families born between 1500 and about 1935) found that as late as the seventeenth century of every 1,000 children born live to male members of the European ruling families, only 664 survived to age 15.[13]

As is well known, the greatest improvement in mortality control has come about through the reduction of deaths in infancy and early childhood. Under Model I conditions, nearly one-half of the population is lost by age 5, whereas in Model V only about 1.5 per cent is gone. For the purposes of relating life expectancy to life cycle, however, it is not the losses in the early years that are of most importance. Death at any time, including the first few years of life, is of course a "waste," but the loss on "investment" at these ages for both parents and society is not nearly so great as for those persons who die at just about the time they are ready to assume adult responsibilities. This is when such significant stages in the life cycle as higher education, work career, marriage, and child-rearing take place. For this reason, the focus of this article is upon

---

[12] Eric Hoffer, *The Temper of Our Time* (New York: Harper & Row, Publishers, 1967), p. 4.

[13] Sigismund Peller, "Births and Deaths among Europe's Ruling Families Since 1500," in D. V. Glass and D. E. C. Eversley, eds., *Population in History* (Chicago: Aldine Publishing Company, 1965), p. 94.

the fifty-year span from age 15 to 65. By age 15 the boy is in the process of becoming the man and is preparing himself either for higher education or entry into the labor force. Fifty years later at age 65 the man either is retired or, if not, his productivity is beginning to decline noticeably in most cases.

In the lower panel of Table 1 the per cent who survive not from birth but from age 15 is given by ten-year intervals to age 65. A comparison of the five models clearly indicates the degree to which man has been able to reduce the risk of death during the so-called "active" part of his life span. More than four of every five males born recently in the United States may expect to live through the entire period. The comparable figure for females is 88.7 per cent. It is improbable that this achievement will be much improved upon in the foreseeable future unless radical improvements in controlling the degenerative causes of death are made.

This achievement, which now permits so large a proportion of those born in advanced societies to pass through virtually all important stages in the life cycle, must surely be counted among man's most impressive accomplishments. George Stolnitz rightly has rebuked demographers for, in effect, ignoring or minimizing this great accomplishment. Their present preoccupation with rapid population growth has sometimes made them appear to almost deplore the plummeting death rates. Whatever the problems occasioned by the great rise in natural increase, no one would ever want to give up the very real gains that derive from the control of mortality that man now possesses. Stolnitz then goes on to state the principal theme of this paper:

> The probably favorable effects of longer survival on worker efficiency, mobility, educational aspirations, family formation patterns and eventually on family size have hardly been studied and receive scant attention in either popular or professional discussions.[14]

Living the "Complete" Life

But what are the consequences of changes that have recently permitted a substantial part of the world's population for the first time to live what Fourastié has called "une vie biologiquement com-

---

[14] "Recent Mortality Trends in Latin America, Asia and Africa," p. 119.

plète" ("a life biologically complete")? We really can't say because as yet there has been no *systematic* effort to follow all of the ramifications of this relatively new condition of man's existence. One technique that holds promise for such an effort is the use of analytic simulation models on electronic computers.[15] What can be the meaning of death in a society where nearly everyone lives out his allotted three score and ten years? Is death beyond the age of 65 or 70 really a "tragic" occurrence? The spectre of early and unexpected death manifested itself symbolically in countless ways in societies with high mortality. In Fourastié's word: "A l'époque traditionelle, la mort était au centre de la vie, comme le cimetière au centre du village" ("Traditionally, death was at the center of life, just as a cemetery was at the center of town").[16] Perhaps the very rarity of death nowadays during adolescence and early youth heightens its poignancy. How else are we to account for the fascination with death, particularly violent rather than natural death, revealed in teen-age cultural mediums such as songs and movies? Even the relationship between much improved life expectancy and its effects upon religious fervor and belief remains to be explored.

Of course, not everyone believes that the great improvement in life expectancy is entirely favorable in its consequences. It is sometimes argued that perhaps advanced societies now allow too high a proportion of those born into them to pass through until advanced ages. "Natural selection" no longer works effectively to eliminate the weak and the infirm. In other words, one consequence of improved mortality conditions is that the biological "quality" of the population declines.

It is reasonable to assume that a number of individuals who can now survive to old age are incapable of making any contribution to their society. The real question is how important a group they represent. There simply is not enough evidence to evaluate the argument, partly because conditions of extremely low mortality are such a recent development. My impression is that their importance generally has been exaggerated by some eugenicists, and that the cost of maintaining these relatively few individuals is far out-

---

[15] For a good example of their potential, see Jeanne Clare Ridley, Mindel C. Sheps, Joan W. Lingner, and Jane A. Menken, "The Effects of Changing Mortality on Natality," *Milbank Memorial Fund Quarterly*, XLV (January, 1967), pp. 77-97.

[16] Fourastie, "De la Vie Traditionelle à la Vie Tertiaire," p. 418.

weighed by the many benefits deriving from high survivorship. In any event, the strong ethical supports for the preservation of life under virtually all conditions are unlikely to be dramatically altered within the next generation or so.

In a paper of this nature only a few of the ramifications of increased life expectancy can be considered. One of the most interesting features is the biological continuity of the "nuclear" family during the period when childbearing and childrearing take place. In most societies the most crucial period, for men at least, is between ages 25 and 55. As shown in Table 1, only a little more than a third of the males under Model I conditions survive from age 15 to age 55. In contrast, almost 94 per cent in Model V reach this age. The fact that until relatively recently there was a high probability that one or both parents would die before their children reached maturity had a profound effect upon family institutions. In "functional" terms, the survival of the society depended upon early marriages, and early and frequent conceptions within those marriages.[17]

Collver has shown this very effectively in his comparative study of the family cycle in India and the United States (see Table 3). The mortality conditions of Benares are rather similar to Model II in Table 1. There are important differences between India and the United States at each stage of the family life cycle with the greatest difference, of course, being age of the death of one spouse, a difference of more than twenty years in the case of either the husband or the wife. Collver sums up his study and the implications for these differences between the United States and India as follows:

The demographic characteristics of the nuclear family in the two societies compared have numerous implications for the structure of kinship groups and households. In the United States, the married couple, assured of a long span of life together, can take on long-term responsibilities for starting a new household, rearing children, and setting aside some provisions for their old age. In India, by contrast, the existence of the nuclear family is too precarious for it to be entrusted entirely with these important functions. The joint household alone has a good prospect for continuity. When two or more couples pool their resources and their labor they are better able to supply their minimum needs than they could separately.

---

[17] This argument is elaborated in Kingsley Davis and Judith Blake, "Social Structure and Fertility: An Analytic Framework," *Economic Development and Cultural Change*, IV (April, 1956), pp. 211-35.

TABLE 3   MEDIAN AGES OF HUSBAND AND WIFE AT EACH STAGE
OF THE FAMILY CYCLE, U.S. AND BENARES, INDIA

	Median Age of Husband		Median Age of Wife	
Stage	Benares, 1956	U.S., 1950	Benares, 1956	U.S., 1950
First marriage*	17.3	22.8	14.6	20.1
Birth of first child	20.9	24.5	18.2	21.8
Birth of last child	39.7	28.8	37.2	26.1
Marriage of first child	36.9	46.0	34.2	43.3
Marriage of last child	55.7	50.3	53.0	47.6
Death of one spouse	42.2	64.1	39.5	61.4

* For Benares this is median age at *gauna*, the consummation of the marriage rather than at *shadi* or the formal wedding that occurs several years earlier.
SOURCE: Adapted from Table 1, Andrew Collver, "The Family Cycle in India and the United States," *American Sociological Review*, XXVIII (February, 1963), p. 88. The Benares figures are based upon a sample survey and those for the United States on Paul Glick's *American Families* (New York: John Wiley & Sons, Inc., 1957), pp. 53-70.

When one adult dies others remain to care for the orphaned children. Aging parents deprived of their sons may still be adequately assisted by grandchildren or nephews living with them. Certainly the degree of independence enjoyed by the nuclear family in America would be out of the question in rural India.[18]

This statement needs to be qualified by the fact that not all societies with high mortality are also characterized by the equal importance of joint households. But all societies of the past in one way or another had to provide for children whose parents died before they reached maturity. One largely uncelebrated consequence of greatly reduced mortality in Western countries has been the virtual disappearance of orphanages because of the marked decline of complete orphanhood (both parents dead) and the marked reduction in partial orphans. In the United States the number of complete orphans declined from 750,000 in 1920 to 66,000 in 1953.[19] In this way a favorite theme of novelists a century or so ago has largely

[18] Andrew Collver, "The Family Cycle in India and the United States," *American Sociological Review*, XXVIII (February, 1963), p. 96.
[19] Louis O. Shudde and Lenore A. Epstein, "Orphanhood—A Diminishing Problem," *Research and Statistics Note No. 33* (Social Security Administration, Division of Research and Statistics; Washington: U.S. Gov't Printing Office, Dec. 27, 1954).

disappeared. Were Dickens writing today, however, he would likely shift his attention from orphans to the children of the divorced or separated parents; families nowadays are rarely broken by death, but are much more likely to be broken by divorce, desertion, or separation. Nonetheless, the consequences of whether homes are broken in the one rather than the other way will not be the same.

The great advantage of increased life expectancy both for the individual and his society in terms of advanced education and consequent professional career is so obvious that it needs little elaboration. Under present conditions, it is now possible for individuals to plan realistically their entire education and work life with little fear of not being able to carry out their plans. Fourastie believes that the change permits a shift from the "état végétative" ("vegetating") of large numbers of people in traditional times to the possibility, at least, of the "l'intellectualisation de l'humanité" ("intellectualization of humanity"). In France of the seventeenth century, only 475 of every 1,000 males born live reached the age of 20, an age when they begin to think independently. In this respect, the developed countries have a considerable advantage over developing countries with their appreciably higher levels of mortality, for the former do not suffer many losses on the training and education provided their youth. But under conditions of Model II that are still typical of a large number of countries, a third of those who have reached the age of 15 never reach age 45, the peak productive period of an educated person's life. In such countries, primary education for everyone may be desirable, but it should be recognized that a part of the investment will be lost for the substantial number who will die during their most productive periods.

Another consequence, perhaps overlooked, of the improvement of life expectancy in advanced countries is that while even the rich and powerful were likely to die at early ages in older societies, now everyone, including the poor, can expect to live throughout most of the life span.[20] Considerable attention in America now is devoted to the demonstration of conditions of social inequality, and it is clear that very large differences exist for characteristics such as

---

[20] Probably the period of greatest class differentials in mortality occurs during the transition from high to low mortality rates.

education, occupation, and income. But in a society where about eighty-five of every one hundred persons can expect to reach their sixty-fifth birthday, it follows that there cannot be extreme differences in longevity among the social strata. This is not to say that mortality differentials do not exist; they do, but not nearly to the degree found for other major socioeconomic variables.[21] For the poor, unfortunately, increased longevity may be at best a mixed blessing for it can only mean a prolongation of ill health, joblessness, dependency, and so on.

CHANGES IN THE SPACING OF KEY EVENTS IN THE LIFE CYCLE

The facts of the worldwide extension of life expectancy are well known even if, as we have just seen, all of the social ramifications are not. What is still not well appreciated are the consequences of this prolongation of life for the life cycle itself. In particular, what effect, if any, has this lengthening had for the spacing of key events in the life cycle? Obviously, there can be no wholesale transformation of the life cycle because most of the events and stages of importance are to one degree or another associated with age. Thus retirement cannot come before a first job. But this does not mean that the life cycle is not subject to important changes. Education, beginning of work career, age at marriage, birth of first and last child, and other stages all are subject to changes that can have marked repercussions on both a societal and an individual level.

Our understanding of such changes is still quite incomplete for

---

[21] For example, in life tables for the United States in 1964 the nonwhite population may be taken as representing the lower stratum. Comparing white and nonwhite in terms of the expectation of surviving to ages 50 and 60 for those who have already reached the age 20 we find the following differences:

	Per Cent Surviving from Age 20 to Ages	
	50	60
White males	91%	80%
Nonwhite males	82	67
White females	95	88
Nonwhite females	90	75

SOURCE: U.S. Department of Health, Education and Welfare, *Vital Statistics of the United States 1964*, II, Mortality, Part A (Washington: U.S. Gov't Printing Office, 1966). Tables 5 and 3.

a number of reasons. As has been remarked, the normative approach to the life cycle has not provided much help because the sociologists, anthropologists, and developmental phychologists working in this field do not often see the life cycle itself as changing; they see the only change as being the people within the system as they move from one status to another.

In addition, one of the difficulties of dealing with the life cycle is that it is rarely seen in its entirety. Generally it is fragmented, depending upon one's particular interest. Specialists on child development concentrate only on the early years, while the period of adolescence has its own "youth culture" specialists. Others concentrate on the family life cycle or on stages in work career. Finally, there are specialists dealing with problems of old age. Few indeed take a perspective that includes the entire life cycle and how it influences their particular specialty. An instructive example of the utility of a perspective of the total life cycle is provided by Belknap and Friedsam. Their problem was to account for the incidence of mental disorders of the aged. They wisely did not restrict themselves to old people but were able to demonstrate that the kinds of transition persons make from one stage of the life cycle to another are very important in determining the probability of mental disorders in later maturity.[22]

A final reason why changes in the life cycle itself have not received much attention is the problem of data. Documentation on a world basis of increased longevity is adequate, and even for countries that have poor mortality statistics model life tables serve as acceptable substitutes. Adequate data for the life cycle, in contrast, are not available even for the most advanced countries. Ideally, life histories would be available so that the timing of each event in the life cycle can be specified, but until quite recently the technical problems in gathering and especially in processing detailed life histories on a large scale were so great as to make the task unfeasible.[23]

Some indirect approximations on an aggregate basis can be made by using census and other official data sources. Until recently, these

---

[22] Ivan Belknap and Hiram J. Friedsam, "Age and Sex Categories as Sociological Variables in the Mental Disorders of Later Maturity," *American Sociological Review*, XIV (June, 1949), pp. 367-76.

approximations have been difficult and tedious to make. Paul Glick has done more than any other demographer to work out ways whereby these kinds of data can be used to show changes in the family life cycle.[24]

In the investigation of the relationship of changes in life expectancy to changes in life cycle it would be worthwhile to consider two groupings of countries: the developed countries, where life expectancy has increased over a considerable period of time, and the developing countries, with their recent very rapid increase. For the latter, an important question for which we have little evidence as yet is how much people are aware at all social levels of the dramatic change in life expectancy. Perhaps it is not generally perceived, and probably few of the implications are recognized or understood. This is due in part to the fact that the change has been so recent that it has not had time to manifest itself in the lifetime of many persons. Because of the great generational difference in life expectancy in Mexico, the son may expect to live almost twice as long as his father; surely this will have considerable impact upon the family and other institutions. But we can only know for certain these changes as the son passes through his life-span, or well into the next century, a time when all of us will be dead. Fortunately, we are not dealing exclusively with the cohort formed in 1965, for changes in life expectancy are continuous, and cohorts formed before 1965 will be helpful in the identification of trends.

A most intriguing question is when and how the institutional arrangements that have evolved over many centuries as a response to high mortality conditions will change in response to the radically altered mortality risks. For example, will the Indian family system as described by Collver remain much the same, even though the mortality threat to the continuity of the nuclear family has been

---

[23] Fortunately, computer technology offers a way of handling large numbers of detailed life histories. At the University of Texas a project sponsored by the Ford Foundation is enabling Jorge and Elizabeth Balan, Alvan Zarate, and the author to explore these possibilities. We have 1,640 life histories of males age 21-60 with detailed information on such topics as migration, education, family formation, and work. Our procedures are described in Jorge Balan, Elizabeth Balan, and Harley L. Browning, "Obtaining Life History Data in the Course of a Sample Survey," mimeographed, Population Research Center.

[24] See Paul C. Glick and Robert Parke, Jr., "New Approaches in Studying the Life Cycle of the Family," *Demography,* II (1965), pp. 187-202.

much reduced? Will the joint family system decline in importance as the need for it becomes less apparent? These are the kinds of questions that need to be investigated. They naturally will differ in some respects from country to country, depending upon various factors.

THE STRANGE CASE OF THE AGE AT FIRST MARRIAGE TREND IN THE UNITED STATES

Rather than attempt in this paper a consideration of all features of the life cycle in developed countries, I want to concentrate on one feature—age at first marriage—and to limit myself to one country—the United States. The data are reasonably good, at least for the last seventy years, and age at first marriage is subject to a fair amount of variation in its timing. It is also of considerable importance in affecting the subsequent course of a person's life and is indicative of changes in social structure.[25]

The trend of age at first marriage in the United States is of particular interest when it is set in the context of increased life expectancy. In the time period of concern to us, 1890-1960, the generational life expectancy at age 20 increased thirteen years for males and eleven years for females.[26] This is not so great an increase as is now occurring in developing countries, but it is still a substantial and impressive gain. Given this appreciable extension in life expectancy, it would be reasonable to believe that the spacing of key events in the life cycle also would be altered in order to take advantage of the longer time span available. In particular, it might be anticipated that age at first marriage would rise. Exactly the opposite has happened, as shown in Table 4. Between 1890 and 1960, the median age at first marriage for males declined about four

---

[25] "An inquiry into the origins of the European marriage pattern will inevitably take one into the fundamental issues of economic and social history." J. Hajnal, "European Marriage Patterns in Perspective" in D. V. Glass and D. E. C. Eversley, eds., *Population in History* (Chicago: Aldine Publishing Company, 1965), p. 132. This is a good review of the European literature. For a longitudinal study of the marriage patterns of a special group see T. H. Hollingsworth, *The Demography of the British Peerage, Supplement to Population Studies*, XVIII.

[26] Paul H. Jacobson, "Cohort Survival for Generations since 1840," *The Milbank Memorial Fund Quarterly*, XLII (July, 1964), Part 1, p. 48.

TABLE 4. TRENDS IN MEDIAN AND QUARTILE AGES AT FIRST MARRIAGE FOR THE UNITED STATES

Census Year	Males					Females				Difference in Male and Female Median Ages
	Median	First Quartile Q_1	Third Quartile Q_3	Interquartile Range Q_3-Q_1		Median	First Quartile Q_1	Third Quartile Q_3	Interquartile Range Q_3-Q_1	
1890	26.1	...	...	...		22.0	...	...	...	4.1
1900	25.9	...	...	...		21.9	...	...	...	4.0
1910	25.1	22.2	31.6	9.4		21.6	19.1	26.5	7.4	3.5
1920	24.5	21.5	30.3	8.8		21.2	18.8	25.9	7.1	3.3
1930	24.2	21.7	29.3	7.6		21.3	18.8	25.7	6.9	2.9
1940	24.4	21.9	29.1	7.2		21.5	19.0	25.9	6.9	2.9
1950	22.9	20.9	26.6	5.7		20.2	18.4	23.0	4.6	2.7
1960	22.3	20.4	25.8	5.4		20.0	18.4	22.4	4.0	2.3

SOURCE: Adopted from J. R. Rele, "Trends and Differentials in the American Age at Marriage," *The Milbank Memorial Fund Quarterly*, XLII (April, 1965), Part 1, Table 1. The figures are derived from census data.

years, a very significant change. For females the decline was only two years, but their age at first marriage in 1890 (22.0) already was quite low. (Note that the interquartile range for both males and females was much reduced, indicating less variability among the population. Also, the difference between male and female median age at first marriage registered a continuous decline. In 1890 the difference was four years, but in 1960 it was only a little over two years.)

Is this not strange? During the same period of an important extension in life expectancy there has been a substantial decline in age at first marriage. Unquestionably, many factors are required to provide an adequate explanation for the pronounced drop in age at marriage since 1890. One of the reasons it was high around the turn of the century was the importance of the foreign born, most of whom originated in Europe where a rather high age at first marriage was characteristic, even among the lower strata. In addition, those immigrants who arrived as single men had some difficulty finding marriage partners, and this delayed their first marriage.

At this earlier time men, especially those who were professional and white collar, were not expected to marry until they had completed their education, established themselves in their careers, and accumulated sufficient assets to finance the marriage and a proper style of living (at least an apartment or a downpayment on a house and furniture). Is it any wonder that many professionals did not marry until they were well into their thirties?

This was the era of the long engagement. Perhaps Freud developed his concept of sublimation during the four years of waiting until his marriage to Martha Bernays could be consummated. Norbert Wiener, the mathematician and son of a European immigrant scholar, as late as 1925 when he was 31 and long a Ph.D., wrote this about his marital prospects:

> For the last few years, the meetings between Margaret and me had been a bit too intermittent to suit us. Her teaching and her continued obligations to her own family kept her fully occupied. For my part, my position was not yet sufficiently secure for me to take on the obligation of a married man. Yet the recognition I was receiving from Germany, together with an improved economic status at M.I.T. consequent upon it, now for the first time made it possible to look the responsibilities of marriage in the face.[27]

How very remote this seems now! The major drop in age at first marriage occurred between 1940 and 1960, especially for females. During this period, a great many changes took place that worked to facilitate early marriages. These include the practice of "going steady" throughout a good part of adolescence, a more permissive attitude to early age at marriage on the part of parents who often help the young couple to get started, the reduced threat of military conscription for married men with children, a period of general prosperity, and an easy credit system enabling newlyweds to have a house, furnishings, and car, all with a minimal downpayment.

As Kingsley Davis has often remarked, all these changes have made marriage a much easier step to take, one that does not require the planning and accumulation of assets as it did a generation or so ago. Marriage is not only easier to get into, it is now easier to get out of because divorce no longer carries the stigma once attached to it.

Of course, many early marriages are not wholly voluntary, and in a substantial number of instances the couple either would never

---

[27]Norbert Wiener, *I Am a Mathematician* (Cambridge: The M.I.T. Press, 1956), p. 110.

have married or would have married at a later age. Goldberg has estimated, on the basis of a Detroit survey, that as high as 25 per cent of white first births are conceived outside of marriage, with a fifth of these being illegitimate. As he puts it:

> We have been accustomed to thinking of the sequence marriage, conception, and birth. It is apparent that for a very substantial part of the population the current sequence is conception followed by birth, with marriage intervening, following birth, or not occurring at all. This may represent a fundamental change in marriage and fertility patterns, but historical patterns are lacking. An increase in illegitimate conceptions may be largely responsible for the decline in marriage age in the postwar period.[28]

There is, unfortunately, no way to determine if the proportion of illegitimate conceptions has risen substantially since 1890. I suspect it has risen, but I do not know to what extent.[29]

The causes of early first marriage are not so important for the purposes of this paper as their implications and consequences for other subsequent stages of the life cycle. For one thing, age at first marriage is closely related to the stability of the marriage. The high dissolution of teen-age marriages by divorce or other means is notorious. This may be appreciated by the following 1890-1960 data on the per cent of those who have been married more than once by age at first marriage:

	14-19	20-24	25-29	30-34	35+
White male	22.0	13.5	10.4	9.4	8.7
White female	23.6	15.4	10.4	8.6	8.3

SOURCE: U.S. Bureau of the Census, *U.S. Census of Population: 1960; Subject Reports, Age at First Marriage* (Final Report PC(2)-4D; Washington: U.S. Gov't Printing Office, 1966), Table 4.

Most of the difference between the groups 14-19 and 25 and over is due to higher divorce rates in the category of lowest age at first marriage. One may or may not wish to term the high proportion of

---

[28] David Goldberg, "Fertility and Fertility Differentials: Some Observations on Recent Changes in the United States," in Mindel C. Sheps and Jeanne Clare Ridley, eds., *Public Health and Population Change* (Pittsburgh: University of Pittsburgh Press, 1965), p. 129.

[29] Pre-marital pregnancy apparently was quite common in rural England in the period between the late 15th and early 19th centuries. Hair, on the basis of a sample investigation of parish registers believes that about one-third of the brides were pregnant before marriage. P. E. H. Hair, "Bridal Pregnancy in Rural England in Earlier Centuries," *Population Studies*, XX (November, 1966), pp. 233-43.

unsuccessful teen-age marriages as wastage, but there is no question about the costs of these unsuccessful unions to the couples involved, their children, and often to the society in the form of greater welfare expenditures.

Not only has age at first marriage taken a downward trend, especially since World War II, but family formation patterns also have changed. For women, the interval between first marriage and first birth has declined somewhat, and the intervals between subsequent births also have been reduced.[30] The result of these changes has been to permit most women to complete their childbearing period by the time they reach age 30.[31]

The effects of these changes on the family cycle are as yet not very well understood. Freedman and Coombs recently made an important contribution to our knowledge of the effect of child-spacing upon family income and economic assets formation.[32] Their concern, it bears stressing, was not the relationship between completed family size and family income (the relationship appears to be of declining significance) but with effects of the timing of births. Their Detroit sample survey data of white women living with their husbands revealed a "strong and consistent" relationship between timing of births and economic position, as measured by current income or accumulation of assets (such as equity in house, savings, investments, and value of cars owned). The sizable minority (20 per cent) of couples in which the wife was premaritally pregnant were "particularly disadvantaged economically," partly because they had their subsequent children more quickly than the other couples. Freedman and Coombs believe their data permit them the following conclusion:

[30] As Whelpton and others have shown, the significant changes in timing of age at marriage and spacing of births have had a pronounced effect upon population growth in the United States. The short-term effect of the speedup has been to increase population growth by several millions over what it would have been had the pattern remained the same as for the female cohort born 1911-15. The long-term effect also promotes population growth because the span of a generation is reduced. Pascal K. Whelpton, Arthur A. Campbell, and John E. Patterson, *Fertility and Family Planning in the United States* (Princeton: Princeton University Press, 1966), Chapter 8.

[31] "New Approaches in Studying the Life Cycle of the Family," p. 191.

[32] Ronald Freedman and Lolagene Coombs, "Childspacing and Family Economic Position," *American Sociological Review*, XXX (October, 1966), pp. 631-48 and "Economic Considerations in Family Growth Decisions," *Population Studies*, XX (November, 1966), pp. 197-222.

Those who have their children very quickly after marriage find themselves under great economic pressure, particularly if they marry at an early age. Opportunities for education or decisions involving present sacrifices for future gains are difficult. They are less able than others to accumulate the goods and assets regarded as desirable by young couples in our society. They are more likely than others to become discouraged at an early point and to lose interest more quickly than others in the competition for economic success.[33]

In effect, the lowering of age at first marriage of men has worked to compress within the brief time span of the early twenties many of the most important steps of the life cycle: advanced education, marriage, first stages of work career, and family formation. (This holds most for the college educated. Since at least four of every ten college-age males will have some college training, this is an important segment of the population.) Each of these stages, to be successful, requires commitment and involvement. If they are crowded together, the time required for fulfillment of each one is to one degree or another reduced. A few energetic and gifted individuals may be able successfully to meet these demands, but for most men the crowding means that one or more of these vital steps must be neglected. There is no opportunity here to follow out all of the implications of this fact, nor can the consequences of the compression of events upon the later years of maturity and of old age be considered.

Prospects for the Planned Alteration of the Life Cycle

Our review of the extension of life expectancy and the timing of stages in the life cycle leads to the conclusion that there seems to be relatively little relationship between the two. Man has been able to push back the threat of death both in developing and developed societies, but as yet he has not seen fit to make much use of this increased longevity. Must this be? In the developing societies, perhaps, the lengthening of life expectancy has happened so recently that the implications and consequences have not had time to manifest themselves. In the developed countries, at least in the case of the United States, there is clear-cut evidence that there has been, via earlier age at marriage and family formation, an increased com-

---

[33] "Childspacing and Family Economic Position," p. 648.

pression of important stages in the life cycle within the span of a few short years. Would the "quality" of the populations in both developing and developed countries be improved by means of a wider spacing of key stages in the life cycle? I believe a good argument can be made that it can.

Let us take the situation in the developing countries first. What would be the consequences of raising the age at marriage several years and of widening the intervals between births? The demographic consequences would be very important for, independent of any reduction of completed family size, these changes would substantially reduce fertility rates. The effects would be the opposite of what has happened in the United States since 1940, as described by Whelpton and others. Raising age at marriage would delay births as a short-run effect and lengthen the span of a generation as a long-run effect. At a time when there is much concern about slowing down the rate of population growth in most developing countries, this would be particularly effective when coupled with a concomitant reduction in completed family size.

Another effect of the raising of age at marriage and widening the spacing of births would be to allow these societies to better gear themselves to the requirements of a modernized and highly trained population. The heavy burdens of dependency brought about by early and frequent childbearing could then be spread over a longer time span. A later age at marriage for women could permit more of them to enter the labor force, and this in itself would probably result in lowered fertility. In most developing societies, the role and position of the woman outside the home must be encouraged and strengthened.

The case of the developed countries, and particularly the United States, is somewhat different. I see very few advantages either for the individual, the couple, or the society deriving from the recent practice of squeezing the terminal stages of education, early work career, marriage, and family formation within the period of the early twenties. There simply isn't enough time to do justice to each of these stages. The negative effects are often felt most by the women. If they are married by age 20, have completed their childbearing before 30, and see their children leave home before they have reached 50, this leaves a long, long time of about thirty years to fill in some manner. We know that many women have difficulty in finding meaningful activities to occupy themselves. The shortening of generations does permit people the opportunity of watching their great-grandchildren grow up, but this has to be balanced against earlier disadvantages of this arrangement. From the standpoint of the society, there are few advantages, if any.

If an argument can be made that little intelligent use is being made of the extension of life expectancy in terms of the spacing of key stages in the life cycle, it is proper to ask, what can be done about it? In any direct way, probably very little. The licensing of people to do certain things at certain ages is, to my mind, appropriate only in totalitarian societies. So far as I am aware, contemporary totalitarian societies have made relatively little effort to actively regulate the timing of events in the life cycle. The Chinese, for example, have only suggested that males defer marriage until age 30. But if people are not to be forced by the state to do things at specified ages, at least they might be educated as to the advantages of proper spacing, and also be made aware of the handicaps to which they will subject themselves by marrying and forming a family too early. Both in developing and developed countries there probably is little direct awareness of how spacing will affect one's life chances and how something might be done about it.

Obviously, if a delay of marriage is proposed, something must be done to accommodate the sex drive. Fifty years ago the solution to this problem seems to have been for the men to visit houses of prostitution and for the women to have periodic fainting spells. Neither solution is very attractive under contemporary conditions. Perhaps Margaret Mead has provided us with an answer to this problem by her proposal that two kinds of marriages be sanctioned, those with and those without children. Her individual marriage would permit young people to enter and leave unions relatively freely as long as they did not have children (this requires effective contraception). This arrangement would provide sexual satisfaction, companionship, and (provided the woman is employed, as would be probable) two contributors to household expenses. This arrangement would not markedly interfere with the careers of either sex. Marriages for the purpose of having children would be made more difficult to enter into, but presumably many couples would pass from the individual into the family marriage. This suggestion, of course, will affront the conventional morality, but so do most circumstances of social change.

Quantity and Quality in Populations of Man and Animals—Comments on Browning

CHARLES J. KREBS

Assistant Professor of Zoology
Dept. of Zoology, Indiana University

DR. BROWNING's paper on life expectancy and life cycles in human populations is important in making an attempt to connect two divergent approaches to population problems—the numerical, statistical aspects of *quantity* and the more subtle, elusive aspects of *quality*. As a biologist, I would like to comment briefly on this matter of quantity and quality, first, in some natural populations and, second, with regard specifically to humans.

For many years in biology we have had a group of people concerned with the quality of organisms—geneticists mainly, but also physiologists and animal behaviorists—and another group strongly concerned with the quantity of organisms—ecologists in their many forms (agricultural entomologists, foresters, fishery and wildlife managers, and so on). We are now beginning to appreciate that these two groups have much in common and that changes in quantity have repercussions for changes in quality, as Dr. Browning has just pointed out.[1]

One example of this has been my field of research on the population "cycles" of lemmings and field mice. Several species of field mice and lemmings go through population fluctuations, reaching peak numbers at recurrent intervals of three to four years, only to

---

[1] L. C. Birch, "The Genetic Factor in Population Ecology," *American Naturalist*, XCIV (1960), pp. 5-24; B. P. Uvarov, "Quantity and Quality in Insect Populations," *Proceedings of the Royal Entomological Society of London*, XXV (1961), pp. 52-59; and W. G. Wellington, "Qualitative Changes in Populations in Unstable Environments," *Canadian Entomoligist*, XCVI (1964), pp. 436-51.

decline again to low numbers. For about thirty years, biologists searched for an explanation of these cycles in terms of epidemic disease, food shortage, predation, and weather catastrophes. None of these factors, however, could be implicated as necessary causes of these recurrent population declines.[2] About fifteen years ago, the search was extended into a new dimension when the question arose: could these cycles be generated by qualitative changes in these populations? Might we be dealing with a circular causal system in which changes in numbers produce changes in the quality of the individuals in the population, which in turn produce changes in numbers?

We have been questioning, if you like, the old belief that "a mouse is a mouse is a mouse" and trying to find out if animals from sparse and dense populations differ qualitatively. For the past fifteen years, we have been searching, unsuccessfully to date, for the relevant qualitative changes. We first thought that these mice might be affected by the "stresses of crowding" we have heard so much about in recent years, but this does not seem to be the case. We are presently looking for possible genetic mechanisms linked with aggressive behavior. We know of significant correlations in these rodents between life expectancy and the events of the life cycle. For example, in dense peak populations of lemmings, where life expectancy is high, the median age at sexual maturity is increased, and this seems to reverse in low populations.[3]

I tell you this not because I think mouse populations will shed any great light on human population problems, but because I am struck by the convergence of aims evident in the paper just presented by Dr. Browning and a substantial independent body of research effort in population ecology.

Let us make no mistake; these are very complex problems which Dr. Browning has touched on. He has not delved into the genetic consequences of changes in life cycles which may accompany changes in life expectancy. In the long run, these genetic consequences may be of primary importance. In the short run and at

---

[2] D. Chitty, "Population Processes in the Vole and Their Relevance to General Theory," *Canadian Journal of Zoology*, XXXVIII (1960), pp. 99-113.
[3] C. J. Krebs, "The Lemming Cycle at Baker Lake, Northwest Territories, During 1959-62," Artic Institute of North America, Technical Paper No. 15 (1964), p. 104.

the present level of ignorance about these problems, the genetic consequences may not be of primary importance in making a total evaluation to pick the best strategy of solving our population problems. They must, however, be considered. For example, if we actively seek to encourage a later age at marriage, we should realize that the incidence of certain fetal anomalies increases with maternal age and that older mothers tend to produce an excess of female offspring.[4] We must also consider physiological and behavioral consequents of changes in the life cycle. Do we know, for example, why first-born offspring tend to be higher achievers, or whether this effect is dependent on maternal age? I am passing here beyond my field of specialization to raise questions which should be answered to appreciate some of Dr. Browning's suggestions. Do we appreciate the effect of maternal age on the well-being of offspring? Are lines of descent which pass from older females to older females as viable as lines which pass via younger mothers?[5] Do we know what effect widening the intervals between births has on child development and maternal well-being?

Dr. Browning has raised enough questions to keep an army of graduate students in projects indefinitely. More important, he has pointed out a unique opportunity which now exists for the study of man: we are rapidly passing through a period of unparalleled demographic changes which will have strong sociological consequences. Will we merely watch these go by and spend the next century describing them *a posteriori,* or will we delve into these opportunities now to investigate and possibly to direct the qualitative changes which are inextricably interwoven with the present world population changes?

[4] P. B. Medewar, *The Future of Man* (London: Methuen, 1961).

[5] A. I. Lansing, "A Transmissible, Cumulative, and Reversible Factor in Aging," *Journal of Gerontology,* II (1947), pp. 228-39, for work along these lines on rotifers.

# DEATH AND BIRTH CONTROLS

Death Control—The Implications of Increased Longevity*

R. L. COIGNEY

*Director, World Health Organization
Liaison Office with the United Nations*

FOR CENTURIES, man was satisfied to be the keeper only of his brother's soul. The statistics of life and death in far-off places, incomplete as they were, caused only minor ripples in the conscience of relatively well-off Western man. But then something happened. Travel, trade, rapid communication, the economic needs of the developed countries, even nineteenth century humanism, all combined to make the world suddenly a very small place indeed. The communicable disease in remote corners of Africa could now find its way overnight to New York, London, Paris, and Rome.

Competitive trade demanded world markets. Instant communication, perhaps most powerful of all the forces for change, gave a sick and hungry world a picture window on a world of relative plenty, and vice versa. As in all communications, both the sender and the receiver are participants. Both are affected.

In the new smaller world of the last several decades, we have come to accept the fact that we are our brother's keeper and that he is ours. We have come to accept the fact that three-fourths of the world cannot and will not go to bed hungry indefinitely, and cannot and will not suffer disease and early death indefinitely. We are now engaged in a race against time. We know that if we are to maintain our own way of life we must extend—and extend rapidly—to other men and other nations the advantages we have won for ourselves.

We must make the world a better place in which to live, not

* The opinions expressed in this paper do not necessarily represent those of the World Health Organization.

just in the advanced nations, but in the whole world. In approaching this problem we were not long in developing solutions. It was obvious that the underdeveloped nations would have to develop their economies; they would have to grow more food, develop more power, and take giant leaps in transportation, communications, and literacy. And, of course, to do all this they would have to achieve a level of health commensurate with the tasks at hand. In fact, as became quickly obvious, none of these things could be done in the face of debilitating disease and premature death. A higher level of health and its concomitant, death control, became a priority in the struggle to make the world fit for men to live in.

It would be pleasant at this point if we could review with pride our accomplishments in this area. Much has been done, but much needs to be done. We have cataloged the causes of death, and we have planned and executed health-saving and life-saving programs that have made it possible to speak of "death control" as a scientific reality. We have put into motion a continuing decline in the mortality rates throughout the world. We now speak not of "underdeveloped" countries, but of "developing" countries. We have, in fact, changed the condition of man in many parts of the world.

But the rest of the problems we set out to solve initially are still with us. The gap between the developed and developing countries is still there and is even widening. The historical problems inherent in this gap are still there. And we have created a vast new problem, as urgent of solution as any of the others—the problem relative to longevity.

Mortality Patterns and Trends—Causes of Death

The Data In discussing the effect of medical science on death, it is essential to consider mortality patterns and trends as well as the major causes of death. An obstacle to the study of world mortality is the scarcity of reliable statistics. So-called complete mortality data are available for less than 40 per cent of the world population. Reliable death registration figures exist for only about 4 per cent of the population in Africa and 7 per cent in Asia. In countries with incomplete vital statistics systems, indexes are based on censuses of population and sample surveys for establishing crude death rates, age-sex specific death rates, and infant mortality rates.

The usefulness of the crude death rate for purposes of international comparison is restricted because of the role played by the age-sex structure of a population in determining mortality; nevertheless, it can provide an indication of trends and of progress achieved. Indeed, the figures of crude death rates, appearing in the World Health Organization's three reports on the world health situation for the ten-year period 1954-1963 and in various United Nations publications, bring out not only the differences that still exist between the developed and the developing countries, but also the significant reductions in death rates that have taken place recently in the latter.

The majority of the countries in Africa, Asia, and Central and South America, where death rates were relatively high in 1954, show a steadily declining trend. Death rates range between 10 and 25 per 1,000 population. On the other hand, in most countries of Europe, North America, and Oceania, where death rates were already relatively low—between 7 and 12 per 1,000 population—there has been a leveling or a small decline. In a few of these countries, there has even been an increase in the annual death rates in the recent past, due in large part to the gradual aging of the population. The reductions that have occurred since 1954 show wide variations in countries for which data are available. In Africa, for example, a decline was registered, ranging from 20 to 40 per cent; in Asia, the reduction varied between 14 and 30 per cent, and in Latin America between 10 and 50 per cent.

In all countries, however, the decline in mortality rates varies according to both sex and age. It becomes evident that in both sexes the reduction is uniformly greater among the younger age groups. Decreases in mortality rates are always less marked for men than for women, but women, although they have greater longevity than men, also have higher demand for medical services.

Causes of Death As in the case of death rate patterns, there are also striking differences in the main causes of death as reported by governments and published in the annual WHO *Epidemiological and Vital Statistics Report*. One study deals with the ten most important causes of death in twenty-three selected developed countries in North America, Europe, and Oceania. It reveals that in the periods under review (1962, 1963, and 1964) heart disease was the leading cause of death in all twenty-three; cancer was second; strokes, third; accidents, fourth; and influenza and pneumonia, fifth. These five categories of disease account for nearly 70 per cent of all deaths in the twenty-three countries and territories under consideration.

The overwhelming importance of cardiovascular disease in the more developed areas of the world is shown by the fact that heart disease alone was responsible for 32.5 per cent of all deaths in the same group of countries in 1964. To heart disease must be added strokes, responsible for 13 per cent, so that, on the average, cardiovascular diseases caused more than 45 per cent of all deaths. In these countries, accidents cause more deaths than anything else up to the age of 45. At 45, the accident rate is no longer highest and cancer moves into first place, followed by heart disease and strokes. After 65, heart disease and strokes are the most frequent causes of death, cancer occupying third place.

One of the most significant developments of the past few decades has been an upward trend in the number of deaths caused by cancer in many countries of the world, mostly due to the increased incidence of malignant tumors of the respiratory system. It has been described as an epidemic, and undoubtedly it has been, or is becoming, manifest in more and more countries and in almost every continent. A number of factors may be involved in this increased incidence, such as better diagnosis, prolonged life span, and increased awareness of the disease.

Another WHO study for the same period, dealing with the ten leading causes of death in seventeen developing countries in Africa, Asia, and South and Central America, reveals that infectious and parasitic diseases (especially gastrointestinal ailments) constituted the most important cause of death, followed by influenza, pneumonia, heart disease, cancer, and accidents. In most of these countries, deaths from infectious and parasitic diseases are responsible on the average for 10.5 per cent of the total mortality, while in the majority of the developed countries, the rate is generally between 1.0 and 2.0 per cent.

Other WHO studies, dealing with community water supplies, indicate that diseases due to consumption of contaminated drinking water (typhoid fever, cholera, dysentery, infectious hepatitis, and others) account for much of the mortality in the developing countries. As late as 1963, about 40 per cent of the urban population and 70 per cent of the total population of seventy-five developing countries had no access to piped water within a reasonable distance. It is estimated that about 500 million people suffer from disabling diseases that are related to the lack of potable water. These studies also show the dramatic improvements affected by the provision of safe drinking water and other environmental sanitation measures. For example, after installation of good quality water supplies in thirty rural areas of Japan, cases of communicable intestinal diseases decreased by 72 per cent and the death rates of infants and young children by 52 per cent. After similar improvements in Uttar Pradesh, India, deaths due to cholera, typhoid fever, and diarrheal disease declined by 72, 64, and 42 per cent, respectively.

Mortality due to communicable diseases has diminished considerably over the past years as a result of prolonged control and eradication activities. For example, great strides have been made in the eradication of malaria. It is estimated that in the early fifties, before the WHO eradication campaign began, there were 250 million cases of malaria throughout the world, with 3.5 million deaths per year. By 1960, the estimated number of cases had fallen to 140 million per year, with 980,000 deaths, and the declining trend, both in morbidity and mortality, continues to this date. It is notable, for example, that malaria, which was a main killer in Guatemala, Costa Rica, and Mexico in 1954-56, had entirely lost its significance by 1960-61, following WHO-assisted antimalarial campaigns. Malaria is, however, still a major health problem in Africa, where approximately 185 million people, out of a population of approximately 207 million in the malarial areas, are not yet benefiting from an eradication program.

Information provided by governments for WHO's *Third Report on the World Health Situation* indicates that at least twenty-seven developing countries consider the diseases connected with malnutrition as a major health problem. It is estimated that between 1 and 10 per cent of infants and children in many of these countries suffer from grave forms of protein-calorie deficiency, with a mortality of between 10 and 20 per cent. Furthermore, respiratory and gastrointestinal infections act synergistically with malnutrition to produce more severe forms of disease than each one acting alone. Other diseases which, despite the progress made, still constitute a major problem in the developing countries include trachoma, yaws, bilharziasis, filariasis, and treponematoses.

Infant Mortality Infant mortality and mortality in early childhood (1-4 years) are considered to be one of the most sensitive indicators of a nation's health and also reflect the effects of environment and social conditions. Statistics for infant mortality are not available in all parts of the world and, where they are, they are not altogether reliable. However, among other sources, the demographic yearbooks of the United Nations and the annual *Epidemiological and Vital Statistics Report* of WHO contain sufficient data to observe levels and trends of infant mortality in most parts of the world. Generally, infant mortality has been on the decline in the last two decades, and in many developing countries the improvement has been substantial. In Africa, Asia, and Latin America, however, conditions remain unfavorable. In the developed countries, where there was a low infant mortality rate already, it is now fairly stationary, and improvements are likely to be less dramatic. In these countries, efforts to reduce the rate still further may have to be directed at particular areas and particular groups of people. For example, infant deaths in the United States per 1,000 population are 21.6 for whites and 41.1 for nonwhites.

Thus, despite the over-all decrease in infant and child mortality, vast differences persist in rates in the various regions of the world. For example, the latest available statistics show an infant mortality rate of approximately 12 per 1,000 population for Sweden, 19 for the United Kingdom, 24 for the United States, 83 for Colombia, while for Mali the rate is 123 per 1,000, and for Morocco it rises to 149. It is estimated that in many developing countries, where statistics are not available, infant mortality rates are much higher, reaching probably 300 or more per 1,000. As for mortality in early childhood, in the highly developed countries only a small fraction of the annual number of deaths occur to children between the ages of 1 and 4 years, while in the developing countries it is estimated that 10 per cent or more of all deaths occur in this age group; in some countries the figures exceed 20 per cent.

The burden of deaths in the first five years of life in the developing countries is mostly due to communicable diseases, such as gastroenteritis, pneumonia, and parasitic infections, and, as I mentioned earlier, to nutritional disorders. Not only is infant mortality extremely high in developing countries, but mortality in the second year of life is also very significant, since weaning is often complicated by a combination of nutritional deficiencies and infectious diarrhea. Although the implementation of certain public health measures—environmental sanitation and disease control—has produced appreciable results, much remains to be accomplished in these countries.

Life Expectancy and Longevity

Efforts to reduce mortality at all ages have led to gains in expectation of life at birth. Here again, the gap in average life expectancy between affluent and less advanced countries is very great indeed. On the basis of UN medium estimates, life expectancy at birth in 1960-65 was 41 years in Africa, 46 in South Asia, 58 in Latin America, 69 in Europe, 70 in the USSR, and 72 in North America.

Low as they are, the figures for life expectancy in the developing parts of the world nevertheless represent spectacular improvements over a relatively short period. For instance, the demographic yearbooks of the UN show that expectation of life at birth for males in Mexico was 37.9 in 1940, 55.1 in 1956, and 56.9 in 1960. In Trinidad and Tobago it stood at 44.5 in 1930-32 and rose to 59.9 by 1957. In India, life expectancy for males was 32.4 in 1941-50 and 41.9 by 1951-60. In Mauritius the figure was 32.2 in 1942-46 and reached 49.8 by 1951-53. According to the latest UN estimates, the trends of increased life expectancy will continue. These estimates forecast that the developed countries will gradually attain by 1980-85 the 74 year life expectancy that is assumed to be the limit in the projections by the UN. From 1985 to the year 2000 the projections assume that life expectancy will remain unchanged in the developed countries. In the developing regions, on the other hand, the projections by the UN visualize substantial increases, raising life expectancy from an average of 45 years in 1960-65 to 55 years in 1980-85 and 62 years in 1995-2000, a level still below that existing in the developed areas.

According to a UN publication entitled *The Aging of Populations and its Economic and Social Implications*, about 6.5 per cent of the world's population would be at age 65 and over by the year 2000. By 1960, the population in the more developed areas was already an "aged" one, with more than 8 per cent at age 65 and over, and this process is expected to continue. The proportion of persons of advanced age is estimated to reach about 11 per cent by 1980 and 11.3 per cent by the year 2000. In contrast, in the less-developed areas of the world, the proportion of the population aged 65 and over is expected to increase from the 1960 figure of 3.3 per cent to only 5 per cent by the end of the century.

It is apparent from these figures that, in both the developed and the developing parts of the world, the burden of old-age dependency is tending to rise and, assuming a declining fertility by the year 2000, the old-age portion within the over-all dependency burden, that is children and old people, will also show an increase. It would seem today (with the relatively high level of fertility in the developing countries, the decrease in mortality, and the rise in life expectancy) that there are two important aspects of the world population problem—the "explosion" and the progressive aging of the population, the latter for the time being affecting the more developed areas of the world.

Implications of Longevity I am not dealing with either problem from the demographic point of view. As a physician, however, and one engaged in international public health, I would like to discuss some of the medical implications of aging and increased longevity.

First of all, does increased longevity raise more health problems than it resolves? It is evident that illness, and especially chronic illness, increases in the older population. Old age and its diseases have therefore become one of the serious social problems of today. There is an increased need for health programs dealing with such diseases as heart diseases, hypertension, and arteriosclerosis; cancer; arthritis and rheumatism; mental and neurological diseases; nephritis; and others.

This incidence of illness in the age group 65 and over necessitates a corresponding and, in fact, disproportionate increase in health resources—installations, professional services, and financial resources. Improved health resources are needed for diagnosis and treatment, long-term hospital care, restorative and rehabilitation services, convalescent and aged-care facilities, and home care. Since the elderly, even when they do not suffer from chronic illness, constitute a vulnerable group, special planning is necessary to meet their housing, hygienic, nutritional, and psychological needs, as well as their occupational, social insurance, and retirement problems.

The principal causes of death in the age group in question are cardiovascular diseases, cancer, accidents, suicides, influenza, and pneumonia, in that order. Intensive research is being carried out in many countries which aims at finding the etiology and cure of the two principal causes of death—the cardiovascular diseases and cancer.

It is impossible to determine how soon a breakthrough in medical knowledge will change the trends in mortality of the aged. Public health has a considerable role to assume in this research because of its concern with man's milieu, and because environmental factors such as air and water pollution, waste disposal, ionizing radiation, food toxicity through use of pesticides, and others could also be among the etiological factors of these diseases. Although expensive and complex, this research is extremely important because of the evolution and gradual changing trend of the causes of death we have already discussed.

From the point of view of medical care, an increase in the proportion of aged in the population implies an increased demand on already inadequate health facilities and on medical and ancillary manpower. We know, for instance, that people over 65 require two and a half times as much hospital utilization as younger age groups. We know, too, that the hospital stay is nearly twice as long, 11+ days as compared to 6+ days. We know that the aged require a disproportionate number and degree of health services, and that if increased longevity is to be anything but a burden both to society in general and to the individual aged themselves, we must pursue solutions to the chronic and degenerative diseases, which at present make longevity a very mixed blessing indeed.

It is impossible to consider health—whether of an age group, a nation, or an individual—as a socially isolated phenomenon. It is, for example, inconceivable to project the state of health of the aged population without taking into consideration the social situation in which the aged will find themselves. The total person is not merely a satisfactorily functioning physical entity. The emotional and social needs of the aged may differ in degree and kind from those of the rest of the population, but the needs exist, and it is drawing a thin line between health and general well-being of either the individual or his society if we ignore these needs.

Unless we are prepared to condemn ourselves and our increasing number of aged to mere custodial care, we must view the problem of longevity in terms of maintaining a useful, personally satisfying function and not just the extension of organic existence. The purpose of medicine is not to augment the number of invalids or semi-invalids in a society. It is not simply to treat pathological conditions in later years of life or to replace deficient organs with artificial ones in order to prolong the life of the sick. The ultimate goal must be to prevent premature aging, the appearance of diseases which add to the wear and tear of body and mind, and to find a way of slowing down the process of aging itself.

Up to now, we have been discussing the problems of longevity—as we know it. While life expectancy figures have increased markedly in the developed countries in the past fifty years, the outer limits or maximum life expectancy have changed very little. If we accept the UN projection, average life expectancy figures in the year 2000 will be roughly those already achieved by the developed countries. This will reflect a gigantic increase for the developing countries. In Africa, for example, the prevailing life expectancy of 41 is already well above that recorded fifteen years ago. However, the year 2000 will bring relatively little change in life expectancy for those who, like ourselves, reside in the developed countries of the world.

Causes of Aging But we must emphasize again that these predictions are based on longevity *as we know it,* and the truth of the matter is that we know very little about the subject. We assume that the cause of death of a living organism may be ascribed to two factors, the *actual process of aging* and *diseases,* which do not directly induce aging changes in the cells, but which may accelerate these processes and at least give rise to organic and tissue damage entailing death.

Now let us investigate these assumptions. What, for example, is the so-called aging process? For the purpose of this discussion, we will define aging as those changes in structure and function that occur following the attainment of reproductive maturity, that result in a decreased ability to do the work necessary to overcome environmental or internal challenges, and that result in an increased probability of death with time—death through aging.

It seems obvious that, if we could eliminate altogether the challenges of the major infectious and deteriorative diseases, we could lengthen life expectancy by a number of years. Without atheromatosis and its cardiac as well as cerebral complications, without pyelonephritis and cancer, man could no doubt live longer. How much longer is a much debated question. Recently, for instance, a brilliant American surgeon stated that, once the remaining disease problems were solved, there was no reason why a person could not live to be 100 or 150 years old. In such an event, we may be dealing with deaths due exclusively to pure aging changes involving cell death, cellular atrophy, and reduced cellular function. We will be faced then, as we are already now, with the question of what, exactly, produces aging and the corollary question of its control, reversal, or elimination. A multiplicity of factors come into play in producing the biological changes that provoke the aging process. I would like to refer to a few theories that have been advanced on the possible role of these factors.

Little is known, for example, about the mechanism of some extrinsic factors which may influence the process of aging. Among these factors, however, we include emotional stress, repeated childbirths, lack of sleep, malnutrition, overnutrition, lack of physical activity, climatic conditions, abuse of stimulants, effect of chemical agents and radiation, as well as chronic diseases and infections.

We know, for example, that life expectancy in humans is strikingly reduced by obesity. Much of this reduction in longevity may be ascribed to an increased incidence of coronary artery disease, but other factors may be implicated. We do not know what these factors are. One day we may. Interestingly, one of the few experiments that have produced a marked increase in longevity of the laboratory rat were those involving caloric restriction conducted several decades ago. In these experiments, longevity of rats was increased from 50 to 90 per cent by a process of semistarvation. While a retarded rate of development may account for some of this increase, the mechanism of the effect is still not understood. Conversely, studies of prisoners in German concentration camps in World War II indicate beyond doubt that severe undernutrition accelerates the aging process. In these instances, however, the semistarvation was far more extreme than that endured by the experimental rats.

There have also been a number of extremely interesting experiments involving the lowering of body temperature, which appear to have an effect on the aging process. Research in another area shows that the average rate of aging is essentially unaffected by environmental factors. The differences in mean length of life in the various regions of the world are ascribable to a greater frequency of events that can cause death rather than to an accelerated rate of deterioration in an inhospitable milieu. It seems that it is not the *climate* of Africa as such that causes early death, but the presence of disease, malnutrition and undernutrition, and the absence of medical care.

Several popularized theories of aging are based on the concept that reactive intermediaries in metabolism, or substances from the environment, combine with enzymes or other functional structures of living systems and alter them in such a manner as to reduce their functional capacity. There are, within biological systems, molecules capable of such reactions. We do not know, however, their amount or, more important, their cumulative effect on function. We also have the work involving injections of procaine or the use of sulfadiazine on senile dogs to indicate that the aging process can be inhibited by the action of various enzyme systems.

There is, however, serious doubt as to how much effect on aging these assumed extrinsic influences actually bring to bear. It is hypothesized by most students of gerontology that the major cause of aging that occurs with time is built into the machine, the cells themselves—not the environment. They consider our deaths to be genetically programmed attributes like the color of our eyes and our other physical and many of our less measurable characteristics—at the time of our conception. We are, as so many computers, set for a certain life span barring the introduction of accidents or disease entities which interfere with our genetic programming.

The major question then is, can we alter this programming? Diet or chemotherapy or altered metabolism, selective breeding, reduction of body temperature, radiation at certain crucial stages of development, or pharmacological intervention in the programmed machinery—can we by any of these methods, or others still unconsidered, slow, reverse, or eliminate the aging process?

A few individuals and groups of investigators speak in terms of eliminating or reversing aging altogether, but they are the Jules Vernes of human biology. The possibilities of slowing down the aging process are, however, no longer the prerogative of the science fictionists. If, today, we do not know all of the questions, much less all of the answers, we know some of them. We have an inkling about others, although real perspectives and implications of longevity fifty or a hundred years from now may be far beyond our imagining.

At the 1961 White House Conference on Aging, it was said that in the United States in the lifetime of today's younger generation, without any further progress in medical science, an average life expectancy of 80 to 85 years will be typical. At this moment there are 1 million Americans 85 and over. There are 17 million 75 and over, an increase of 60 per cent in this age group since the 1950 census. The aged are the fastest growing part of this nation's population.

Regardless of future achievements in the control of aging, but with full realization that such achievements are a probability, we are faced now—not tomorrow—but *now* with the necessity of directing an ever increasing attention to the implications of longevity. Our traditional approaches are inadequate in view of the magnitude of the problem. A systematic, coordinated outlook and action policy, in which all gerontological branches—sociological, clinical, and biological—play a part, is increasingly urgent.

MAN HAS today the knowledge and the means, if not the organization and will, to control death in an increasing number of clinical situations. Premature death, barring accidents and war, is no longer inevitable. Communicable diseases, gastrointestinal disease, and problems of nutrition and diseases attributable to environmental factors *can* be controlled, and in fact are in the process of being controlled, however unevenly.

It remains for us to increase our knowledge of the chronic diseases which affect man in his middle and older years to solve the problems of cardiovascular diseases, cancer, mental illness, and accident prevention. No one who has followed medical progress in the past several decades can doubt that similar progress will be made in these areas in the next several decades.

But all of this progress will provide an empty victory if we do not organize our medical and social capabilities toward understanding and solving the problems inherent in increased longevity. If it is true that man does not live by bread alone, neither does he live by his vital signs alone. Unless we tackle the *quality* of life of the aged, we may one day look back on the customs of the ancient Eskimos, who set their old people afloat on ice blocks, as a period of comparative delicacy of feeling and consideration. This is the challenge that faces not only medicine, but other social disciplines—not simply that we make it possible to live longer, but that we make life worth living longer.

BIBLIOGRAPHY

Council of Europe. *Official Documents of the European Population Conference*, II, III. Strasbourg, Aug. 30-Sept. 6, 1966.

Hauser, P. M. *The Population Dilemma.* Englewood Cliffs, N.J.: Prentice-Hall, Inc., 1953.

Hinds, S. W. "The Personal and Socio-Medical Aspects of Retirement," *Royal Society of Health Journal*, LXXXIII, 281-85.

Logan, J. "The International Municipal Water Supply Programme," *American Journal of Tropical Medicine*, IX (1960), 469.

Merrill, M. H. "An Expanding Populace in a Contracting World," *Journal of American Medical Association*, CXCVII (Aug. 22, 1966), 632-36.

United Nations. *The Determinants and Consequences of Population Trends.* Population Studies, No. 17. New York: United Nations, 1953.

United Nations. *The Aging of Population and Its Economic and Social Implications.* Population Studies, No. 26. New York: United Nations, 1956.

United Nations. *Proceedings of the World Population Conference*, II. Belgrade, Aug. 30-Sept. 10, 1965. New York: United Nations, 1967.

United Nations. *Statistical Yearbook 1962.* New York: United Nations, 1963.

United Nations. *Demographic Yearbook 1961.* New York: United Nations, 1962.

United Nations Economic Commission for Europe. "Housing for the Elderly, Proceedings of Colloquium, Belgium and the Netherlands," Document 19, II. New York: United Nations, 1966.

World Health Organization. *First Report on the World Health Situation 1954-1956*, Official Records, No. 94. Geneva: United Nations, 1959.

World Health Organization. *Second Report on the World Health Situation 1957-1960*, Official Records, No. 122. Geneva: United Nations, 1963.

World Health Organization. *Third Report on the World Health Situation 1961-1964*, Official Records No. 155. Geneva: United Nations, 1967.

World Health Organization. *Epidemiological and Vital Statistics Report, 1967*, XX.

World Health Organization. *Expert Committee on Mental Health, Sixth Report, Mental Problems of the Aging and the Aged*, Technical Report Series, No. 171. Geneva: United Nations, 1958.

World Health Organization. *Urban Water Supply, Conditions and Needs in Seventy-Four Developing Countries*, Public Health Papers, No. 23. Geneva: United Nations, 1963.

World Health Organization. "The Public Health Aspects of the Aging of the Population; Report of an Advisory Group," *Document EURO-112.* Geneva, Dec. 17-19, 1956. Copenhagen: United Nations, 1959.

World Health Organization. "Seminar on the Health Protection of the Elderly and the Aged and the Prevention of Premature Aging," *Document EURO-245.* Kiev, May 14-22, 1963. Copenhagen: United Nations, 1963.

Prospects for World Population Control

J. Mayone Stycos

Director, International Population Program
Chairman and Professor of Sociology
Cornell University

The deliberate restriction of birth, either by means of postconception or preconception controls, is an aspect of human culture that appears to be common to all societies. What vary are the conditions under which birth control is legitimately employed, the pervasiveness of its utilization throughout the society, and the efficiency of its utilization.

In the past decade, extraordinary developments have occurred in all these spheres. The pious prayers for "cheap, safe, and effective contraceptives," intoned almost ritualistically at every planned parenthood meeting prior to the 1960's, have been answered. The use of contraceptives, once viewed as more appropriate for houses of prostitution than for houses of decent people, is now espoused by champions of everything from human rights and responsible parenthood to economic development and social modernization. Indeed, that controlled fertility is here to stay in the developed countries, for members of all religions, is a thesis that should no longer merit serious debate. That it will also be characteristic of the peoples of the underdeveloped nations is also not in question. The only question is, how long will it take?

A decade ago, the population debate centered around resources and population growth, with the optimists insisting that resources and technology would keep well ahead of population. Such optimists are fewer in number today, and the debate is now centered around the question of *how* or how soon widespread birth control practices will be effected in the underdeveloped areas. The optimists see the ideological, technological and organizational explosions in family planning as at least matching the population explosion—and soon overtaking it. They believe that, just as contemporary mortality levels can be achieved by modern medical science with a minimum of social and economic change, modern fertility levels can be achieved with minimum change. Opponents of this view feel either that birth control *will not* really take hold until broad socioeconomic changes occur in underdeveloped areas, or that it *should not* be encouraged until such changes occur. A brief historical review should clarify this.

Under the conditions of high mortality characteristic of most of man's history, sheer replacement of the population (plus a margin of safety for catastrophes) requires high fertility. Accordingly, we would not expect a successful society to show a high incidence of birth control practices prior to the achievement of modern mortality levels. On the other hand, the reduction of mortality would appear to be a necessary but not sufficient cause for widespread fertility reduction. In Europe the gradual reductions in mortality that occurred in the last two centuries were a consequence of such broad social changes as the agricultural, industrial, and scientific revolutions, and the improvement of socioeconomic conditions. These general forces directly affected not only mortality but fertility, probably by altering the perceptions of costs and benefits of children. Although the transition from high to low levels of fertility lagged considerably behind mortality declines and often took as long as 150 years, it is noteworthy that they were generally achieved without modern birth control technology, without systematic publicity on family planning, and in the face of opposition from church and state.

In the underdeveloped areas today, declines in mortality are not normally the product of broad social changes, but they are much more efficiently being effected by the application of medical technology. That high fertility has in fact persisted for decades in countries with rapidly declining mortality (for example, many Latin American countries) lends some empirical evidence to the argument that basic socioeconomic changes are necessary preconditions for fertility decline. The unique case of Japan, with its successful demographic transition and socioeconomic modernization, would also support this hypothesis.

More optimistic experts, however, view the contemporary situation as ripe for rapid declines in fertility prior to modernization. They can point to: (1) recent breakthroughs in contraceptive technology; (2) improved methods of disseminating information; (3) the legitimation of birth control by churches and states; and (4) the desire for small families on the part of even poorly-educated populations around the world.

Technology

There is little doubt that modern methods of contraception represent a major advance in technology. If pills, intrauterine devices, and sterilization had been available to European women over the past two centuries it might be assumed that the decline in fertility would have been much faster. On the other hand, it is probable that the decline of European and American birth rates was more attributable to male than to female contraception, namely by means of coitus interruptus and the condom. The new contraceptives are almost exclusively female, as were the methods unsuccessfully promoted by planned parenthood groups in the first half of this century.

There is no doubt that modern female methods require far less motivation than was ever the case with classical technology. Contrasting the IUD with the diaphragm, for example, the former requires only one decision every year or two, is not associated with the sexual act, and, since it is inserted by physicians, shares both the glamour and the medical neutrality of an inoculation. In these respects, it has all the advantages of sterilization, without the disadvantages of irreversibility and possible post-operative complications. Just as Puerto Rican women responded enthusiastically to sterilization prior to the development of IUD's, so many women in other regions can be expected to respond to IUD's. It is not likely, however, that current modern methods alone will be adequate to bring fertility down rapidly in the underdeveloped areas.

Quite aside from the question of the number of women for whom such methods are not advisable (because of side-effects, medical contraindications, expulsions, and so forth), there is the question of whether there is a "hard core" of women who cannot be influenced, or who cannot be influenced early enough. The hypothesis should be entertained that it would be cheaper and more effective to reach their husbands, and to reach them with male contraceptive methods—new and better ones when they are developed, but the classical male methods in the meantime. It is entirely possible that after the first enthusiastic group of higher parity, older, and better-educated women have been reached, that the second round efforts might profitably be directed at males, who are more likely to see the salutary economic consequences of early spacing than are their wives. Clearly there is an important area here for research, involving both technological and sociological considerations.

COMMUNICATION

In earlier days, information on birth control was spread almost entirely by word of mouth, often surreptitiously. This was the case not only because of illiteracy, but because birth control was not a permissible subject for the printed page. There is some evidence, however, that on the few occasions when literature on birth control was widely read, it was not without effect. British sales of Knowlton's *Fruits of Philosophy* jumped from about 1,000 per year to over 100,000 per year in the years immediately following the Bradlaugh-Besant trial in 1877, and one cannot help but wonder whether the long-term decline in British fertility that began in 1876 was not accelerated by the huge increase in public information.[1] And one cannot help but wonder whether, in nonpuritanical and highly literate postwar Japan, the more precipitous decline in birth rates was not in part due to the greater dissemination of printed information via newspapers and women's magazines.

In more than half of the Latin American countries today, better than 50 per cent of the adult population is literate, and the potential for the printed page is greater than in England of the 1870's. It is generally believed that the subject of birth control is unmentionable in Latin American publications. In what he believed to be a crusading article in 1964, the ex-President of Colombia and editor of *Vision* magazine complained that the subject of population and birth control was the "great taboo" of our time. If the

---

[1] Parker G. Marden, "The Bradlaugh-Besant Trial: A Case Study in Declining Fertility," unpublished M.A. thesis, Brown University, 1964.

subject was ever tabooed in the press, it was a taboo fast disappearing, for during the year in which Lleras made his statement, the Cornell International Population Program collected from Latin American newspapers no less than 6,000 articles dealing with population; over three-fourths of them mentioned birth control. Of those articles that mentioned birth control, less than a fifth were unfavorable to it. There is no doubt that those who read today are learning far more about fertility control than readers of newspapers in any previous point in history.

Further, and in the light of the current legitimation of family planning, mass media never before available for such purposes are at the disposal of family planning programmers. A good example is provided by the media treatment of a three-day visit of a Mexican priest to Costa Rica in January, 1967. Father Orozco, who named overpopulation as the number one world problem, and who maintained that the right to limit births is absolute and unconditional, received no less than three and one-half hours of national TV time and recorded three fifteen-minute radio programs. (In addition, he received 609 inches of newspaper publicity.)[2] Of greater long-range significance are the thirteen episode soap-opera series on problems of excessive family size sponsored by the Population Reference Bureau and currently being broadcast by at least twenty Central American radio stations.

When the imminent arrival of a seventh child into an already crowded household becomes known, the topic of abortion is raised and counsel is sought from a social worker who advises that the mother seek further advice from a doctor and a priest. The dialogues bring to light sound medical thinking on the topic of abortion and responsible parenthood, as well as liberal Catholic counsel. For the latter dialogue, actual advice given for use in the program by a Catholic priest is incorporated in the script.[3]

In Eastern countries everything from puppet shows to popular songs are utilized as educational media. In a family planning program in East Pakistan, "Publicity and information were disseminated by a singing team . . . recruited from local artists who performed in towns, villages and bazaars . . . the troupe composed songs

---

[2] *Planifamilia* (Costa Rica), February, 1967.

[3] Alvaro García-Peña, "National and International Informational Programs on Population Problems," mimeographed, PASB Conference on Population Dynamics, February, 1967.

in the local medium, some in a question and answer format [emphasizing] the economic and family health aspects of family planning."[4] Such an approach has received the highest blessings. Last month the *New York Times* reported that Pakistan's president Ayub Khan urged that Pakistan produce "songs in simple language on subjects like 'growing more food,' 'family planning and national integration.' "

LEGITIMATION

While the Eastern religions have never been a major stumbling block to family planning, the Christian churches have traditionally bitterly opposed it. The consequences for fertility, however, have not been particularly striking. All the Catholic countries of Europe have low levels of fertility, and in the United States and Latin America both the ideal family size and contraceptive practice of Catholics is surprisingly close to that of non-Catholics.

Nevertheless, because many Protestant churches have declared themselves in favor of family planning, and because many Catholic churchmen have become more permissive, the situation in Christian underdeveloped nations is much more propitious for family planning than was ever the case in the past. Probably the major impact of the more liberal views characteristic of this decade will be in drawing public attention to the problem, in allowing free discussion, and in softening governments' attitudes toward national policies.

At the same time, the indecisiveness of the leaders of the Catholic Church leaves the door open for the more conservative bishops to take a hard line that can put obstacles in the way of government programs. While such actions will at least slow the pace of government programs, they may also crystallize public opinion and mobilize pro-family planning groups in a way not possible without opposition. In the past the battle was so one-sided that it was suicidal to elicit church opposition. At the present time, some countries, particularly in Latin America, *need* to make birth control a public issue in order to make the matter salient through the mass media, and to arouse courageous public spirited citizens to take political and social action. An interesting test case is being provided in Colombia, where the announcement of a government pro-

---

[4] Harvey M. Choldin in *Studies in Family Planning*, No. 13, August, 1966, pp. 8-9.

gram of family planning caused a concerted attack by the Catholic Church, which had previously been quite permissive. Two entire issues of the influential Catholic weekly, *El Catolicismo*, were devoted to presenting a conservative Catholic position; in March of this year, Cardinal Concha had a pastoral letter read in all of the nation's Catholic churches, condemning all forms of contraception and strongly reaffirming the traditional Catholic position. While at first sight these actions were damaging to the cause of birth control, they in fact will probably accelerate the program. As a result of the opposition, leaders of the family planning movement became "news," they were interviewed at length, and their side of the story was given far more coverage in the press than would ever have been possible without the creation of an issue. However, in other countries, where the birth control movement is only beginning, such opposition could crush rather than strengthen it.

In the long run, it may be that the Catholic Church will legitimate the use of modern birth control techniques. In the short run, it seems more likely that what can realistically be expected is a legitimation of the *goals* of contraception (that is, responsible parenthood) and a relaxation of the insistence on the illegitimacy of mechanical and chemical means of curbing reproduction. The papal encyclical of March, 1967, which recognizes both the population problem and the legitimacy of governmental activity to solve it, is consistent with this expectation.

The greatest shifts in the legitimacy of family planning, however, are being made more by states than by churches. Up until the last decade, the only nations in the world with any experience in attempting to influence fertility were those European nations that tried, and continue to try, to *increase* it. Comparable in importance to the revolution in contraceptive technology is the growing trend for nations to formulate explicit policies for the reduction of fertility. Perhaps the most remarkable document of the century was published on Human Rights Day, Dec. 10, 1966. The heads of twelve national states, subsequently joined by at least four others, declared their belief that "the population problem must be recognized as a principal element in long range national planning," that ". . . the opportunity to decide the number and spacing of children is a basic human right," and that "family planning . . . frees man to attain his individual dignity and reach his full potential."

Signed by the leaders of nations as diverse as Ghana, the Netherlands, United Arab Republic, Morocco, and Colombia, the statement was a clear indication that the worldwide legitimation of birth control is not far off. In the same century, what sent Margaret Sanger to jail is extolled as a basic human right by the leaders of the world.

While words do not necessarily mean action, they can certainly hasten it. An increasing number of nations are adopting national programs specifically designed to curtail human fertility. Whether or not they can succeed depends in part on the demand for the services they supply. What do we know about this demand?

Popular Demand for Family Planning

Over the past decade, an unusually large number of studies of attitudes toward family size and contraception have been conducted around the world. Uniformly, they have disclosed that women would prefer a moderate number of children and know little about birth control, but they would like to learn. Such studies have utilized public opinion polling techniques, and typically include such questions as "Do you want any more children?" and "If you could live your life over, how many children would you like to have?" It is usually found that women regard as ideal about one-fourth fewer children than they in fact have by the end of their childbearing period. The responses to such questions have led to great optimism on the part of family planners concerning the probable outcome of contraceptive programs. Critics of these studies feel that such questions often fail to tap the true attitudes of people, who may be much more indifferent to the question of family size than their responses to simple queries indicate.

My own studies have produced convincing evidence that uneducated women in underdeveloped areas do not in fact give much thought to these matters, and that the intensity of their desire for a small to moderate number of children is not great. But I do not regard as tenable the hypothesis that they are merely trying to "please the interviewer" by saying they want few children. One measure of this is provided by data on stated intentions to use birth control. If respondents *want* to please the interviewer, they should overstate their interest in or intention to use birth control, since this is usually the direct aim of much action research in this field. Of course, a failure to realize one's intentions can be due to many factors other than the intention itself, but there should be some correspondence between the verbal statement and subsequent behavior. Thus, while it should come as no surprise to find that not everyone who says he wants birth control in fact uses it when it is made available, there is nevertheless a strong correlation between the expressed attitude and actual behavior.

In a study in Korea, while only 14 per cent of those who said they did not want contraception actually accepted it subsequently, 48 per cent of those who did express an interest accepted it.[5] In Jamaica, under less favorable conditions, while only 6 per cent of those who said they had not thought of using birth control in fact reported use six weeks later, 25 per cent of those who had thought favorably subsequently reported its use. (The two urban counterpart figures were 6 per cent and 35 per cent.) The women who were not using birth control in the latter period were asked about their intention to use it in the future, and were followed up two years later. Less than 10 per cent of those who had no intention of using birth control measures, but 30 per cent of those who did so intend, were found to be using birth control two years later. Finally, a check of clinic records showed that 97 per cent of those women who reported that they had attended the family planning clinic had in fact done so.[6] In short, people's stated intentions and statements of behavior are predictive of their behavior, though the predictability falls short of 100 per cent.

In the absence of public discussion of the question, and in the light of general ignorance about the "controllability" of human fertility, it is not surprising that women's attitudes are not intense, not crystallized, and not unswerving. But at the same time, there is little doubt that there is a latent preference for a moderate family size rather than for a large one.

---

[5] B. Berelson, "KAP Studies on Fertility" in B. Berelson, et al., eds., *Family Planning and Population Programs* (Chicago: Chicago University Press, 1966).

[6] J. Mayone Stycos and Kurt W. Back, *The Control of Human Fertility in Jamaica* (Ithaca: Cornell University Press, 1964), pp. 233-235. All differences reported are statistically significant at the .05 level. For more detailed considerations of methodological problems of the KAP survey, see K. W. Back and J. M. Stycos, *The Survey Under Unusual Conditions—Fertility Research in Jamaica*, Human Organization Monographs, 1960, No. 1.

At least three things can be done with such a latent preference. First, we may leave it as is and make the technology so easy that little more motivation is required. For example, if there were a temporary sterilizing pill which could be taken annually, accompanied by an effective system of distribution, I believe that most of the women in the world would take it after having three or four children. Second, we may wait for the latent preference to become activated "naturally" as a product of social and economic changes that will alter aspiration levels. Third, by means of direct education the latent preference may be reinforced, crystallized, and intensified to the extent that the individual will act.

The "great debate" today is between the last two alternatives. In the scientific world, the hypothesis that the demographic transition can be achieved by means of direct educational techniques is typified by Bogue:

> Most [traditional demographic theories] are based on correlations between fertility and other variables that are incapable of being manipulated rapidly. . . . Family planning research . . . begins with the assumption that by the discovery of new principles we may be able to devise programs that can accomplish the desired results more quickly than would be possible if we waited for the solution along the lines of increased literacy—rising urbanization, improved levels of living, increased contact with technological-cultural change.[7]

We should note that Bogue is propounding not only a theory of social change, but an *ideology*. It is not surprising that it collides with at least one other combined theory of social change and action ideology—Marxism.

IDEOLOGICAL CONFLICT

Throughout most modernizing countries, and especially in Latin America, we can distinguish at least three major ideological types—the conservative, the social reformist, and the revolutionary. The conservative puts the *status quo* first and revolution last, with social change a reluctant second. The reformer puts social change first and the *status quo* last, with revolution occupying second place. The revolutionary puts revolution first and social change last. He prefers the *status quo* to social change because the latter might

---

[7] Donald J. Bogue, "Family Planning Research: An Outline of the Field," *Family Planning and Population Programs,* p. 724.

stem the revolution, while the former, the more intolerable it becomes, can only precipitate it.[8]

Increasingly, economists are of the opinion that population control can accelerate economic development by such means as decreasing the dependency ratio, reducing the cost of social services, decreasing unemployment, and raising per capita product. In addition to spreading the benefits of economic development less thin, there should be positive generation of economic development as a result of increased savings for investments in capital-producing enterprises. Finally, by alleviating food shortages and other pressures attributable to population increase (for example, rural overcrowding and urban migration) social tensions might be eased. It should be noted that the gains from population control can occur without any basic changes in the economic and social structure, that is, without any radical change in the distribution of wealth, ownership of the means of production, and so forth. Strictly rationally, population control should be of the highest priority to conservatives, of importance but secondary importance to social reformists, and anathema to revolutionaries.

As usual, the revolutionaries have reacted most consistently, and have resisted population control as another palliative of the social reformist that will ease the pressures leading to revolution, diverting attention from the true source of society's ills—the capitalist economic system. More recently, some communist spokesmen have softened the traditional Marxian hostility to Malthusian theory to the extent of admitting that population growth can impede economic progress, and that birth control can alleviate population growth. They feel that birth control, however, will be and *should* be a natural response to the necessary revolutionary changes in society. That Communist nations have some of the most efficient birth control programs in the world while condemning population control is proof that they are not opposed to birth control per se, but only to the *ideology* of population control and to its proposed sequence in the development of societies.

The conservatives, who should be most enthusiastic about birth control, are split because of conflicting ideologies and credos. In Latin America, they tend to be the more traditional and orthodox

---

[8] Albert O. Hirschman, *Journeys Toward Progress* (New York: The Twentieth Century Fund, 1963), pp. 276-297.

Catholics who may have moral objections to family planning, and they are also from the business world that sees more consumers and a cheap labor supply as the very fuel of industry. An example of how these conflicting ideologies lead the conservatives to a negative position on population control is provided in the recent report of the Inter-American Council for Commerce and Production. It maintains that "population growth should be considered a sign of progress . . . a legitimate and welcome price for improvement in sanitary and living conditions." A dim view of birth control is taken, and the report notes somberly that "Relations between young people are acquiring great freedom under protection of modern means and for purposes, needless to say, that are not those mentioned when economic development is being discussed." It concludes that "the solution is not birth control but increased food production and economic development."[9] Finally, many conservatives are strongly nationalistic, and they view with pride a populous nation, regarding population control as a new method of the colonial powers to emasculate the nations they hope to continue to dominate. A good example of the blend of economic conservatism and nationalist "populationism" is provided by the following statement by the editor of El Salvador's *Diario de Hoy*, Napoleon Viera Altamirano. He warns against

> . . . the true conspirators against our America, who come with a plan of massive destruction! The plan to destroy the capital of Latin America, to frighten away private investment, to socialize us before we have capitalized, and to block our growth, cutting the wombs of Latin mothers, castrating Latin males, before we have grown sufficiently or taken possession of the vast empty lands of the continent.[10]

In point of fact birth control is making greatest headway among the liberals or social reformers who are gradually becoming convinced that it can speed the economic development they desire without jeopardizing any of the social reforms they espouse. Of equal or even greater importance, they see birth control as a social measure, as a means of reducing abortion and illegitimacy, and as

---

[9] Committee for Economic Development, *How Low Income Countries Can Advance Their Own Growth*, September, 1966, pp. 45-46.

[10] *Diario de Hoy* (El Salvador), cited in J. M. Stycos, "Opinions of Latin-American Intellectuals on Population Problems and Birth Control," *Annals of the American Academy of Political and Social Science*, CCCLX (July, 1965).

a way of increasing human freedom and control over man's nature. Since they tend to be nominal Catholics or leftist activist Catholics, moral-religious considerations are not of paramount importance. Their main preoccupation about family planning is with respect to its suspiciously enthusiastic promotion by the United States. The more they are convinced, by President Johnson and others, that $5 invested in birth control is worth $100 invested in economic development, the more concerned they are that the bargain-loving United States will choose the $5 investment. In addition, unaware that the conservatives are confused on the issue, they are afraid that both American and local conservatives will substitute Lippes loops for agrarian reform. These concerns have led to the performance of a verbal ritual, performed whenever population control is advocated, which seems to relieve anxieties somewhat. A recent report of the United Nations *ad hoc* Committee of Experts on Programmes in Fertility provides us with a good example. Advisory services in family planning, they warned, "should not be regarded as a substitute for energetic efforts to expand production, reduce unemployment and underemployment, and provide adequate facilities for education, public health, and other essential social services."[11]

In sum, there is not only academic debate over whether or not direct education and services can bring down birth rates, there are definite ideological differences concerning its desirability, sequence, and over-all place in the strategy of development. Given the present trajectory of technological and communications advances in birth control programs, I believe that such ideological obstacles will loom larger in the future, even affecting the vitality of family planning programs among the countries where these are initiated.

In this context, it is important to understand that the task of family planning programs of the future will become more difficult. This is due to the fact that in the underdeveloped areas there is still a great deal of slack in mortality. In many of them the declines in fertility foreseen by family planners may be offset by declines in mortality. As infant mortality approaches insignificance, the three to four children desired by most couples in the modernizing countries will be too many to keep world population growth at a

---

[11] United Nations Economic and Social Council, Population Commission, December, 1966. E/CN9/203.

low level. At the present time, since fertility performance is in excess of people's wishes, the task of planned parenthood is relatively simple—that of activating people's own goals and teaching them how their own goals can be realized. But assuming the goals do not change, the task of the future will be not only teaching people to have less, but to *want* less—a matter not only more difficult operationally, but subject to even greater ideological controversy than is characteristic today.

The sample surveys of the past decade have taught us a great deal about people's actual fertility, their knowlege of contraception and their attitudes toward it, but they have taught us much less about human motivation, and nothing about political or other ideologies. Further, they have taught us little about the moral context of birth control. As religious objections to birth control decline in importance, planned parenthood groups become more and more utilitarian and technocratic, adopting a "Let's get the cookies on the shelf" approach. The hardheaded approach to the distribution of contraceptive devices will undoubtedly be as effective in this area as it has been in the commercial world generally; but if birth control is a way to increase the freedom and dignity of man, one wonders whether it should not be viewed in a broader context of sexual, conjugal, and familial love. If this be the case, then research should go well beyond the technological, and even beyond the motivational and ideological, to include broad moral considerations. One obvious example would be to evaluate the effects on family and other interpersonal relations of birth control education that is purely technical as opposed to that which places it in a context of human morality.

The weakest part of such a research design would be precisely the moral context. So long has Christianity, for example, stressed the negative morality of fertility control that it is unprepared, in my opinion, to offer us a comprehensive positive morality. Even the most liberal religions can go little beyond the abstractions of responsible parenthood. I present this challenge then to the great religions. Rather than follow the world on this issue, lead it. If birth control is more than plastic and pills, then show us how it is. And if the lives of the peoples of the world can be enriched by such knowledge, then teach them.

Comments on Stycos

CHRISTOPHER TIETZE

Associate Director, Bio-Medical Division, The Population Council, and Lecturer on Obstetrics, Columbia University

I have read my friend J. M. Stycos' evaluation of prospects for world population control with great interest and, indeed, with great admiration. This reaction has been a recurring experience for me over a number of years. Whenever I read one of his papers, I cannot help wondering how he manages to express himself cleverly, forthrightly, and even pungently—exactly the way I would like to.

My next reaction is to say, loudly and clearly, "Amen, and more power to you," and then to sit down and speak no more. But I suppose that would not do. As an alternative course of action, I propose to address myself, first, to a few of the points raised in the paper, where my own background in biology and medicine would seem to provide the opportunity for a useful contribution.

I am in full agreement that family planning programs should pay more attention to the male of the species, not only because of the historical importance of such contraceptive methods as coitus interruptus and the condom, but also because most societies offer a far wider range of alternative satisfactions to men than to women, for whom childbearing is often defined as the primary social function and source of joy, self-esteem, and status in the community. It is regrettable that biologists have not yet developed a modern contraceptive for the use of the male, comparable to Dr. Pincus' pink pill or the IUD. This failure may reflect, in part, the fact that most biologists are males and that most males, at least in our culture, would rather have their womenfolk use the pill than use it themselves, not to mention the IUD.

In any event, it is worth remembering that the condom started its career as an adjunct to extramarital pleasure, and while the earliest recorded instance of coitus interruptus was apparently associated with the circumvention of a tribal custom relating to inheritance, it does not appear likely that Onan invented the procedure for the occasion. I do not know when a male pill or injection will be ready for use, but I suspect that it would be more acceptable to men if its early image were one of amatory dalliance and dashing virility than of mere prudence and responsible parenthood.

In the absence of a modern male contraceptive, it may be useful to review the prospects for further improvements in technology, which would make female methods easier to implement and, therefore, more acceptable. There is every reason to anticipate early advances in this area. The next step ahead will probably be the development and perfection of a contraceptive regimen under which very small amounts (250 to 500 micrograms) of a progestin are given by mouth, not cyclically, but every day without interruption. No estrogen is involved.

The mode of action of this treatment is not yet fully understood. It is known, however, that ovulation is not suppressed, and it appears likely that the medication changes the consistency of the cervical mucus, making it inhospitable to sperm. The method is less effective than other forms of oral contraception, but pregnancy rates among clinic patients have been comparable to those achieved with the most successful IUD's. The utter simplicity of the regimen —one pill a day—should make it attractive to those whose ability to count is limited; the minute dosage of the active principal reduces the need for medical supervision; and the low price will recommend this method to the chancellor of the exchequer.

My own organization, the Bio-Medical Division of The Population Council, has recently embarked upon an ambitious program to investigate these compounds and to study their application in a large group of women, perhaps as many as 10,000, over a period of several years. This program is a direct continuation of the council's work since 1962 in the evaluation of the IUD's. By late 1968 we hope to have a product and procedure ready for the use of governments and voluntary family planning organizations, especially in the developing regions of the world.

Beyond the daily "mini-pill" we are looking toward the development of contraceptive implants. It is possible to dispense a small amount of the progestin into a soft silicone capsule which is then installed subcutaneously. This has been done experimentally in rats. The progestin moves through the capsule at a very slow rate, but in sufficient quantity to protect the animal against pregnancy. It has been estimated that protection would last for twenty years in the case of the rat, longer than the life span of this animal.

We hope to have the first implants in humans accomplished by next year. Later on we hope to be able to reduce the size of the implants and to insert them by means of a hypodermic needle. It is too early to guess the life span of the implants that will be done in the human female. When will they be ready? Once more, it's too early to be precise, but 1972 is our unofficial target.

In summary, then, there are distinct possibilities of making the effective practice of contraception a simpler task and thus overcoming weaknesses of motivation. I am under no illusion that these technological advances, by themselves, will suffice to bring population growth under control, and I heartily agree with Stycos that a major task of social engineering lies ahead. I am sure no one in this room expects it to be easy, especially if control is to be achieved within the limitations imposed by respect for individual freedom and human dignity, which we cherish for ourselves and profess to cherish for all mankind.

It has been said that the present generation may be the last one to adopt voluntary family planning, that one more generation of unrestrained or inadequately controlled growth may force at least some governments to impose compulsory family limitation. This is not a pleasant prospect, but it should be faced at least as a contingency to be avoided.

Where does one draw the line between persuasion and coercion? Between bonuses paid to those who refrain from reproduction, as proposed by Stephen Enke, and a graduated surtax on families with more than three children, as proposed by nobody so far? Or at some other point along the continuum that extends from taking no stand and no action to the application of fiscal force in attacks on large families, as proposed by Dr. Spengler, I suspect with tongue in cheek? These are some of the questions raised by Stycos' paper.

ETHICAL ISSUES OF CONTROL

The Ethics of Population Control in the Light of Biology and Theology

JOHN ROCK

*Director, Rock Reproductive Clinic, Inc.,
and Clinical Professor of Gynecology, Emeritus,
Harvard Medical School*

POPULATION EXPRESSES the difference between the number of births and the number of deaths. So long as we think human life is sacred, the death rate must be brought as low as possible. Therefore, human welfare demands that the birth rate must not exceed that level which makes harmful to mankind the disparity between the birth rate and the unavoidable death rate. Since human life starts with conception, and this results from expression of sex—which is a biological constituent of the human animal—the ethics of conception must be considered in the light of biology.

We have three indestructible basic instincts: hunger, defense, and sex. As McLean has pointed out, the first two pertain to individual survival, but pure animal-sex concerns itself with only species survival.[1] Emphasizing the significance of this goal difference to the human animal, endowed with discretion and will, John Money states that sex is but "loaned" to the individual man and woman; they are but agents for its ultimate application to the welfare of mankind. Since reason and spirituality are the specific qualities unique to humanity, sex is properly manifested toward human welfare only in ways that, while doing man no harm, enable and induce him not only to procreate but also to maintain and develop in his offspring his peculiar intellect. It is his cortex that substantiates reason and affords him increasingly accurate apperception of his spiritual destiny.

---

[1] Paul D. McLean, in John Money, ed., *Sex Research* (New York: Holt, Rinehart & Winston, 1965), p. 197.

With these assumptions, the ethics of conceiving or not conceiving—of the individual's exercise of his procreative ability—from the purely biological point of view is determined by the effect of his product, not only on the birth rate that is determined by numbers, but also on the human quality of each unit. The ethical use of sex is biologically directed to preservation of species. Hence, it is restricted, not simply in the numbers procreated but, rather, in the number of procreated that, at a given time, can be assured the education and culture required to enable them to qualify as reproductions of healthy, rational, spiritual adults. This is the criterion of the truly biological fulfillment of the human sex instinct: that it contribute to the welfare of the species, *Homo sapiens*. Expression of this instinct is biologically evil if it leads to the procreation of more young than are good—not only for the individual parent or family, but also for all of society. These young cannot be good for society unless they are reared in health and in cultured intellectuality.

Ethics of the means used to limit births to the socially useful number is also restricted by biology. Our intrinsic defense instinct forbids use of any method that is injurious to the parent organism. Sterilization by radiation, before or after procreation of the proper number, is an example of unethical choice by either man or woman. One thinks also of surgical castration. Both of these agents, radiation and surgery, rob the body of sex hormones that are intended to contribute much more than sexuality toward the health of the individual. They play a very useful role in the general metabolism that preserves the integrity of many tissues and organs. Is our biologically fixed defense instinct not also violated by that degree of willful suppression of sexuality that seriously disturbs the smooth functioning of the psychosexual dynamo described by Freud? Indeed, any birth control method, be it medicinal or mechanical, may be biologically unethical for one or another individual man or woman.

I have mentioned man's peculiar inborn spirituality. This leads me to the theological implications of birth control. But, first, what is this "spirituality"? I think of it as what emanates from man's motivating awareness of an all-pervasive force beyond and above him. This is found only in the human animal, but always in him, however primitive he may be and wherever he is found. Man's spirituality expresses itself in the intrinsic aspiration of man to participate in this perceived force. Modern man has rather anthropomorphized this extra- and supernatural force, which we Judeo-Christians call God. Now the theology that affects the ethics of birth control is the formulation of what a given social group believes to be God's will in regard to it.

Let me limit myself, here, to Judeo-Christian theology. This is derived basically from the interpretation, made by recognized teaching authorities of any denomination, of what they consider to be God's direct revelation of His will as found in the Bible. Theology also includes what is called tradition. This comprises what the early fathers of the church taught and is taken to be their inspired insight into the will of God. Until the beginning of this century, Christian theology equated any coital use of sex with procreation and decreed that anything willfully done that would prevent coitus from inducing conception was unethical.[2] Furthermore, coitus was obligatory in marriage and forbidden to all others. About 1930, the Catholic Church taught that a married couple who, for justifiable medical reasons (dignified by the defense instinct), felt in conscience that it should not procreate, was, for this reason, not obliged to—perhaps should not—have intercourse during the fertile phase of the menstrual cycle. Any other method of avoidance of conception was sinful. About the same time, by most Protestant denominations, it was allowable for the married partners to prevent what was considered the primary purpose of coitus, conception, by any harmless method, so long as during their reproductive years they tried to have as many children as they could safely rear. In this matter their consciences were their guides.

Gradually, the Catholic authorities extended the acceptable indication for birth control to the limits of what is called "responsible parenthood." Parents could take advantage of allowable continence during what they considered the fertile period, if, in good conscience, they felt possible parentage could not be converted to good parenthood. This latter, of course, is merely the rearing of young to become healthy, rational adults. Parents need not procreate if they sincerely believe they cannot reproduce themselves in each

---

[2] John T. Noonan, Jr., *Contraception: A History of Its Treatment by the Catholic Theologians and Canonists* (Cambridge, Mass.: Belknap Press of Harvard University Press, 1965).

of their offspring. In theory, all married adults were assumed to be constructive members of society.

Indeed, this more recent, broader Catholic view of legitimacy for marital continence, beyond medical indications, therefore seems merely to correspond with the Catholic Church's basic traditional teaching of parental responsibility. The great difference is in the limiting qualification of parental responsibility to good parenthood, not just parentage. It is of great importance that, in Pope Paul's latest statement, he extended the indications beyond the purely medical ones. He emphasized the obligation of parents to limit offspring within the bounds of their ability to supply, directly or indirectly, the education and culture that constitute good parenthood. Significantly, he also spoke of freedom of conscience. Promptly, then, he reverted not to revelation or even ancient tradition, but rather to the medieval theological principle that a "good conscience" was only one that included the authoritative teaching of the Church as to what was the moral method of contraception. As yet there has been no papal word that there is any such, except periodic continence; the "period" becomes permanent for the parents whose fertile phase cannot be determined.

Of tremendous import, also, was the Pope's extension of parental responsibility beyond the immediate family. It now includes concern for social welfare as well. Good parenthood now is restricted to the family size that does not endanger society's ability to nourish and culture the young in general. Population must be limited within available resources, particularly of food and shelter and all that these imply. Of equal significance is Pope Paul's extension of responsibility for proper restriction of births to governments, which now should promulgate parental social obligations and facilitate use of the moral means to restrict conception. He allows that the consciences of others than Catholics are not restrained by the Catholic authoritative teachings on the morality or sinfulness of method.

It appears, then, that the ethics of birth control are the same, whether appraised by biology or by theology, with the exception of the enfeebling Catholic Church doctrine on methods. Coitus within marriage is a good by itself, and, with only the one Catholic limitation mentioned, any harmless method to prevent its resulting in conception is licit. Furthermore, both biologically and theologically, population growth must be kept within the bounds of social welfare.

Playing God

ROBERT C. COOK

President, Population Reference Bureau

WHAT ANTHROPOLOGIST Ralph Linton called "The Age of Faith and Epidemics" suddenly began to end when Jenner discovered vaccination in 1800. A half-million years of terror-impelled and fruitless efforts to deal with death by prayer, incantation, incense, and magic went into the rubbish heap as the genius of the human mind began to be applied to fundamental life processes. In less than a century, this application changed utterly the pattern of man's dying.

The "vital revolution" had begun. It was not enthusiastically received. Clerics were understandably dismayed at what to them seemed blasphemous arrogance—a sacrilegious tinkering with God's plan of survival. Since Eden, the Lord had given and the Lord had taken away. The giving and the taking were the perquisite of Deity. No wonder men asked who these bumptious nobodies were, and how they dared to meddle with the divine plan.

The preachers were not alone in their dismay. Law, medicine, and the press rallied to the defense of tradition. But times were changing. The burning of heretics was out of fashion, and opposition to Jenner lacked sales appeal. If a child could be spared smallpox by a scratch on the arm, what were these worthies fussing about, thought the mothers. Then, in 1801 the king and queen of England had themselves vaccinated, and the first round went overwhelmingly to Jenner. In 1805 the number of deaths from smallpox in London dropped from over 2,000 to about 600.

The first phase of the vital revolution was over. A generation passed before Parliament enacted a compulsory vaccination law in England. Jenner's discovery was only the beginning. Why vaccination worked he did not know; it was Pasteur who established that infections were caused by "tiny beasties." Thereafter, the causes and the timing of death were removed from the exclusive purview of divine Providence and turned over to the Bureau of Public Health.

At the other end of the equation of life, matters arranged themselves differently. Throughout all those millennia of the age of faith and epidemics, very high levels of fertility were essential to survival. Pre-Jenner existence was a horrendous gamble against a multitude of killers whose special target was the young. If half of the babies born in any particular year managed to survive to have children of their own, it was a veritable miracle. In some years, half of the babies born did not even live to celebrate a first birthday. The consequence of this ghastly slaughter of the innocents by the microscopic Herods of the bacterial and viral worlds was that human fertility had to be sustained at flood level if the human species was to have any hope of surviving. Mores and superstitions intended to guarantee an abundant human harvest were legion, a part of every culture everywhere on earth. Any society that took a casual attitude toward the necessity to "be fruitful and multiply" had long since disappeared. Those fertility imperatives were backed by the most august sanctions; they were essential to survival of the human race during the vast reaches of time before the pre-Jenner era.

The next step does not require the genius of an Einstein to figure out. The modest intricacies of human population dynamics were foreign to practically the entire human species. Hence, nobody had any inkling that Jenner and those who followed him were initiating one of the great cultural revolutions of all time.

As long as man was at the mercy of an apparently blind and indifferent Providence, he could only fight back by trying frantially to outbreed the ravening regiments of the apocalyptic cavalry: war, famine, and pestilence. Jenner changed all that, but nobody had any idea that winning at long last a round with death could be anything but a blessing. It never occurred to anyone that, in upsetting a fundamental demographic balance, humankind was off on a numbers game that today threatens the most dire consequences.

Put in its simplest terms, Jenner's momentous discovery opened up a frightening new era in which it became necessary to review some fundamental morals, taken for granted, and to engage in a most difficult game of truth and consequences. Man, having to a great extent elbowed Providence out of the timing of life's end, had opened up a veritable Pandora's box of most difficult formulations and decisions; he must forsooth apply all his wit, will, and wisdom to the basic facts of human arithmetic. Compassion, too, would be required. The arduous task of dealing with this power to prolong life has until very recently been shunned. In the game of truth and consequences a fantastic and disastrous dichotomy developed. Man disposed of disease and death to the best of his rapidly growing powers, and thus postponed the ravages of the Grim Reaper. Divine Providence, with the cooperation of that rather moronic bird, the stork, continued to be looked upon as the arbiter of who was born, when, where, and to whom.

This, in a nutshell, presents the background of the ethical problem man must face in the mushrooming population crisis. The preachers, physicians, and other defenders of the *status quo* were right in 1800. Jenner was definitely upsetting the vital applecart. The opposition sensed that Jenner's arrogant meddling with age-old patterns of survival was dangerous, but the nature and scope of the danger escaped them.

With the opening of the vital revolution, man took the first steps toward becoming the master of his own destiny. Charles Darwin had shown how, over the ages, blind forces could create forms so varied, so beautiful, and yet so admirably adapted that they could function in many environmental contexts. Out of this process of natural selection had grown the human mind. And this mind had the power to probe the mysteries of entwined matter and energy, to plumb the depths of space, and to unlock the secrets of life and death.

In a real and challenging sense, the increasing power to control mortality and the timing of births puts mankind in the position of playing God, of facing the frightening reality that he must—or else.

The coin of life has two sides, birth and death. It may be—though it is not likely—that those who opposed Jenner recognized that mankind lacked the wisdom, the insight, the compassion, and the guts to play God all across the board. To purchase progress with only one side of the coin of life is to buy a ticket to disaster, as we are finding out today. The oft-repeated story engraved on rocks and fossils tells us that many species have reached their highest levels of specialization just before they were cast into the evolutionary rubbish heap. The human experiment centering around the emergence of mind has reached the point where we human beings must face both our potential for power and our responsibility for using it wisely. Ultimately, the alternative is extinction.

Do we have the intelligence, and with it the humility, to make the vital revolution work? Can we become the architects of our own evolution? Indeed, dare we do any less? That is the challenge of this particular and unique age of man in which we find ourselves. The possibilities are limitless, and the difficulties, complexities, and dangers terrifying.

If we dare—and we can hardly not dare and still survive—the problem that confronts us is basically ethical. Heretofore, ethics have always been abstracts and reconstructs from tradition, revelation, and experience. Today, in the era of the vital revolution, there are fundamental ethical challenges for which the past can give no answers. The Jennerian dilemma is an example. Superficially viewed, the power to avert death could only be conceived as an absolute good. Yet, given an equation wherein time is a coordinate, the vital imbalance can prove in the end to be a prelude to disaster.

The population crisis is a case in point. Annual rates of population increase of 3.5 or even 4.0 per cent a year are even now pushing vast areas and many hundreds of millions of human beings to the verge of famine—and beyond. Such rates of population growth are due to human action. In the end they are bound to be destructive to the very lives that Jenner and those who followed him hoped to save. The correction of man-induced changes that are catastrophic in their implications is obviously and basically a moral imperative.

The ethical considerations involved are complex enough to tax the wisdom and the conscience of man. Since the issues are related to sex with its high emotional octane, solutions will be difficult. Fundamental consideration of evolutionary serendipity will also loom large. A classic example of this principle is illustrated, as Dr. F. Frazer Darling has pointed out, in the evolution of feathers, which started out as an adaptive expedient to make possible a high and stabilized body temperature. With the passage of ages, feathers became an essential component of organs of flight. In the fantastic plumage and coloring of some genera of birds, feathers also came to have an important sexual function. These benefits accrued over a long and zig-zag course as they amplified the original function of merely keeping the creature warm.

Sex itself has been enriched by a comparable evolutionary change. Initially, the function of sex was reproduction. This became specialized in various ways with the passage of evolutionary time. Modern science recognizes that sex contributes abundantly to the fundamental emotional components of personality. The spectrum of this complex chain reaction is much too long to catalog here. Nevertheless, with the technology of fertility control becoming highly developed, the tangled emotive functions of sex can be—and indeed are being—divorced from the reproductive.

This whole area of human experience demands searching ethical reevaluation. The current wide-ranging revolt against assumedly divinely ordained moral codes and traditional standards of conduct is not unrelated to the revolt that Jenner innocently set off over a century and a half ago. Events since that time underline the far-ranging consequences of upsetting an ecological balance. Humankind can never go back to the imposed absolutes of the past. But mere revolt against the dead hand of the past is not enough. In this new kind of world, the elaboration of a code tailored to this time of crisis demands the orchestrating of many skills and insights and more than a tincture of genius. The challenge is tremendous and the prospect is disturbing.

Sex is a powerful creative force, and at its best one of the great sacramental experiences of life. Albert Ellis recently described the American attitude toward sex as "addled, straddled and spraddled." This is hardly a state of mind likely to apprehend and to deal effectively with the extremely varied and complex moral and ethical issues involved.

An ethical code for the age of the vital revolution must center around three major objectives. It must do a better job of enabling human beings to pursue happiness in an atmosphere of adventure than our present moral assumptions and imperatives permit. Beyond that, it must ensure that man recognize the responsibility entailed in the ultimate game of truth and consequences as it is now beginning to be revealed. Finally, a moral code for tomorrow must challenge the best in man to accept with courage and compassion the great undertaking of becoming master of his own evolutionary fate.

No other species has ever had the opportunity of thus mastering and guiding its destiny. The king of the hominids has the intelligence to write the necessary new rules, but has he the wisdom as well? "And Jehovah God said: Behold man is become as one of us, to know good and evil." The fellowship with the Deity which this knowledge conferred, as recorded in Genesis, can no longer be evaded. Nothing more difficult has ever challenged the mind, the finest aspirations, and the genius of man.

Birth Control—Ethical and Theological Implications

PHILIP APPLEMAN
Profesor of English, Indiana University

DR. COOK, Dr. Rock, and I were asked to address ourselves specifically to the ethical and theological implications of birth control; however, as most of you have no doubt noticed, moral and spiritual concerns have not been altogether neglected by previous speakers. For instance, Dr. Spengler concluded his paper on agricultural development with the assertion that some current views of technological promise are not adequate for actual world problems because they fail to devote attention "to the purpose of life, to man's aspirations."

Part of Mr. Landsberg's paper dealt with the human values that underlie economic development. Dr. Hauser remarked on the tendency of large and densely packed populations to "devalue personal and familial relationships" and to break down informal social controls of thought and behavior. Dr. Browning's paper was explicitly concerned with matters of human "quality" or human value. Dr. Stycos called, in his conclusion, for a new "comprehensive positive morality" as regards fertility control. And various remarks in the ensuing discussions referred to patently moral matters, such as attitudes toward famine and starvation, the question of enforced family limitation, ideological obstructions to humanitarian foreign aid, and so on.

The moral aspects of the population question remind me of a remark of Samuel Johnson's to the effect that we are perpetually moralists, but mathematicians only by choice. Everyone at this conference is aware of the awesome mathematics of population growth and its increasingly grim significance for humanity. If our world were a more rational place, such knowledge would have led, years ago, to broadly based and energetic campaigns of population limitation in all of the critically affected countries. That campaigns have not even yet been launched in any effective way is perhaps evidence that people tend to be governed more by their conjectural moralizing than by their most precise mathematics.

The particular moralizing we now tend to associate with birth control is, of course, that of the Roman Catholic Church, the only major religion in the world officially opposed to contraception. Catholics, who constitute about 15 per cent of the world's population (a percentage that daily decreases under the impact of Asian growth rates), should presumably have little influence on the population policies of countries like India, where Catholics make up less than 1 per cent of the population. Unfortunately, however, countries like India are often largely dependent for aid in fertility control programs upon the wealthier nations and upon international organizations; in these centers of power and potential assistance, Catholic political influence has, for the past two decades, been partly responsible for enforcing a minority veto over any effective action in this field.

THUS the central question of morality as regards birth control is this: why, in the face of the human tragedy that we dramatically call the "population explosion," has the Catholic Church continued to oppose what it terms "artificial" birth control? Part of the answer (and a rather peripheral part) is that many Catholic clergymen have long held that the easy availability of contraceptives stimulates "immorality." One of my assigned tasks is to offer a critical perspective on the Catholic position; I hope I will not offend anyone if I am quite forthright about doing so.

On the question as to whether contraceptives stimulate immorality, I must respond that this proposition seems to me to confuse morality with behavior. A moral choice is a decision among certain alternatives on the basis of their rightness or wrongness, not a compulsion to act in a certain way because of the fear of consequences. A woman who refrains from illicit sexual activity only because of the fear of pregnancy is not in a Christian sense a moral woman; she is merely a cautious one.

Even from the point of view of behavior, and ignoring the question of morality for the moment, I find it impossible to accept the proposition that easy access to contraceptives necessarily has a degrading influence on people; there are too many complicating factors in human experience to warrant that conclusion. Consider, for instance, the behavior of many nominally Catholic women in Latin America. Catholic influence has made contraceptives difficult to obtain in many Latin American countries. According to the familiar Catholic argument, then, if other things are equal, the behavior of Latin American women should be of a comparatively exemplary character—and yet, in parts of Latin America we find some of the world's highest rates of abortion and illegitimate births.

Or consider similar behavioral problems in our own country. In the United States, there are probably more than 1 million illegal abortions every year. Does this behavior occur because the women involved are using contraceptives, or because they are not? In the United States, every year, there are about a quarter of a million unwed mothers. Is this because they are using contraceptives, or because they are not? In the United States today, one in every six brides is pregnant on her wedding day—because they use contraceptives, or because they do not? The obvious answers to these questions illustrate, surely, that matters of morality and behavior are not as simply and causally linked to contraceptives as some Catholic moralists would have us think.

But discussions of morality and behavior are really of secondary importance to Catholic theologians, as regards birth control. Fundamentally, the Catholic Church rests its opposition to contraceptives on the theory of natural law. According to this idea, a correct understanding of natural phenomena will lead reasonable men to a clear idea of the proper use of these natural phenomena. With respect to sex, the Catholic Church has traditionally held that God has made it clear that it is in the essential nature of sex to be reproductive; therefore, to employ sex in a nonreproductive way must be against the law of nature, and necessarily sinful, whether so used by Catholics in Castille, by Buddhists in Bangkok, or by Hindus in Hyderabad.

Again, speaking for myself, I find it impossible to accept this argument for a number of reasons. Due to lack of time, I can only outline them briefly here. First, if God had really indicated something clearly essential regarding the use of sex, then it would necessarily follow that reasonable people everywhere would see the purpose of sex and agree upon it; but of course they do not. Second, it is precisely the natural order of things that man is forever thwarting nature for his own benefit (the very roof over our heads is an example of this). If nature can be altered for one beneficial purpose, why not for another?

Third, if natural law is to be an infallible guide, then it goes without saying that its proponents must have an infallibly accurate conception of nature; but the Catholic Church's treatment of Galileo (to use only the most memorable example) is a constant reminder that the Church is something less than infallible on this subject. Dr. Rock, by the way, who really does know something about nature, tried to help the Church out of its birth-control predicament by writing a thoughtful book called *The Time Has Come*; but that book, I believe, was not greeted with any marked enthusiasm in Rome. My fourth objection to the natural law theory is that nature is at best an ambiguous guide to morality. If any man acted as ruthlessly, as destructively, as murderously as nature often does (as it did when it recently ravaged the magnificent city of Florence), that man would be considered a moral monster. It seems clear to me, then, that natural law is in fact useless as a guide to human behavior. Natural law is, as Episcopal Bishop James Pike recently put it, "simply a holy noise."

UP TO THIS point, I have been talking as if all Catholics thought alike on this subject; that, of course, is not the case. We have it on no less authority than Gilbert and Sullivan that

> every boy and every gal,
> That's born into this world alive
> Is either a little Liberal
> Or else a little Conservative,

and clergymen are not exceptions to this rule. The conservatives and the liberals in the priesthood are widely and sometimes bitterly opposed on the subject of birth control. The British liberals at the Vatican Council were supposed to have invented a little parody in which the conservative prelates stood around singing "Should old Aquinas be forgot?"

Just two weeks ago, the liberal newspaper, the *National Catholic Reporter*, published in full the texts of the liberal majority and the conservative minority on the Pope's so-called "birth-control commission." I have dutifully read through these texts, and I feel I should warn you scientists, social scientists, and other realists who might be tempted to read them—particularly the conservatives' document—that you should be prepared to emerge from them with a feeling of having escaped from Wonderland one jump ahead of the Red Queen. The conservatives on the commission maintain that the Church is and always has been right in its strict interpretation of natural law as regards birth control. *"Is contraception always seriously evil?"* they ask (in italics); and many paragraphs later, their answer is of course *yes:* reproduction is "subject to the all-holy, inviolable, and immutable laws of God."

Their answer was to be expected; what came as a surprise to me (and apparently to some others) was that for the first time, to my knowledge, the conservatives relinquished the old claim that man's reason alone can lead him to a proper understanding of natural law. "If we could bring forward arguments which are clear and cogent based on reason alone," the conservatives wrote, "it would not be necessary for our commission to exist." And they followed that axiom with the all-important corollary: ". . . in this matter men need the help of the teaching of the Church, explained and applied under the leadership of the magisterium."

The direction of that line of reasoning should be clear; here as elsewhere, it introduces a restatement of the Catholic Church's claim to ultimate authority on all matters of faith and morals. Until one understands this basic reliance upon authority, one has simply not understood the Church's position on birth control. It is this fundamental belief in ultimate rightness that made it possible for the Pope to come to New York and stand up at the United Nations, not very long ago, and insist, in the presence of delegates of malnourished peoples, that we welcome more and more babies to what he termed the "banquet of life"—and barely a month later, apparently with totally unconscious irony, to call for a war on world hunger.

The liberal clergy in the Catholic Church are largely a keen-minded group, some of whom I have been privileged to know, and whose work is often a pleasure to read. Their majority report for the birth-control commission does not reject the arguments from natural law; rather, it reinterprets them to mean nearly the opposite of the conservatives' opinion. "There is a certain change in the mind of contemporary man," the liberals wrote. "He feels that he is more conformed to his rational nature, created by God with liberty and responsibility, when he uses his skill to intervene in the biological process of nature . . . than if he would abandon himself to chance."

We on the outside don't yet know how the Pope will decide this momentous argument, but most reports coming from the inside have indicated that he will probably align himself with the conservatives. If this happens, the already sufficient difficulties of initiating effective programs of fertility control may be compounded. For while the Pope's recent encyclical, *Populorum Progressio,* gave with one hand approval of public programs of fertility control, he effectively took it all back with the other when he reiterated that such programs would have to operate by "suitable measures . . . in conformity with the moral law"; in other words, to interpret him strictly, only the ineffective "rhythm" method could be contemplated for use in public health programs of fertility control. Past experience with the "rhythm rosary" in India has demonstrated the utter inadequacy of this approach.

To ME, a most unattractive feature of the conservatives' report to the Pope is that it sometimes seems to be based more upon *Realpolitik* than upon either theology or morality. The conservatives retreated from reason to authority partly because reason had simply failed them, but partly also from an apparent fear of admitting error and of losing, thereby, the appearance of infallibility in moral teaching. The Catholic Church, they insisted, "could not have so wrongly erred during all those centuries of its history. . . . If the Church could err in such a way, the authority of the ordinary magisterium in moral matters would be thrown into question. . . . If contraception were declared not intrinsically evil, in honesty it would have to be acknowledged that the Holy Spirit, in 1930, in 1951, and 1958, assisted Protestant Churches. . . ."

There is unquestionably a great deal of honest (and anguished) doubt in the Catholic Church on the subject of birth control, and there is a great deal of uncertainty among all of us as to just what kind of role contraceptives will be able to play in the stupendous task of rescuing the world from the population explosion; but I would submit that the kind of self-serving rationalization I have just quoted is outside intellectual honesty. Considerable study has convinced me, in fact, that the recalcitrance of the Catholic conservatives is based less on logic than on temperament. Such recalcitrance, probably beyond the reach of reason or persuasion, will simply have to be ignored and bypassed if anything is to be accomplished in this field at all. With the welfare of most of the world at stake, it seems to me that there is no other choice.

And that (to end on what I consider a relatively cheerful note) is what seems now to be happening. One of our participants, Father Hanley, is on record as supporting the idea that even a conservative Catholic decision on birth control need not prevent government action in this field. That is a comforting thought which, to judge from past actions of our Congress and of various organizations in the UN, has had all too little implementation. But now, it is true, Congress and our national Administration are at last beginning to take meaningful actions toward assisting underdeveloped nations with fertility control; the February issue of Dr. Cook's indispensable *Population Bulletin* calls 1966 the "year of the breakthrough" on population problems at the UN; he refers to two recent UN documents that take firm positions in favor of fertility control. It has taken twenty years, Dr. Cook notes, but at last the "ideological logjam" on this issue seems to have been broken. Let us fervently hope so.

Participants

JOHN F. ADAMS
Temple University

PHILIP APPLEMAN
Indiana University

MARSHALL C. BALFOUR
Population Council

HARLEY L. BROWNING
The University of Texas

ROBERT F. BYRNES
Indiana University

ANSLEY J. COALE
Princeton University

R. L. COIGNEY
World Health Organization

ROBERT C. COOK
Population Conference Bureau

JOHN D. DURAND
University of Pennsylvania

M. A. EL-BADRY
United Nations

RAYMOND EWELL
State University of New York
 at Buffalo

RICHARD N. FARMER
Indiana University

W. DEAN FRASER
Indiana University

T. J. GORDON
Douglas Aircraft Company

MARK R. GREENE
University of Oregon

DEXTER L. HANLEY, S.J.
Georgetown University

PHILIP M. HAUSER
University of Chicago

EDGAR M. HOOVER
University of Pittsburgh

BERT F. HOSELITZ
University of Chicago

PAUL H. JACOBSON
Metropolitan Life Insurance Co.

JOHN F. KANTNER
University of West Ontario

BRYANT E. KEARL
University of Wisconsin

CHARLES J. KREBS
Indiana University

SIMON KUZNETS
Harvard University

HANS H. LANDSBERG
Resources for the Future, Inc.

NORMAN LAWRENCE
U.S. Bureau of the Census

FORREST E. LINDER
University of North Carolina

JOHN D. LONG
Indiana University

MILOS MACURA
United Nations

E. WAINRIGHT MARTIN, JR.
Indiana University

JOHN F. MEE
Indiana University

ROBERT I. MEHR
University of Illinois

JOSEPH J. MELONE
McCahan Foundation

ROBERT H. MENKE
Styline Corporation

JEROME W. MILLIMAN
Indiana University

PAUL F. MYERS
U.S. Department of Commerce

CHARLES B. NAM
Florida State University

IRVING PFEFFER
University of California
 at Los Angeles

GUSTAV RANIS
Yale University

ROSS M. ROBERTSON
Indiana University

JOHN ROCK
Rock Reproductive Clinic, Inc.

HOWARD G. SCHALLER
Indiana University

H. WAYNE SNIDER
Temple University

JOSEPH J. SPENGLER
Duke University

GEORGE J. STOLNITZ
Indiana University

J. MAYONE STYCOS
Cornell University

CHRISTOPHER TIETZE
The Population Council

HILDE WANDER
Institut fur Welwirtschaft

L. L. WATERS
Indiana University

VINCENT H. WHITNEY
University of Pennsylvania

EDGAR G. WILLIAMS
Indiana University

GEORGE W. WILSON
Indiana University

LOWDON WINGO, JR.
Resources for the Future, Inc.